CAMBRIDGE LIBRARY COLLECTION

Books of enduring scholarly value

Travel and Exploration

The history of travel writing dates back to the Bible, Caesar, the Vikings and the Crusaders, and its many themes include war, trade, science and recreation. Explorers from Columbus to Cook charted lands not previously visited by Western travellers, and were followed by merchants, missionaries, and colonists, who wrote accounts of their experiences. The development of steam power in the nineteenth century provided opportunities for increasing numbers of 'ordinary' people to travel further, more economically, and more safely, and resulted in great enthusiasm for travel writing among the reading public. Works included in this series range from first-hand descriptions of previously unrecorded places, to literary accounts of the strange habits of foreigners, to examples of the burgeoning numbers of guidebooks produced to satisfy the needs of a new kind of traveller - the tourist.

The Voyages of William Baffin, 1612-1622

The publications of the Hakluyt Society (founded in 1846) made available edited (and sometimes translated) early accounts of exploration. The first series, which ran from 1847 to 1899, consists of 100 books containing published or previously unpublished works by authors from Christopher Columbus to Sir Francis Drake, and covering voyages to the New World, to China and Japan, to Russia and to Africa and India. This 1881 volume contains accounts by William Baffin (1584–1622) and others of Baffin's voyages exploring the coasts of Greenland and Spitsbergen, and his search for the North-West Passage. Although he did not find a route east, he got considerably further north than previous navigators, and provided much useful information on the conditions and natural resources of the area. His meticulous chart making and record keeping, and his use of lunar observations to calculate longitude, were groundbreaking and remarkably accurate, as later explorers found.

Cambridge University Press has long been a pioneer in the reissuing of out-of-print titles from its own backlist, producing digital reprints of books that are still sought after by scholars and students but could not be reprinted economically using traditional technology. The Cambridge Library Collection extends this activity to a wider range of books which are still of importance to researchers and professionals, either for the source material they contain, or as landmarks in the history of their academic discipline.

Drawing from the world-renowned collections in the Cambridge University Library, and guided by the advice of experts in each subject area, Cambridge University Press is using state-of-the-art scanning machines in its own Printing House to capture the content of each book selected for inclusion. The files are processed to give a consistently clear, crisp image, and the books finished to the high quality standard for which the Press is recognised around the world. The latest print-on-demand technology ensures that the books will remain available indefinitely, and that orders for single or multiple copies can quickly be supplied.

The Cambridge Library Collection will bring back to life books of enduring scholarly value (including out-of-copyright works originally issued by other publishers) across a wide range of disciplines in the humanities and social sciences and in science and technology.

The
Voyages
of William Baffin,
1612-1622

EDITED BY CLEMENTS R. MARKHAM

CAMBRIDGE
UNIVERSITY PRESS

CAMBRIDGE UNIVERSITY PRESS

Cambridge, New York, Melbourne, Madrid, Cape Town, Singapore,
São Paolo, Delhi, Dubai, Tokyo

Published in the United States of America by Cambridge University Press, New York

www.cambridge.org
Information on this title: www.cambridge.org/9781108011556

© in this compilation Cambridge University Press 2010

This edition first published 1881
This digitally printed version 2010

ISBN 978-1-108-01155-6 Paperback

The original edition of this book contains a number of colour plates, which cannot
be printed cost-effectively in the current state of technology. The colour scans
will, however, be incorporated in the online version of this reissue, and in printed
copies when this becomes feasible while maintaining affordable prices.

Additional resources for this publication at www.cambridge.org/9781108011556

WORKS ISSUED BY

The Hakluyt Society.

———◆———

THE

VOYAGES OF WILLIAM BAFFIN.

No. LXIII.

The Honourable Sr Thomas Smith Knight, late Embaſſador from his Maⁱ to y̆ great Emperour of Ruſſie, Gouernour of y̆ Honᵇˡᵉ and famous Societyes of Marchantᵗˢ tradinge to y̆ East-Indies, Muſſcovy, the French and Somer Ilands Company: Treſurer for Virginia. etc.

Simon Paſſeus ſculp: Lond: Aᵒ 1616.

Jo:Woodall exc:

THE

VOYAGES

OF

WILLIAM BAFFIN,

1612–1622.

EDITED,

𝔚ith 𝔑otes and an 𝔦ntroduction,

BY

CLEMENTS R. MARKHAM, C.B., F.R.S.

LONDON:

PRINTED FOR THE HAKLUYT SOCIETY.

MDCCCLXXXI.

COUNCIL

OF

THE HAKLUYT SOCIETY.

CONTENTS.

ILLUSTRATIONS.

INTRODUCTION.

WILLIAM BAFFIN, the narratives of whose voyages are now for the first time collected in a single volume, occupies a deservedly high place in the list of our early navigators. Although he is only known to us during the last twelve years of his life, and his previous history is an absolute blank, yet the record of those later achievements secures for him an honourable niche in England's temple of fame. He was a daring seaman, a scientific observer, and a great discoverer.

I propose, in this Introduction, to consider Baffin's position successively in those three capacities. But it will, I believe, be alike an act of justice to those who enabled Baffin to perform his work, and conducive to a more thorough appreciation of that work, if I devote my opening pages to a notice of the grand old Merchant Adventurers, who were the munificent patrons of discovery during the Elizabethan age.

Baffin gratefully immortalised the names of the generous patrons who set forth the voyages in which he served; of Sir Thomas Smith, Sir Francis Jones, Sir Dudley Digges, Sir John Wolstenholme, and Sir James Lancaster; and among these pillars of

England's commercial greatness, Sir Thomas Smith takes the foremost rank. To his wisdom and patriotism, to his disinterested zeal for discovery, and adventurous boldness, the marvellous extension of our trade, and the honour of many of our maritime exploits, are mainly due.

Thomas Smith of Westenhanger, in Kent, better known as "Customer Smith", was the son of a yeoman, of long descent in Wiltshire, and was for many years one of the Farmers of the Queen's Customs. By his wife Alice, daughter of the Lord Mayor, Sir Andrew Judd, he had four sons who survived him, and three daughters. Alice Judd was descended from Sir Robert Chicheley, through whom her children were Founder's Kin of All Souls, and she was a first cousin of Sir Henry Cromwell, grandfather of the great Protector.[1] Customer Smith died in 1591, and was buried at Ashford. Of his four sons, the eldest, Sir John of Westenhanger and Ashford, was father of Thomas Smythe, first Viscount Strangford. His line became extinct with that accomplished geographer, the eighth Viscount, who was Vice-President of the Royal Geographical Society, and died in 1869. Sir Thomas, the second son, was the Merchant Adventurer. Simon, the third, was slain at Cadiz in 1597. The fourth, Sir

[1] Sir Thomas Murfin, Lord Mayor, had a daughter Alice, wife of Sir Andrew Judd and mother of Alice, who married "Customer" Smith; and another daughter, Frances, who married Sir Richard Williams, alias Cromwell, and was mother of Sir Henry Cromwell of Hinchinbrook, and great grandmother of Oliver Cromwell.

Richard Smythe, was of Leeds Castle, which his daughter sold to Sir Thomas Colepepper of Hollingbourne. Of the three daughters, Catharine married Sir Rowland Hayward, Lord Mayor of London; Elizabeth married Sir Henry Fanshaw, and Jane was wife of J. Fanshaw, of Ware Park.

Thomas Smith,[1] the second son, succeeded his father as Customer to Queen Elizabeth, and became a successful London Merchant. He inherited, from his father, the manor of Bidborough, and an estate in the parish of Sutton-at-Hone, in Kent, called Brooke Place, where he built a large house. He also had another house at Deptford, and town houses in Philpot Lane, and in Gracechurch Street. He became wealthy and influential, and it was his great merit to have encouraged maritime enterprise and discovery throughout a long life, not mainly for the sake of gain, but for the honour of his country.

Sir Thomas Smith was an active Member of the Muscovy Company, and was among those adventurers who despatched the first voyages to Spitzbergen. He also took a leading part in the found-

[1] He must not be confused with his contemporary, the learned Sir Thomas Smith, who was born at Saffron Walden in 1514, and whose life was written by Strype. This Sir Thomas Smith was of Queen's College, Cambridge. In conjunction with Cheke he brought in a new way of pronouncing Greek, and was University Orator. He was Secretary of State in the reign of Edward VI, sent ambassador to France by Queen Elizabeth, again Secretary of State in 1572, and died in 1577. He must have been many years the senior of his namesake the Merchant Adventurer. His descendant is Sir W. Bowyer Smijth, Bart., of Hill Hall, in Essex.

ation of the East India Company, and was elected
its first Governor in 1600. He was Sheriff of London
in the same year, and was knighted by James I, at
the Tower, on May 13th, 1603. In 1604, he was
sent Ambassador to Muscovy, sailing in June, and
arriving at Archangel on the 22nd of July. Thence
he proceeded to Moscow, and succeeded in obtaining
privileges for English merchants from Boris Go-
dunof.[1] He returned in the following year, and was
afterwards employed, on several occasions, in affairs
of State connected with commerce.

Sir Thomas Smith was re-elected Governor of the
East India Company in 1607, and again in 1609 ;
when, for his great services, and for having procured
the first and second charters, a sum of £500 was
voted for his acceptance. But he refused to take
the oath of Governor until the Company took back
£250. "The residue his Worship kindly yielded to
take." The East India Company flourished mightily
under his wise and energetic administration ; and in
1610, the largest merchant vessel that had ever
been built, was launched in presence of the King.
She was named by James I, the "Trade's Increase",
and at the same time his Majesty, with his own
hands, placed a gold chain, worth £200, with his
portrait hanging to it, round the neck of Sir Thomas
Smith.

[1] The narrative of the Embassy was published unknown to Sir
Thomas Smith and without his consent. *"Sir Thomas Smith's
Voyage and Entertainment in Russia, with the Tragical Ends of
Two Emperors and One Empress within one month of his being
there,"* London, 1605. See also *Purchas*, iii, 747.

The great Merchant Adventurer, while thus deve-
loping the trade with India, was ever mindful of
Arctic discovery. As a manager of the Muscovy
Company, he despatched Jonas Poole to Spitzbergen,
in 1609; and he had previously induced the East
India Company to send Captain Weymouth in search
of a North-West Passage, in 1602. But there were
men of less patriotic aims in the direction; and
when Weymouth returned unsuccessful, it was resolved that the attempt should utterly be left off.
Sir Thomas Smith was, however, a true friend to
Arctic discovery, through good report and evil report. He resolutely and persistently advocated the
glorious cause, and at length, in 1611, he once more
induced the East India Company to adventure £300
towards the discovery of the North-West Passage.
Again, "the business did not succeed according to
desire". Still, Sir Thomas remained true. In 1614,
he urged the Company "not to refuse to adventure
again, somewhat more, considering it were dis-
honourable to withdraw from so worthy a work".
Grudgingly it was resolved to adventure £200, "so
that there may be no expectation of any further
supply".

But, in the meanwhile, a new Company had been
formed in 1612, with the special object of Arctic
discovery, and Sir Thomas Smith became its first
Governor. It was called "the Company of Merchants of London, Discoverers of the North-West
Passage", and Sir Thomas gathered round him, as
colleagues, Sir James Lancaster, Sir Dudley Digges,

Sir William Cockayne, Sir Francis Jones, Sir John Wolstenholme, Richard Wyche, Ralph Freeman, and William Stone, all names well known in Arctic geography. They had already, before they were actually formed into a Company, despatched Henry Hudson, in 1610, on his last fatal voyage; and in 1612, Sir Thomas Button's expedition started, under the special patronage of Henry, Prince of Wales. The voyages of Bylot and Baffin followed.

Both Arctic discovery and Indian trading ventures received the unceasing and laborious attention of Sir Thomas Smith during many years, and he wore himself out by his incessant work in the service of the great trading Companies. In 1615, he was again re-elected Governor of the East India Company; again, in 1618, though old, and wishing to retire; and again, in 1620, by special wish of the King. His house at Deptford was accidentally burnt to the ground in 1619, nothing being saved, except the people, who escaped narrowly. He was at the very time engaged, with Sir Dudley Carleton, in negotiating with Commissioners from the States General, on matters relating to trade. He feasted them in his house in London, in July 1619.

At length, in July 1621, Sir Thomas Smith was allowed to retire from the Governorship of the East India Company, after serving for upwards of twenty years. He resigned from weakness and old age; after having created and fully established the prosperity of a famous body which, in after years, was destined to found a great Empire. Sir Thomas had

himself adventured £20,000; he had closely attended
to details respecting the equipment of ships, training
of officers, and regulation of trade; and had in-
stilled his own enthusiasm, and desire to advance
the honour as well as the wealth of his country, into
the Company's servants. He encouraged the scientific branches of a seaman's profession, and lectures
on navigation were delivered at his house by Dr.
Hood,[1] and Edward Wright. At the same time, he
was careful to ensure the permanent record of the
voyages sent out under his auspices, by furnishing
historical materials to Hakluyt, and afterwards to
Purchas. He was the perfect model of an enlight-
ened and patriotic Merchant Adventurer, a type
which has now, alas! disappeared from this country.

Sir Thomas Smith died on the 4th of September
1625, and was buried in the church of Sutton-at-
Hone, in Kent. A monument to his memory may
still be seen in the south aisle, with the following
inscription:—

M. S.

To the glorie of God and to ye pious
Memorie of the ho^nble Sr *Thomas Smith* Kt.

(late *Gouernour* of ye East-Indian Muscovia French and Sommer-
Island *Companies: Treasvrer* for the Virginian Plantations: Prime
Vndertaker in the year 1612 for that noble Designe the Disco-
uerie of the *North-West Passage:* Principall *Comissioner* for the
London-expedition against y^e *Pirates:* and for a Voiage to y^e
Ryver *Senega* upon ye Coast of *Africa:* one of ye cheefe Comis-

---

[1] The speech made by Dr. Hood in the house of Sir Thomas
Smith in Gracechurch Street, in November 1588, was published in
the same year. There is a copy in the British Museum.

sioners for ye Nauie-Roial and sometime *Ambassadour* from y
Matie of Gr. *Brit.* to ye Emperour and great Duke of *Russia* and
Moscovia etc.) who hauinge iudiciously, conscionably, and with admirable facility managed many difficult and weighty affairs to y^e
honour and profit of this *Nation* rested from his labours the 4th
day of Septem. 1625, and his soul returning to Him that
gaue it, his body was here laid vp in ye hope of a
blessed Resurrection.

> " From those large *Kingdomes* where the Svn doth rise ;
> From that rich newefound-world that westward lies ;
> From *Volga* to the floud of *Amazons;*
> From vnder both the *Poles*, and all the *Zones ;*
> From all the famous *Ryuers, Landes*, and *Seas*,
> Betwixt this *Place* and our *Anti-Podes;*
> He gott intelligence, what might be found
> To giue contentment, through this massie *Round.*
> But finding earthly things did rather tire
> His longing *Soul*, then answer her desire ;
> To this obscured Village he withdrewe :
> From hence his Heauenlie *Voiage* did pursue.
> Here, sum'd vp all, and when his *Gale* of Breath,
> Had left becalmed in the *Port of Death*,
> The soules fraile *Barke* (and safe had landed her
> Where *Faith* his *Factor*, and his *Harbinger*
> Made place before), he did (no doubt) obtaine
> That wealth wch here on Earth wee seek in vain."

There was a portrait of Sir Thomas Smith, en-
graved by Simon Passe.[1] The original print is very

---

[1] Simon Passe, the son of another famous engraver, Nicholas
Passe, a native of Utrecht, was employed by Hilliard, and was
ten years in England. His father, whose works are numerous,
was in England for several years, and drew many of his portraits
from life. This was also the practice of Simon Passe, whose
earliest works were James I and his Queen, Prince Henry with a
lance, Raleigh, Buck, Gondomar, Archbishop Abbot. He also en-
graved the Earl and Countess of Somerset, the Earls of Arundel,
Dorset, and Pembroke, Sir E. Cecil and Sir T. Smith.

rare. Its date is 1617. It is bound up in the Grenville copy of the embassy to Russia, and in some copies of the *Surgeon's Mate*, a book dedicated to Sir Thomas Smith, and published in 1617. It is a half length figure, in hat, ruff, and furred robe, holding a map in the left hand, with the words— " Russia" and " Oceanus" on it. A second, and very inferior edition, appeared in 1707. The portrait which forms the frontispiece of the present volume is taken from the copy in the Grenville library.

Sir Thomas Smith was married three times. His first wife was Judith, daughter of Richard Culverwell. I have not been able to ascertain the name of the second; but the third was Sarah, daughter of William Blunt. She was the mother of his children, and she married secondly Robert Sydney, Earl of Leicester. There were two sons born to Sir Thomas Smith and Sarah Blunt. The eldest, Sir John Smyth, succeeded to Brooke Place, in the parish of Sutton-at-Hone, and married Isabella Rich, a daughter of Sir Philip Sydney's "Stella". The second son married another daughter of "Stella" by the Lord Mountjoy, in November 1618, but he left England in the following year, under some cloud. The male descendants of Sir Thomas Smith became extinct, on the death of the Chief Baron, Sir Sydney Stafford Smythe, in 1778.[1]

---

[1] The eldest son of Sir Thomas Smith, Sir John Smyth of Brooke Place, had, by Isabella Rich, a son, Robert, and a daughter, Isabella, married to John, Lord Robartes of Truro, in 1646. Robert Smythe (for he adopted this way of spelling the name) of Brooke

One of the most active among Sir Thomas Smith's
colleagues, in the encouragement of maritime enterprise, was Alderman Francis Jones. This Merchant Adventurer was of a Shropshire family, citizen
and haberdasher of London, Alderman of Aldgate
Ward, and Lord Mayor. He was also one of the
Farmers of Customs, and was knighted on March
12th 1617. He resided at Welford, and had a
town house in the city, in the parish of St. Andrew
Undershaft. Sir Francis died at Welford, in 1622.

A still more eminent encourager of Arctic enterprise, and one who should take rank next to Sir
Thomas Smith, although he was a much younger
man, was Sir Dudley Digges. He came of an emi-
nently learned and accomplished family. Roger
Digge was living at Mildenhall, in Suffolk, in the
reign of Henry III, and his descendant, James
Digges, came to Kent, and settled at Digges Court,
in Barham. Here his son Leonard, the grandfather
of Sir Dudley Digges, was born. Educated at Uni-

Place, married in 1652 the Lady Dorothy Sydney, widow of that
Earl of Sunderland who was slain at the battle of Newbury in 1643.
She was born in 1620, and was the "Saccharissa" of the poet
Waller. By this marriage there was one son, Robert Smythe,
Governor of Dover Castle, who died in 1698. By Catherine,
daughter of William Stafford of Blatherwicke, he had a son,
Henry Smythe, married to Elizabeth, daughter of Dr. Lloyd,
Canon of Windsor. Henry sold Brooke Place in 1699 to Sir
John le Thuillier, who pulled down the old house built by Sir
Thomas Smith. Dying in 1706, Henry Smythe left an only
child, Sydney Stafford Smythe, who was called to the bar in
1728, was Chief Baron in 1772, and died childless in 1778. Thus
the male line of Sir Thomas Smith became extinct.

versity College, Oxford, Leonard became an accomplished mathematician, architect, and surveyor. He was the author of several learned works,[1] some of which were edited by his son. Leonard Digges, who was of Wootton Court, in Kent, married Bridget, sister of those two gallant soldiers, James and Thomas Wilford, by whom he had a son Thomas. He died in 1574. This Thomas Digges inherited his father's tastes, and was one of the most eminent mathematicians of his time. He was Muster Master to the Queen's Army in the Netherlands from 1585, and prepared exhaustive reports on several important military positions, and on their fortification, with plans. Thomas Digges was as remarkable for his piety as for his learning.[2] He married Agnes, daughter of Sir William St. Leger, by Ursula, daughter of George Neville, Lord Abergavenny, by whom he had a son Dudley, and a daughter Margaret, married to Sir Anthony Palmer. The

[1] He wrote *Tectonicum*, a book on land surveying, 4to., 1556; second edition, edited by his son, 1592; third edition, 1597. Also, *Pantometria*, a geometrical treatise, published by his son, folio, 1591; and *Prognostication*, rules to judge the weather by sun, moon, and stars, 1555; new edition by his son, 1592.

[2] His works were, *Alae sive Scalae Mathematicae*, 4to., 1573; *Arithmetical Military Treatise*, 4to., 1579; "*Stratioticos*, a geometrical treatise requisite for the practice of soldiers", begun by his father. At the end there is a report of the proceedings of the Earl of Leicester for the relief of Sluys, from his arrival at Flushing in June 1587, proving that his Excellency was not in fault for the loss of the town, 4to., 1579, second edition, 1590; *Perfect Description of the Celestial Orbs*, 4to., 1599; *England's Defence*, a treatise concerning invasion, written 1589, published 1686, folio.

great mathematician died on August 24th, 1595,
and was buried in the church of St. Mary's, Alder-
manbury. His monument was destroyed in the great
fire of London, but the inscription is preserved in
Strype's edition of Stowe.

Dudley Digges was born in 1583, and was educated at his grandfather's old college at Oxford,
under Dr. Abbot, afterwards Archbishop of Canterbury. He took his degree in 1601, studied at
the Inns of Court, travelled on the Continent, and
was knighted on his return. In 1615, Sir Dudley
Digges published a reply to an attack on the East
India Company,[1] in which he gave an interesting
account of their ships, and of the progress of their
trade ; and from this time he appears to have been
intimately connected with Sir Thomas Smith's pro-
jects, and to have been his friend and worthy dis-
ciple. Sir Dudley was sent on an Embassy to
Russia, in 1618, and an account of his voyage to
Archangel is preserved in manuscript at Oxford.[2]

[1] *The Defence of Trade, in a Letter to Sir Thomas Smith,
Knight, Governor of the East India Company, from one of that
Societie,* London, 1615, pp. 50 ; signed " Dudley Digges". It is a
reply to a pamphlet entitled, *Increase of Trade.*

[2] *MS. Ashmole,* vol. 824, xvi, p. 175. " A Viag of Ambasad
undertaken by the Right Honnorable Sr Dudlie Diggs in the
year 1618." The narrative commences with the embassy leaving
the Thames in June 1618. The ship reached Archangel on July
14th, sailed for England again on August 5th, and reached St.
Katherine's, near London, on the 22nd. The manuscript ends
with notes on " Things by me observed", describing the Samoyeds,
the houses, carts, farms, and vegetation round Archangel, and
the Russian boats and sailing vessels. Pp. 22.

Next he was employed, in 1620, at the Hague, to obtain restitution of goods taken by the Dutch from English merchants in the East Indies. In the following year he entered Parliament, but he was so little compliant with Court measures, that he was sent to Ireland on a commission, but really as a punishment. He was again returned to Parliament, for the county of Kent, in 1626, and was one of the eight chief managers of the charges against the Duke of Buckingham, the others being Sir John Eliot, Pym, Selden, Wandesford, Glanvile, Sherland, and Herbert. Sir Dudley Digges, by way of prologue, made a short and eloquent speech, and read the preamble of the charges, while Sir John Eliot's speech concluded the impeachment. For these bold measures, both Sir Dudley Digges and Sir John Eliot were committed to the Tower, by command of Charles I. Buckingham accused Archbishop Abbot of instigating Sir Dudley and, in reply, the good old man spoke manfully in favour of his former pupil. "Ever since the days of Queen Elizabeth", he said, "I have been nearly acquainted with him. He was my pupil at Oxford, and a very towardly one. He calleth me father, and I call his wife my daughter, his eldest son is my godson, and their children are, in love, accounted my children." Digges continued to uphold the rights of the people. In 1627, he was appointed by the Commons to manage a conference with the Lords respecting the resolutions touching the liberty of the subject, and the right of every man to a writ of Habeas Corpus.

He opened the proceedings with an introductory historical speech of great ability, and was followed by Selden, Littleton, and Cook. In 1628 he was a member of another conference respecting the Petition of Right, and he boldly protested against the King's command to the Speaker, that no member should speak against the Government.[1] In April 1636, Sir Dudley Digges succeeded Sir Julius Cæsar as Master of the Rolls, and he died on March 18th, 1639.[2]

Sir Dudley Digges married Mary, daughter of Sir Thomas Kempe, the heiress of Chilham, near Canterbury; where he built a stately mansion. His wife was a kinswoman of Sir Thomas Smith, both being descendants of Philippa Chicheley, and therefore founder's kin of All Souls. Sir Dudley and Lady Digges had ten children, of whom the eldest, Thomas Digges, succeeded to Chilham, married Mary, daughter of Sir Maurice Abbot, and died in 1687. His son Leonard Digges died in 1718, leaving a son, Thomas, whose eldest son died at Cork in 1787. The second son, West Digges, was a well

[1] *Rushworth*, vol. i, pp. 55, 302, 356, 360, 361, 450, 451, 521, 527, 546, 606.

[2] Besides the *Defence of Trade*, Sir Dudley Digges was the author of the *Compleat Ambassador*, London, folio, 1665, which contains the correspondence between Sir F. Walsingham, Burleigh, Leicester, and others respecting the two treaties of the intended marriage of Queen Elizabeth. The frontispiece consists of engravings by Faithorne of Elizabeth, Burleigh, and Walsingham. He also wrote, *Digiti Lingua*, the most compendious way of silent converse ever yet discovered, London, 12mo., 1693.

known comedian, and here I have lost touch of the descendants. Chilham had long before passed away to Colebrookes, Herons, Wildmans, and is now the property of Mr. Charles Stewart Hardy.[1] But the old house, built by Sir Dudley Digges, is still standing. It is beautifully situated on a hill, sloping away on every side. The village of Chilham, consisting of old-fashioned thatched houses, is built round a green, at one end the church, at the other a short avenue, leading to the old manor house. The mansion was finished in 1616, and the names of Sir Dudley Digges, and of his wife Mary Kempe, are carved over the hall door. It is a brick structure, with stone doorway and dressings, square turrets at each angle of the front, and a beautiful oriel window over the carved doorway. The two wings are at an obtuse angle to the front, a peculiar arrangement giving increased space, and the means of arranging most picturesque vistas and angles in the interior. Behind is the ancient keep of the feudal castle of the Badlesmeres, with enormously thick walls. A series of terraces with wall fruit, slope down to a well timbered park, and there are lovely views from the windows. Truly, this patriotic Merchant Adventurer, and bold asserter of his country's liberties, had a most lovely English home. Here, surrounded by wife and children, he retired from the cares of State, and here he died at the age of fifty-six.

Sir Dudley Digges was buried in Chilham church,

[1] In 1724, Thomas Digges sold Chilham to a mercer of London named Colebrooke, whose son sold it to Heron in 1775.

a cruciform edifice with double aisles. Over his
grave was erected a magnificent tomb. On a square
pedestal of white marble are seated four life-size
female figures, and in their midst rises a pillar of
black marble surmounted by an urn, with four
shields of arms hanging round it.[1] On each side
of the pedestal there are black marble tablets with
inscriptions. That on the western side preserves
the memory of Sir Dudley Digges himself, "whose
death the wisest men doe reckon amongst the publique calamities of these times". On the south side
there is a genealogical account of his family in
Latin. The eastern tablet bears an inscription to
the memory of Lady Digges, the heiress of Chilham,
while the northern tablet records her virtues. Sir
Dudley left £20 yearly to keep this monument in
repair, the surplus to be given to the poor. The
name of this noble promoter of voyages of discovery
is also immortalised by the Cape, on the coast of
Baffin's Bay, which is so often mentioned in modern
Arctic voyages.

Baffin's most immediate patron, to whom he addressed his letters, was Sir John Wolstenholme.
His father, John Wolstenholme, was a native of
Derbyshire. He came up to London, and after
making a fortune, established himself at Stanmore
Magna, near Harrow. His son, Sir John, born in
1562, was a Farmer of the Customs, and a most
active promoter of voyages for the discovery of the

---

[1] The arms of Digges, of Kemp, of Kemp and Digges impaled,
and a fourth which I could not make out.

North-West Passage. He was knighted by James I
at Whitehall, on March 12th, 1617. He built the
church at Stanmore, which was consecrated by Archbishop Laud in 1632, at his sole expense. He died,
aged seventy-seven, on November 25th, 1639, and
was buried in Stanmore church, where there is a
handsome monument to his memory. His second
son, Henry, was slain in the Palatinate, while serving under Lord Vere. The eldest, Sir John, was
knighted by Charles I, on May 18th, 1633. He succeeded to Nostell Priory, in Yorkshire, which had
been purchased by his father. He was a great suf-
ferer during the civil war, having joined the Royalist
side, but was created a Baronet at the Restoration,
and, dying in 1670, he was buried at Stanmore.
His eldest son, John, who died before him, married
Dorothy, the daughter of Lord Vere, and sister of
Lady Fairfax, but had no children. Both were
buried under a stately monument at Stanmore.[1]
His second son, Henry, was slain at Marston Moor.
The baronetcy became extinct with Sir Francis Wolstenholme, who died in 1780.

Sir William Cockayne, Sir James Lancaster, and
Mr. Richard Ball,[2] were also among those liberal
patrons of Arctic discovery whose ventures enabled
the ships to be fitted out, and whose patriotic zeal

---

[1] For an account of monuments in Stanmore Church, and ex-
tracts from the registers, see Lysons' *Environs of London*, first
edition, 1795, vol. iii, pp. 395-400.

[2] See notices in foot notes at page 3.

infused a similar spirit into the hearts of the gallant seamen whom they employed.

In Baffin's first recorded voyage, the wealthy adventurers wisely associated with themselves the commander of the expedition; and it is, therefore, necessary to give some account of the brave seaman in whose company our discoverer first appears. James Hall was a Yorkshireman, and almost certainly a native of Hull.[1] We first hear of him as chief pilot of an expedition sent by Christian IV, King of Denmark, to discover the lost colonies of Greenland. It consisted of three ships: the *Trost*[2] (Comfort), with the admiral on board, a Scottish officer named John Cunningham, and James Hall as chief Pilot, was the leading vessel. The second, named *Löven*, was commanded by a Dane—Godske Lindenov; and the third was a pinnace, called *Kathen*, under an Englishman named John Knight. The expedition sailed from Copenhagen, on May 2nd, 1605, and sighted Greenland on the 30th. Soon afterwards, the *Löven* parted company and went home, after hot words. The *Trost* pressed onwards, and came to land under a hill named Mount Cunningham, between the headlands which were called Capes Anne and Sophia, after the Queen and Queen Dowager of Denmark. They were in the neighbourhood of the modern Greenland settlement of Holsteinborg. The Danes had much communication with the Eskimo, and Hall gives an interesting account of them. The *Trost* and *Kathen* safely re-

---

[1] Luke Fox.   [2] Purchas calls her the *Frost*.

turned to Elsinore on August 10th.[1] John Knight then went back to England, but Hall continued in the Danish service. Knight commanded an expedition in the year 1606, in which he perished. I printed the narrative of Knight's voyage, from the original manuscript at the India Office, in 1877.[2] The King of Denmark fitted out a second expedition in 1606, consisting of five vessels. There were the *Trost* of sixty tons, with Godske Lindenov as admiral, and Hall as chief pilot ; the *Löven*, of seventy tons, under John Cunningham ; the *Ornen* (100 tons), commanded by a Norwegian named Hans Brun, a Scotch vessel of forty tons, called the *Gilliflower*, under Corsten Richardson, and the pinnace *Kathen*, of twenty tons, under Anders Nolk[3] of Bergen. Sailing from Copenhagen on May 27th, 1606, they were beset by mighty banks of ice, and

[1] Hall's account of the voyage is given in *Purchas*, iii, lib. iv, cap. xiv, p. 814. There is another brief account in a Danish work, "*Reiser til Grönland om de vigtigste reiser som i nyere tider ere foretagne fra Danmark og Norge for igjen at opsöge det tabte Grönland og at undersöge set gjenfunde*, af C. Pingel," Kjobenhavn, 1845. Pingel quotes a manuscript written on board the *Kathen*. The original is now in a quarto volume, containing various papers about Greenland, in the Royal Library at Stockholm (K. 29). The manuscript was captured by Charles X in the library of Soro in Zealand, and taken by him to Sweden. It consists of six quarto leaves, with the title, "*Sanndferdigh Berettningh om thenn Groenlanndez reise som Konng May 3 Skiff giorde*, anno 1605." It is in the form of a ship's journal, and is signed "Alexander Leyell".

[2] At the end of the Hakluyt Society's volume, *The Voyages of Sir James Lancaster, Knight, to the East Indies*, p. 281.

[3] Purchas calls him Noll.

did not reach Greenland until July, anchoring off Cunningham Fiord, to the north of Cape Sophia. The glittering mica, occurring in the gneiss, was mistaken for silver ore, and the idea of unbounded mineral wealth was indulged in by the explorers. As on the former voyage, several Eskimo were seized with their kayaks, to be taken to Denmark, and some were killed. These outrages led to fatal retaliation when Hall appeared among the Eskimo in a subsequent voyage; while the wretched captives pined away and died. The Greenland expedition returned in October 1606;[1] but King Christian still persevered. In the following year a third expedition, under Carsten Richardson, was despatched with Hall on board the *Gilliflower* as pilot, and "styrmand". But the crews mutinied, and the vessels never got beyond Iceland. Purchas had the journal of this third voyage in his possession, with curious drawings by Josias Hubert[2] of Hull, but he says that he omitted to print it because of the mutiny.[3] Christian IV then gave up his attempts to re-discover old Greenland.

James Hall consequently returned to England, eager to embark once more on discoveries in the

[1] Pingel gives a narrative written by Hans Brun, captain of the *Ornen*, of the second expedition, the manuscript of which is also in the Royal Library at Stockholm.

[2] Afterwards pilot in the *Resolution* in Sir Thomas Button's expedition.

[3] There is a brief account of this third voyage in the work of Claus Christophersen Lyschander, Royal Historiographer of Denmark, entitled, *Den Grönlandsche Chronica* (Kbhvn., 1808).

direction of Greenland, and full of ideas respecting silver ores and other mineral wealth. His faithful follower, a Scarborough lad named William Huntriss, who had accompanied him in all his voyages, and had become so proficient as a navigator that King Christian had granted him a special allowance, came back with Hall. There is, in the British Museum, a manuscript report on Hall's voyages to Greenland, with several coloured maps and sketches of coast lines, which is addressed to the King of Denmark. When Christian IV abandoned the work, Hall probably withheld this report, brought it with him to England, and presented it to King James.[1]

James Hall induced four great Merchant Princes to be venturers with him in a voyage of discovery to Greenland in 1612. His partners were Sir Thomas Smith himself, Sir James Lancaster, Sir William Cockayne, and Mr. Ball. Two vessels, called the *Patience* and the *Heart's Ease*, were fitted out at Hull, and William Baffin first appears in history as pilot on board Hall's ship, the *Patience*.

We are thus first introduced to WILLIAM BAFFIN as an experienced seaman, in the prime of life, and I have been baffled in all my attempts to discover even a single fact respecting his former history. The name is very uncommon, and I am indebted to the

[1] *MS. Bibl. Reg.*, 17 A, xlviii, p. 261. The manuscript contains a narrative, a coloured map of King Christian's Fiord in Greenland, another of Cunningham's Fiord, a third of Brade Ranson's Fiord, a fourth of the "coast of Greenland, with latitudes of havens and harbours as I found them".

obliging kindness of Colonel Chester, to whose research I also owe many facts and dates relating to the Merchant Adventurers, for the very few entries where it occurs. There is no trace of the name at Hull, the place where Baffin first appears to us. From the Parish Registers of St. Margaret, Westminster, Colonel Chester has supplied me with the following entries :—

Baptized 1603. Sept. 30.	Richard, son of John Baffin.	
Buried 1609. June 8.	Joseph Baffin.	*Plague.*
„ „ 22.	Elizabeth Baffin.	„
„ July 11.	William Baffin.	„
1612 June 8.	Margaret Baffin.	*Child.*

In the Register of the church of St. Thomas Apostle, in the city of London, there is one entry of the name.

Baptized 1609. Oct. 15.   Susan Baffen, daughter of William Baffen.

Colonel Chester has kindly looked at the indexes to his collections from parish registers and monuments, extending all over the kingdom, in more than one hundred folio volumes, comprising upwards of a million and a half of names, and the only instances of the name of Baffin are the above. We are, therefore, justified in the conclusion that it is extremely uncommon. Between 1603 and 1612, we find five individuals named Baffin, three men, a woman, and a child, dying in St. Margaret's parish, Westminster, the three adults of the plague. One is named William Baffin. A child named Richard Baffin is born in St. Margaret's parish in 1603.

Lastly, the child of a William Baffin is baptized
in 1609, in the church of St. Thomas the Apostle,[1]
in Vintry Ward, within the city of London. This
ward includes Queenhithe, a landing-place frequented by sailors, and not an unlikely locality for
a seaman to take up his abode in, while on shore.

These meagre facts lead to the conjecture that
William Baffin was a native of London or Westminster, that he had relations living in the parish
of St. Margaret, and that he himself had established
a home for his wife, and for himself when on shore,
in the city, in the parish of St. Thomas, and probably in a street near Queenhithe, where his daughter,
named Susan, was born in 1609. But Baffin himself must have been constantly at sea, and probably
raised himself, by his good conduct and talent, from
a very humble position. I gather that Purchas intended to convey such an idea, when he speaks of
Baffin as "that learned-unlearned mariner and mathematician, who, wanting art of words, so really
employed himself to those industries, whereof here
you see so evident fruits".[2] If he was not a Hull
man, he probably was not known to Captain Hall,
and it may, therefore, be conjectured that, when
Hall induced the great London merchants to join
in his venture, one of them recommended Baffin to
him, as an accomplished seaman. Accordingly, William Baffin was chief pilot of Captain Hall's ship,
the *Patience*, when, in company with the *Heart's*

[1] The church of St. Thomas Apostle was burnt at the great
fire and was not rebuilt.   [2] See page 154.

Ease, she was hauled into Hull Road on April 10th, 1612. Andrew Barker, the master of the *Heart's Ease*, the mate, William Huntriss, and the quartermaster, John Gatonby, were all Yorkshiremen. The expedition finally left the Humber, and made sail for Greenland on the 22nd of April.

The narrative of this voyage was written by Baffin himself, though Purchas has only preserved a fragment, commencing on July 8th in Cockin Sound, on the coast of Greenland. But, in Churchill's *Collection of Voyages and Travels*, there is a journal of the voyage kept by one of the quartermasters named John Gatonby, a native of Hull, and dedicated to Sir Christopher Hildyard of Winestead. I have, therefore, printed the portion of Gatonby's journal from the commencement of the voyage to July 8th, the time when Baffin's fragment, in Purchas, commences. Thus the whole story of the voyage is presented, though only the last half is in Baffin's own words. Captain Hall himself was murdered by the Eskimo, in revenge for the kidnapping perpetrated by the Danes, with whom he served in the two previous voyages, and the expedition returned in charge of Andrew Barker. Baffin relates the events of the voyage while the ships were on the Greenland coast, including the death and burial of Hall, and concludes with some account of the Greenland Eskimo and their country. He examined the west coast, from Godthaab northward to Cunningham Fiord, and, as was his wont, made numerous astronomical observations.

As soon as he returned from Greenland, William Baffin entered the service of the Muscovy Company. This enterprising body of merchants, under the lead of Sir Thomas Smith, began to send ships to fish for whales near Spitzbergen, in 1597. In 1607 and 1608, the Company despatched Henry Hudson on his two important voyages to Spitzbergen and Novaya Zemlya. In the years 1609 and 1610, they sent Captain Jonas Pool, who carefully explored the whole of the west coast of Spitzbergen, naming Bell Sound, Ice Sound, and several other positions. He wrote interesting journals, which are given in Purchas, and had a prosperous career before him. But it was his ill-fate to be "miserably and basely murdered betwixt Ratcliffe and London", after his return in 1611. In the following year the Muscovy Company obtained a charter, excluding all others from the Spitzbergen fishery, native and foreign. The concession of this charter was followed by very high-handed proceedings on the part of the English, and in 1612 a fleet was sent out by the Muscovy Company, which drove away from the Spitzbergen coast fifteen sail of Dutch, French, and Biscayans.

It is remarkable that, although the Biscayans, when in their own ships, were hunted away, the English were obliged to learn the craft and mystery of whale fishing from Biscayans whom they entered on board their own ships. In the middle ages there was a great whale frequenting the Bay of Biscay, and the Atlantic, which is now extinct, known to

naturalists as the *Balæna Biscayensis*.[1] The fishermen of Biscay and Guipuzcoa had been engaged in
pursuing this whale from time immemorial, and the
dangerous occupation had trained up a most expert
and daring race of sailors along those coasts. A
whale figures in the arms of the Guipuzcoan towns
of Fuentarrabia, Guetaria, and Motrico; and the
whale fishery was long the chief source of wealth
to all the ports from St. Jean de Luz to Santander.
The King of Spain, in conceding privileges to San
Sebastian, and other whaling ports, retained his own
right to a strip of blubber from the head to the foot
of the whale, as the royal share.[2] But gradually the
Biscayan whale became more and more scarce, and
the Basque fishermen began to frequent the Newfoundland banks, where 41 vessels, and 298 boats,
employing 1,470 sailors, were annually sent from
Guipuzcoa and Biscay, in the early part of the
seventeenth century.[3] The Biscayans were still the
most expert whale fishers when the Moscovy Company began to send whaling ships to Spitzbergen,
and it was the practice to enter a Basque boat's
crew, from St. Jean de Luz or San Sebastian, on
board one or more of the vessels of each fleet.
Orders were given that they were "to be used very

---

[1] A complete skeleton was found in the peat of Jutland, and
is now in the Museum at Copenhagen.

[2] "Et si mactaveritis aliquam ballenam detis mihi unam tiram
a capite usque ad caudam sicut forum est."—*Grant of San Fer-
nando*, 1217-1232.

[3] The privileges of the Biscayan fishermen on the Newfoundland banks were recognised by Article 15 of the Treaty of Utrecht.

kindly and friendly, being strangers, and leaving their own country to do us service". At the same time, the Biscayan vessels were forcibly driven from Spitzbergen waters.[1]

A fleet of seven ships was fitted out by the Muscovy Company in 1613, the command of which was given to Captain Benjamin Joseph. He was on board the *Tiger* of 260 tons, with William Baffin as chief pilot; and twenty-four Biscayans were engaged for the voyage. One ship of St. Jean de Luz had permission from the Company to fish, perhaps in return for the two dozen expert whalers. The English found as many as seventeen foreign ships on the Spitzbergen coast—four Dutch, two Dunkirkers, four hailing from St. Jean de Luz, and seven from San Sebastian. All submitted to the English, most were ordered away, a few being allowed to fish on condition of surrendering half their catch to the English ships. The Company's fleet returned safely in September, with full cargoes. The narrative of this voyage was written by Baffin himself, and is given in Purchas. There is a second narrative, probably by Robert Fotherby, which remained in manuscript until it was printed by the

---

[1] " Todavia la celebre compania de ballenas sostenia en el mayor esplendor el comercio de San Sebastian y aun de toda la provincia, empero los Ingleses, rivales de los Vascongados para alzarse en el beneficio de la pesca de las ballenas, y con tal objeto, enviaron en 1613 dos galeones armados a las costas de la Groenlandia, en cuyo punto se hacia a la sazon, abundante pesca de ballenas, y apresaron doce barcos de Guipuzcoanos."—*Madoz*, ix, p. 163.

American Antiquarian Society.[1] I have reprinted
both these accounts of the voyage of 1613, one following the other. Fotherby concludes his journal
by giving an interesting description of Spitzbergen,
and of the whale fishery.

Baffin served again in the Spitzbergen voyage
of 1614, which was also commanded by Benjamin
Joseph. This time the fleet consisted of no less
than eleven ships and two pinnaces. Fotherby and
Baffin were together in a ship called the *Thomasine*,
and the former wrote the narrative, which is given
by Purchas. During the summer, very persevering
attempts were made by Fotherby and Baffin to extend discovery to the eastward, along the north
coast of Spitzbergen. Leaving their ship in a harbour, they provisioned two shallops, and, on several
occasions advanced eastward, until they were stopped
by the ice. At length, in August, they reached
Wiches Sound (*Wiide Bay* of modern maps), and
walked thence until they came to the entrance of
Sir Thomas Smith's Inlet (Hinlopen Strait), encountering much danger on their return. Finally, the
ship sailed, towards the end of the season, twenty
leagues E.N.E. from Cape Barren (*Vogelsang* of the
Dutch), being nine or ten leagues off shore, which
brought her off Sir Thomas Smith's Inlet. Such a
course and distance from Vogelsang would bring a
vessel off Hinlopen Strait; and this identifies the
Sir Thomas Smith's Inlet of our old navigators with
the Hinlopen Strait of the Dutch. It was the

_____
[1] For an account of this manuscript see p. 54 (*note*).

furthest point reached by Baffin. The year 1614 was very unfavourable for navigation, the ice having been close down on the north coast during the greater part of the season. Baffin returned to London on the 4th of October with the whole crew in perfect health.

After his second voyage to Spitzbergen, Baffin took service with the Company for the discovery of the North-West Passage, which was directed by Sir Thomas Smith, Sir Dudley Digges, and John Wolstenholme. These princely adventurers had, in 1610, furnished out the gallant explorer Henry Hudson, to try if, through any of those inlets which were seen by John Davis, a passage could be found. His ship was named the *Discovery*, and, after discovering the great inland sea which bears his name, and wintering on its shores, he was abandoned to his fate in an open boat, by the villainous crew. The well known story was told by a servant of Sir Dudley Digges, who remained on board, named Abacuk Prickett. The Company next sent out Sir Thomas Button, with Robert Bylot and Abacuk Prickett under him, who had both been with Hudson in his last voyage. Henry, Prince of Wales, took special interest in this expedition. Sir Thomas Button, a talented officer, was selected by the Prince, who drew up the instructions.[1] Button commanded the *Discovery*, and the second ship, under Captain Ingram, was named the *Resolution*. They sailed in

---

[1] The poor young Prince died on November 6th, 1612, aged eighteen years and a half, before Button returned.

May 1612, and wintered at Port Nelson, on the
eastern side of Hudson's Bay. Sir Thomas Button
thus made an important discovery, and he returned,
in the autumn of 1613, strongly impressed with the
idea that a North-West Passage existed. The *Discovery* was sent out, for a third time, under the
command of Captain Gibbons, who had been with
Button in the previous year. He sailed in the
spring of 1614, but only reached the coast of Labrador, where he took shelter in a bay, and remained
there so long that his crew named it *Gibbons his
hole*. He returned home in the autumn.

This was the record of the Company's proceedings
when Baffin took service under it. Three expeditions had been sent out under Hudson, Button, and
Gibbons. The two first had made great discoveries,
and the Company was not discouraged. The adventurers resolved to fit out the *Discovery* for a
fourth voyage. Robert Bylot, who had been in
the three previous voyages, was appointed master,
and William Baffin was pilot of the expedition. An
excellent system of keeping log books, inaugurated
by Sebastian Cabot, was enforced by the Muscovy
Company, and the officers of its ships were expected
to take frequent astronomical observations. Baffin,
who had a natural love for such work, was given an
excellent training while serving under the Company
in his two Spitzbergen voyages, and he continued
the same admirable system in his western enterprises under the North-West Passage Company.
The whole history of the expedition of 1614 was

written by Baffin himself. It is printed by Purchas, but the manuscript, preserved in the British Museum, is fuller. This manuscript was first edited by Mr. Rundall, who very carefully collated it with the narrative in Purchas. Mr. Rundall's edition has now been reprinted, the matter omitted by Purchas being printed in italics, and alterations and additions, in the Purchas version, being noticed in the foot-notes.

Baffin begins with a letter addressed to his patrons, Sir Thomas Smith, Sir Dudley Digges, and Sir John Wolstenholme. He describes his method in preparing the tabulated log book, and in delineating the coast on his map, which is also preserved with the manuscript. As it is the only map, by this accomplished seaman, that has come down to us, it has been thought desirable to reproduce it, as a *facsimile*. It shows Baffin's style of drawing, and is very interesting as a real specimen of his handiwork. The letter to his employers is introductory to a tabulated log book, called *The Breefe Journall*. Then follows "A true relation of such things as happened in fourth voyage for the discovery of a passage to the North-West, performed in the yeare 1615."

In this voyage Baffin carefully examined Hudson Strait and the western end of Southampton Island. Sir Edward Parry passed over the same ground in 1821, and noticed the places named by Baffin with interest. Parry's observations on the tides confirm those of Baffin, and the latitudes of the older navigator were found to be nearly correct. On August 6th, 1821, Parry was nearly on the spot where Baffin left off his search for a passage. Baffin's reasons for relinquishing the attempt in that direction were the increased quantity of ice, the water becoming less deep, and his seeing land bearing N.E. b. E., which led him to conclude that he was at the mouth of a large bay. Parry gave this land the name of Baffin Island, "out of respect to the memory of that able and enterprising navigator". Here Parry's own discoveries commenced.[1]

Returning in the autumn of 1615, Baffin prepared for his fifth and most important Arctic voyage, during which he discovered the great bay which bears his name. The enterprise was again undertaken by Sir Thomas Smith, Sir Francis Jones, Sir Dudley Digges, and Sir John Wolstenholme, and the same good ship *Discovery*, of 55 tons, with 16 men, was fitted out, with Robert Bylot (or Bileth) as master, and William Baffin as pilot. They set sail from Gravesend on the 26th of March 1616, and on the 1st of June, having passed Hope Sanderson of Davis, they entered upon new discoveries. It is an irreparable misfortune that Baffin's papers and maps should have fallen into the hands of old Purchas. It was upwards of two centuries before the mischief done by his suppression of the journal and maps was repaired. We must, however, be thankful for what

---

[1] *Journal of the Second Voyage for the Discovery of a North-West Passage*, by Captain W. Edward Parry, R.N., F.R.S. Murray, 1824, p. 33.

the Rev. Samuel has spared. He printed Baffin's *Briefe and True Relation*,[1] and his interesting letter to Sir John Wolstenholme,[2] and certainly these two precious documents furnish us with the main incidents of Baffin's great discovery, and with his opinions and conclusions. But when Baffin tells us that "all these sounds and islands the map doth truly describe", we are treated to the following exasperating marginal note by Purchas :—"This map of the author, with the tables of his journall and sayling, were somewhat troublesome and too costly to insert". I shall have to refer to this conduct of Baffin's injudicious editor further on, when we come to consider its consequences.

Baffin had now made five voyages to the Arctic Regions. The fiords and islets of West Greenland, the glaciers and ice floes of Spitzbergen, the tidal phenomena of Hudson's Straits, and the unveiled geographical secrets of the far northern bay, were all familiar to him. He had practically sought out, and deeply pondered over the absorbing questions of polar discovery. As an astronomical observer and navigator, his unwearied diligence was as remarkable as his talent, and in this branch of study he was certainly in advance of his contemporaries. If he was a self-taught man, who had risen from a humble origin, he had so far educated himself as to be able to write letters which are not only well expressed, but graced with classical allusions. He was probably past middle age when, in August 1616,

[1] See pages 138 to 149.   [2] See pages 149 to 155.

he returned from his great discovery, and sought for some new employment.

It was not to be expected that the Arctic problems, so fascinating to all who study them, could be effaced from Baffin's mind. It would appear that the bold navigator, like John Davis before him, conceived the idea of attempting the passage from Japan, and the coast of Asia ;[1] and this ambitious hope led him to seek service under the East India Company. The seventh joint-stock voyage was to be undertaken in 1617; and the fleet, which was to be commanded by Captain Martin Pring, was being fitted out during the winter. Baffin obtained an appointment in it, as master's mate on board the *Anne Royal*.

In 1616, the trade of the East India Company was well established; the profits had been very large, and the enterprise was already a great success. Fleets had been annually sent out since 1601; and ships, of a size hitherto unknown, had been built to bring home the rich cargoes from the East. The fleet which was prepared in the winter of 1616, to make the seventh joint-stock voyage, was under the chief command of Captain Martin Pring. The Admiral was a ship called the *Royal James*, of 1,320 tons, with Captain Pring on board, and Rowland Coytmore as master. The *Anne Royal*, of 1,057 tons, was commanded by Andrew Shilling, of whom there was a good report, and who "was not inferior

[1] See page 156.

to any man for government". William Baffin served
under him as master's mate. The other ships of
the fleet were the *New Yeere's Gift*, of 867 tons,
"new built of Irish timber",[1] of which Nathaniel
Salmon was master; the *Bull*, of 400 tons, Robert
Adams, master; and the *Bee*, of 15 tons, John
Hatch, master.

In those days the chief commander of a fleet was
called the General, and his ship was the Admiral,
and the second in command was the Lieutenant-
General, sailing in the Vice-Admiral. The captain
conducted warlike operations, and the master was
responsible for the navigation and safety of the ship,
and for the merchandize; but frequently the two
offices were united. The purser was also held ac-
countable for the cargo, under sureties, and for the
provisions. The *Romager* regulated the stowage.
The ordinary food for the sailors consisted of bread,
meal, dry salted beef, pickled beef and pork, peas,
beans, cod, and stock fish, beer, and cyder. Other
articles, coming under the head of "victualling ex-
traordinarie", were cheese, butter, sweet oil, vinegar,
aquavitæ, honey, mustard, rice, lamp oil, candles.
Great attention was paid to the quality of the meat,
the Company slaughtering their own beasts at
Blackwall. Special instructions were given for diet
and discipline, and strong injunctions were issued on
the necessity for cleanliness, and other precautions
for preserving health. The most terrible scourge,
in the early voyages to India, was the scurvy. In

[1] Sir Dudley Digges' *Defence of Trade*.

a curious little book, called the *Surgeon's Mate*,[1] the prevention and cure of this disease are very fully discussed. The causes of scurvy are said to be infinite and unsearchable; but the chief exciting causes were believed to be long continuance of salt diet, want of sufficient food, and of wine and beer to comfort and warm the stomach, want of changes of clothes, not keeping the clothes clean and dry, and not keeping the cabins sweet and clean. The men were attacked on the voyage from England to the Cape, and on landing they grew strong again, cured by fresh air and fresh food. When deprived of fresh food, the surgeon is recommended to use wine, sugar, and spices, to see that the men's sleeping places are clean and sweet, and to provide themselves with juice of oranges, limes, and lemons, wherever they touch. A quantity of lime juice was always sent on board, by the good care of the merchants; and the instructions were that it should be

---

[1] " *The Surgeon's Mate,* or a treatise discovering faithfully and plainly the due contents of the surgeon's chest, the uses of the instruments, the virtues and operations of the medicines, the cures of the most frequent diseases at sea, namely wounds, apostumes, ulcers, fractures, dislocations, with the true manner of amputation, the cure of the scurvie, the fluxes of the belly, of the collica and *illica passio*, the callenture, with a briefe explanation of sal, sulphur, and mercury, with certaine characters and tearmes of arte. Published chiefly for the benefit of young sea surgeons imployed in the East India Companies affaires, by John Woodall, Master in Chirurgery." London, printed at the Tyger's Head in Paul's Churchyard, 1617, pp. 348, small 4to.

" To the farre renowned, vertuous, and worthy knight, Sir Thomas Smith, Governor of the East India Company, my singular good patrone."

given daily to the men in health, as a preservative. "To that terrible disease of the scurvy, how excellent hath it been approved".[1]

When an East Indian fleet was fully equipped, it was usually inspected by Sir Thomas Smith, or his deputy, before sailing. The fleet, commanded by Martin Pring, left Gravesend on February 4th, 1617, and Maurice Abbot, the Deputy-Governor of the East India Company, with divers Commissioners, came on board on the 6th, mustered the men, and paid the wages. On the 5th of March, the ships weighed anchor in the Downs, and after a prosperous voyage, they arrived at Saldanha Bay on the 21st of June. Captain Pring was obliged to use force, to get a supply of cattle and sheep; but a number were obtained, which overjoyed the hearts of the sick men. In September 1617, the fleet arrived at Surat.[2]

---

[1] *Surgeon's Mate*, p. 194.

[2] There are three accounts of the proceedings of this fleet in *Purchas*.

    I. "Relations and Remembrances taken out of a large Journall of a voyage set forth by the East India Societie, wherein were employed the *James*, the *Anne*, the *New Yeere's Gift*, the *Bull*, and the *Bee*, written by John Hatch, master of the *Bee*, and after of the *New Yeere's Gift*, and lately came home in the *James*." Vol. i, p. 168, lib. v, cap. iiii.

    II. "Voyage of the *Anne Royall* from Surat to Mocha in the Red Sea for settling an English trade in those parts, 1618, extracted out of Master Edward Heynes, his Journal." Vol. i, lib. v, cap. v, p. 622.

    III. Second voyage of Captain Pring. Vol. i, lib. v, cap. vii, p. 601.

In the India Office there is a manuscript journal written by Robert Adams the master of the *Bull* (No. 20). A very meagre log.

It was then determined to send Captain Shilling
to the Red Sea, "for settling an English trade in
those parts". Instructions were drawn up by Sir
Thomas Roe, the Ambassador at the Court of the
Mogul, and three merchants, named Joseph Salbanke, Edward Heynes, and Richard Barber, were
selected to conduct the business. The *Anne Royal*
sailed from Swally Roads on March 17th, and anchored off Mocha on the 13th of April 1618. The
merchants then went on shore with presents to the
Governor, and eventually Captain Shilling succeeded
in obtaining a Firman from the Pasha, for English
merchants to trade at Mocha and Aden. In May,
the *Anne Royal* crossed the Red Sea to the bay of
Assab, on the African side, for the benefit of the
sick men, to procure ballast, and also with a view to
exploring the coast ; and Baffin was very diligently
employed in surveying and preparing charts. On
July 21st, the ship returned to Mocha, and on the
20th of August Captain Shilling sailed for India.
Later in the year the *Anne Royal* was in the Persian
Gulf, and Baffin again made good use of his time,
observing and surveying the coasts. Returning to
Surat, the *Anne Royal* commenced her homeward
voyage in February, and arrived in the Thames in
September 1619. She was ordered to unlade at
Woolwich.

Baffin had been absent on this voyage to the East
Indies for more than two years, from 1617 to 1619,
and had won both the confidence of his immediate
superior, and the approbation of the Company. In

the Court's Minutes of October 1st, 1619, there is the following entry : " William Baffyn, a master's mate in the *Anne,* to have a gratuity for his pains and good art in drawing out certain plots of the coast of Persia and the Red Sea, which are judged to have been very well and artificially performed ; some to be drawn out by Adam Bowen, for the benefit of such as shall be employed in those parts."[1]

Captain Andrew Shilling commanded the *Anne Royal* so ably, and conducted important negotiations with such discretion and zeal, that he was selected to have charge of the fleet in the following year. It consisted of four new ships, the building of which was only completed in the end of 1619. The great ship, built at Deptford, was named the *London,* and Captain Shilling was allowed to choose her as his Admiral. The *Harte,* commanded by Captain Blithe, was the Vice-Admiral. The other two ships were the *Roebuck,* under Captain Richard Swan, and the *Eagle,* whose master was Christopher Browne.

William Baffin, at the special recommendation of Captain Shilling, was appointed master of the *London,*[2] and he thus received the command of a ship for the first time. He had worked his way zealously and resolutely, and had become one of the

---

[1] *Calendar of State Papers (Colonial), East India,* 1617 21, p. 257, para. 748.

Adam Bowen was a clerk in the Company's counting house, and was also employed to draw up sailing directions from the journals, and to prepare fair copies of charts.

[2] *Calendar of State Papers (Colonial), East Indies,* 1617-21, para. 758.

best astronomical observers of his day, a daring and skilful navigator, and even a great discoverer, before his distinguished services were recognised, and he at length became the master of a large ship.[1]

On the 4th of February 1620, the *London* set sail from Gravesend, and on the 25th of March she departed from the Downs, with the rest of the fleet in company.[2] On June 25th they reached Saldanha Bay, and on July 20th Baffin was present at a consultation on board the *London,* as to whether it would be better to go within or without the island of St. Lawrence or Madagascar. After a long voyage they anchored in Swally Road, on the 9th November. Here news was received that a combined force of Portuguese and Dutch ships was waiting off Jáshak, near the entrance of the Persian Gulf, to intercept and attack the English ships. The fleet, therefore, left Swally on November 19th, and went in search of the enemy. On the 16th of December, Captain

[1] Officers of the *London*—William Baffin, master ; Bartholomew Symonds, surgeon ; Nicholas Crispe, purser; John Woolhouse, chaplain ; Robert Jefferies, John Barker, Edward Monox, merchants ; Archibald Jennison, master's mate ; Edwyn Guy, purser's mate.

[2] There are two journals kept on board ships belonging to this fleet, among the manuscript logs at the India Office.

No. 24. "The journal of Archibald Jennison on board the *London,* commanded by Captain Andrew Shillinge, from 1620 to 1622." Thirty-seven and a quarter MS. pages.

No. 25. "The journal of Captain Richard Swan of the *Roebuck* (300 tons) from 1620 to 1622." Sixty-eight pages. This journal of Richard Swan is also given by *Purchas,* vol. i, lib. v, cap. 16, p. 723.

Shilling, with his four ships, came in sight of two large Portuguese ships, and two smaller Flemish vessels, forming a fleet under the command of Ruy Frere de Andrado, with Joam Boralio as Vice-Admiral. The fight commenced at once, and continued, without intermission, for nine hours. The Portuguese then anchored to repair damages, and the English ships, after raking them, put into Jáshak Roads, on the Mekran coast. The two fleets watched each other for ten days, and a second and more decisive encounter took place on the 28th of December.

Captain Swan, in the manuscript journal at the India Office, gives a lively account of the second fight. He says :—" Our broadsides were brought up, and the good ordinance from our whole fleet played so fast upon them that, doubtless, if the knowledge in our people had been answerable to their willing minds and ready resolutions, not one of the galleons, unless their sides were impenetrable, had escaped us. About three in the afternoon, unwilling, after so hotte a dinner, to receive a like supper, they cutte their cables, and drove with the tide until they were without range of our guns, and then their frigate came to them, and towed them away, wonderfully mangled and torn. Their Admiral, in the greatest fury of the fight, was enforced to heale his ship to stop his leakes, his main topmast overboard, and the head of his mainmast. In the *London*, our Admiral and Peter Robinson were wounded ; Henry Grand and John Coard slain ; in the *Hart*, Edmund Okely wounded, and Walter

David killed. The shot spent in both fights was 1,382 by the *London*; 1024 by the *Hart*; 815 by the *Roebuck*, and 800 by the *Eagle*; total, 4,021." The calm prevented the two latter vessels from joining in the first part of the battle.

"Our worthy Admiral, in the beginning of the fight, received a great and grievous wound through the left shoulder, by a great shot, which hurt he with such courage and patience underwent, that it gave great hope to us all of his most wished recovery. But having, besides the wound, two of the uppermost ribs on the left side broken, this day, about noon, he departed this life, showing himself, as ever before, a resolute commander; so now, in his passage through the gates of death, a most willing, humble, constant, and assured Christian. His body was interred at Jasques[1] on the 9th, with all the solemnity, decency, and respect the time and place afforded."

Captain Shilling died at noon, on the 6th of January 1621. In the afternoon, "white box No. 1" was opened, and Captain Blithe, according to order, assumed the chief command. It was then arranged, by a consultation, that William Baffin should continue master of the *London*, that Swan should be removed from the *Roebuck* to the *Hart*, that Christopher Browne should go to the *Roebuck*, and that Thomas Taylor should be master of the *Eagle*.

The merchants on board the *London* had a quarrel while the ship was in Jáshak Roads; Mr. Monox

[1] Jáshak.

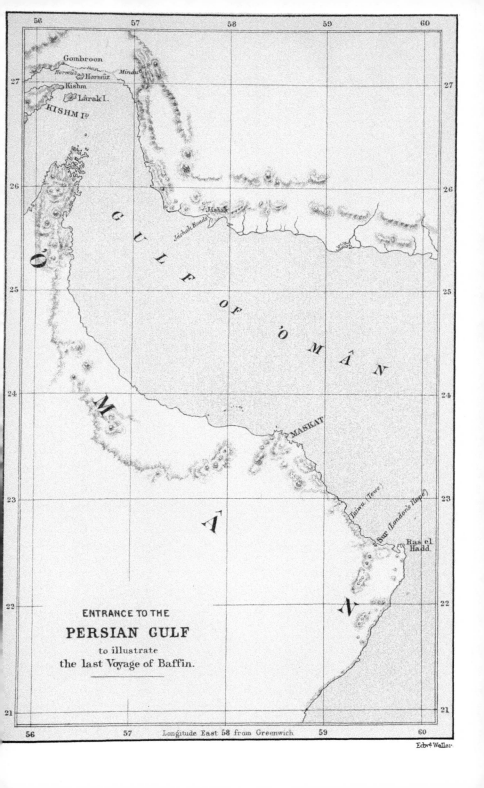

ENTRANCE TO THE

PERSIAN GULF

to illustrate
the last Voyage of Baffin.

trying to disgrace and excite dis-esteem against his colleague, Mr. Jeffries, which led to a certificate on the subject being signed by William Baffin the master, and countersigned by the Chaplain and the Surgeon.[1] In February the ships returned to Surat.

The fleet, under Captain Blithe, was then to have proceeded to the Red Sea ; but it was found to be too late in the season, and the ships shaped a course to the coast of Arabia. The *Hart* and *Roebuck* went to the barren island of Masirah, while the *London* stood onwards, in the direction of Ras al Had, which the English then called Cape Rosselgate. Baffin put into the little port of Súr, on the 'Omân coast, and found water and palm trees. The other ships were ordered to join company, and Súr received the name of "London's Hope". The latitude was found to be 22° 32′ N.[2] Here they appear to have remained at anchor until the 15th of August, when they all set sail for India.

The English now agreed with Shah Abbas the Great, of Persia, to drive the Portuguese out of Ormuz, by a joint attack. The great Viceroy, Albuquerque, had occupied this island in 1515, built a

[1] *Calendar of State Papers, Colonial (East Indies)*, 1617-21 p. 414, para. 972.

[2] Lieutenant Wellsted gives the latitude of Súr at 22° 37′ N.; longitude, 59° 36′ E. He was there in November 1835. Súr is the port of the district of Jailan, a large collection of huts neatly constructed with the leaves of date palms, and erected on either side of a deep lagoon, which also serves for its harbour. During the S. W. monsoon the coast of Arabia is a dead lee shore.— *R. G. S. Journal*, vii, p. 104.

strong fort, and exacted an exorbitant tribute from
the people, but retained the succession of native
kings. The commerce and importance of Ormuz
began to decline from the date of the Portuguese
occupation, partly owing to their rapacity, and partly
on account of the new channel for trade by the Cape
of Good Hope. Still, the place was wealthy at the
time of the Anglo-Persian attack. The Shah agreed
to give the English, for their help, a share of the
plunder, and half the customs duties at Goimbroon
(Bandar 'Abbasi). The English fleet assembled at
Surat, and consisted of the *London*, with Captain
Blithe and William Baffin on board, the *Jonas*,
Whale, *Dolphin*, and *Lion*. On the 23rd of December
1621, they arrived at an open roadstead on the
Persian coast, near Minab, Ormuz being in sight
about ten leagues W.N.W. Here the news was
received that the Portuguese had erected a fort on
the island of Kishm, to protect some wells, to which
the Persians had ineffectually laid siege for some
time. On the 19th of January 1622, the English
fleet anchored off the town of Ormuz, expecting
that the enemy's ships, under Ruy Frere de Andrada,
would come out to fight. But it was found that
Ruy Frere was in the fort at Kishm, an important
post, because it defended the wells for supplying
Ormuz. This fort had been built out of the stones
of a fine town, containing tombs and mosques, which
had been pulled down for the purpose. The wall
was of great height, with half moons, and flankers,
and a deep dry moat. The Portuguese were already

beleaguered by a Persian army, and the English
fleet arrived on the 20th of January 1622.

The first operation was to land a certain number
of guns from each ship, and to throw up batteries.
The siege then commenced, and after two days,
William Baffin went on shore with his mathematical
instruments, to take the height and distance of the
castle wall, so as to find the range " for the better
levelling of his piece. But as he was about the
same, he received a shot from the castle into his
belly, wherewith he gave three leaps, and died im-
mediately". Purchas says :—" In the Indies he
dyed, in the late Ormus businesse, slaine in fight
with a shot, as hee was trying his mathematicall
proiects and conclusions."[1] The death of the great
navigator took place on January 23rd, 1622. On
February 1st the fort of Kishm surrendered, and
the fall of Ormuz followed a few days after.[2]

[1] See page 156.

[2] The " Ormuz businesse", as it was called, is related by Master
W. Pinder, in *Purchas*, ii, lib. x, cap. ix, p. 1787. Also in a
letter to Sir John Wolstenholme from T. Wilson, chirurgeon ;
and in the journal of the merchant, Edward Monox, both given
in *Purchas*.

In the fort of Kishm seventeen guns were captured, and Ruy
Frere de Andrada was sent as a prisoner to Surat on board the
Lion. On the 9th of February, the rest of the English fleet,
with about 200 Persian boats laden with soldiers, sailed from
Gombroon to Ormuz. About 3,000 Persians landed, occupied
the town, and drove the Portuguese into the castle. The English
planted batteries, and directed the siege operations, a practicable
breach was formed, but the Persian assaults were repulsed. On
the 23rd, the Portuguese offered to surrender to the English ;
and, on the 27th, the garrison embarked for Goa in two of the

Baffin does not appear to have made a will, and he probably left no surviving children, or we should have heard of them, either as claimants of his property, or as recipients of the charity of the Company.[1] But his old widow lived to make claims which were considered troublesome. She is described as a "troublesome impatient woman" who had received £100, and Sir John Wolstenholme, her husband's patron, was moved to cause her to have patience awhile. This was in August 1623. On November 7th of the same year the Court's Minutes record a letter on behalf of Mrs. Baffin for the money due to her deceased husband. The Court "are ready to pay what is due for wages, but to pay £800 which cannot but be gotten by private trade, the Company will not do it. Nevertheless, Mrs. Baffin shall expect their further answer". On the 21st she came in person, accompanied by a Mr. Robert Bourne, and "made demand of her husband's estate, who deceased in the Indies in the Company's service". The Court told them that "if Baffin's estate were questioned it might prove dangerous to the widow, especially if it be true, which she pretends, that he carried £600 out in money, a thing utterly unlawful". The Court proposed arbitration, and Mr. Bourne desired time to consider it.

---

prizes. It was not until September that the English ships left Ormuz in possession of the Persians and returned to Surat. Ormuz was utterly ruined, and has ever since remained desolate.

[1] As in the case of Henry Hudson's son, and scores of other children of men who had served the Company well.

On the 28th, two arbitrators were chosen on either side. The matter lingered on for three years, and, in January 1628, it was ordered that Mrs. Baffin should have £500 in full of all demands, provided that she herself, her friend Mr. Bourne, and her second husband, should join in a discharge to the Company. It was said that Mrs. Baffin was then advanced in years and deaf, and "had made an unequal choice of a man not of the best governed". The Court, therefore, promised so to work with the husband that some honest means might be allotted her out of this grant. This is all that is preserved to us concerning the gallant old sailor's family.[1]

We only know the history of Baffin in the last ten years of his life, from 1612 to 1622. During that period he was engaged in seven important voyages. In the first (1612) he explored the west coast of Greenland. In the second and third (1613 and 1614) he navigated along the coasts of Spitzbergen. In the fourth (1615) he examined Hudson's Strait. In the fifth (1616) he discovered the great bay which bears his name. In the sixth (1617-19) he made valuable surveys in the Red Sea and Persian Gulf. In the seventh (1620-22) he took part in a well sustained sea fight, and fell gloriously in the service of his country. We have seen the place he holds as a brave and able seaman; we will now con-

[1] *Calendar of State Papers, Colonial (East India)*, 1622-24, pp. 140, 175, 181, 184, 189, 219, 231; *Court Minute Book*, vi, pp. 248-267.

sider the position he takes as a scientific observer
and as a great discoverer.

We first became acquainted with Baffin in July
1612, at Cockin Sound, on the coast of Greenland,
and he is then actively employed on an experimental
observation for obtaining the longitude by moon's
culmination.[1] The fact of his attempting to take an
observation of this kind, the care with which he
made all his arrangements, and the interesting remarks with which he accompanied their record,
prove him to have been a man who had already
devoted much time to self culture, and who was
alike thoughtful and ingenious. In the fragment of
his journal of this voyage that has been preserved,
Baffin records sixteen observations for latitude, and
eight for variation of the compass, besides this observation for longitude. In his first voyage to
Spitzbergen, Baffin observed for dip as well as for
variation; and he tells us that he used a quadrant
of four feet semidiameter in taking his altitudes.[2]
But his most interesting observation during this
voyage of 1613 was for sun's refraction, although
there appear to be several mistakes in the record of
it. Baffin's method of finding the refraction is most
ingenious. He first obtains the latitude, and then
takes the difference between the co-latitude and the
declination, corrected for the instant when he observed the sun on meridian below the pole to have
one fifth of its diameter above the horizon. Then
dividing the whole diameter of the sun into fifths,

[1] See page 20, and *note* at page 122.   [2] Page 44.

he calculates that the sun's centre was three-tenths[1] of its whole diameter below the horizon. Subtracting three-tenths of the difference between the co-latitude and the declination from that difference, he gets the approximate refraction.[2]

The second Spitzbergen voyage is recorded by Fotherby, so that the personal work and remarks of Baffin are lost to us; but, during the voyage up Hudson's Strait in 1615, we find him again as active and intelligent as ever. He records twenty-seven observations for variation of the compass, and daily observations for latitude. He also describes a complete lunar observation, the elements being observed altitudes of sun and moon, and angular distance probably measured by difference of azimuth. These elements, cleared from the effects of parallax and refraction, would give the true distance, and the longitude could be found by using the right ascensions of the sun and moon, without the aid of the tables of lunar distances now given in the *Nautical Almanack*.[3] Of course, the distance must have been very roughly observed, and the whole attempt was merely experimental and tentative. But it shows that Baffin was acquainted with the method of finding longitude by observing the altitude of the moon and some other heavenly body, and measuring the angular distance between them; a method first suggested in 1514 by Werner, and again in 1545 by Gemma Frisius. It enables us to claim for Baffin

[1] At page 51 (line four from bottom) "foure five" is obviously a misprint for three-tenths. [2] See p. 51. [3] See p. 122.

the honour of being the first who ever attempted to take a lunar at sea. Baffin also records, during the voyage up Hudson's Strait, another attempt to find the longitude by lunar culmination.[1] He took tidal observations, and the correctness of his deductions from them was long afterwards confirmed by Sir Edward Parry.[2]

In his fifth voyage, when he discovered Baffin's Bay, the great explorer was especially diligent in observing for variation of the compass, but unfortunately his tabulated journal was injudiciously thrown aside by Purchas, into whose hands it fell. In his narrative he only gives the variation of Smith Sound. Enough has been preserved, however, to show that Baffin takes rank among the foremost scientific seamen of his day, and that he combined perseverance and diligence with painfully acquired knowledge, and remarkable ingenuity and originality of conception. His magnetic observations are of permanent value, for they enabled Professor Hansteen to construct the first of his series of variation maps. His style of drawing is shown in the *facsimile* map which illustrates the present volume ; and the great value of his surveying work in the East Indies earned for him special recognition from the East India Company.

As a geographical discoverer, Baffin explored a portion of the west coast of Greenland in 1612, and the west coast of Spitzbergen in 1613. In 1614, Fotherby and Baffin made several attempts to ex-

---

[1] Page 124.   [2] See *note* at page 132.

tend discovery eastward, along the north coast of Spitzbergen. The season was very unfavourable, the ice being close down on the north shore. But they persevered, and useful work was done, by means of expeditions from their ship in open boats, and by climbing up high hills to obtain more extensive views. In this way they examined the coast from Hakluyt Headland to Wijde Bay of modern maps, and saw a more distant point of Spitzbergen, about sixty miles E.N.E. of the furthest point they reached. Finally, at the end of the season, the ice allowed them to take the ship a distance of about sixty miles E.N.E. from Vogelsang of modern maps, which they called Cape Barren. They were then off the entrance of Hinlopen Strait, and nine or ten leagues from the land.[1]

---

[1] But there is not the slightest foundation for Dr. Petermann's theory, that Baffin saw the western shore of Franz Josef Land. There is not a word or a syllable in the narrative to justify the notion.

In the *R. G. S. Proceedings*, vol. xix (1874-75), p. 177, Dr. Petermann says :—" I consider it also highly probable that that great Arctic pioneer and navigator, William Baffin, may have seen the western shores of Franz Josef Land as long ago as 1614, for in that year he proceeded to 81° N. latitude, and thought he saw land as far as 82° to the north-east of Spitzbergen, which is accordingly marked in one of Purchas's maps." See also *Mittheilungen*, 18 Band (1872), p. 112, and the map facing page 392 in 20 Band, 1874. From the *Mittheilungen*, it would seem that this notion was conceived by Dr. Petermann, not by referring to the narrative in Purchas, where nothing of the sort is to be found, but by misinterpreting a loose, second-hand statement made by Daines Barrington.

Fotherby and Baffin climbed a high hill at the entrance of Wijde Bay, and saw the coast line of Spitzbergen to the E.N.E.

Baffin's work in Hudson's Strait does not amount to discovery, but it was a painstaking and valuable survey, and was recognised by Sir Edward Parry as praiseworthy and highly creditable.

The fame of Baffin mainly rests upon the discovery of the great bay extending north from Davis Strait. Passing Hope Sanderson, the furthest point reached by Davis, Baffin came to the Women Islands, and the Baffin Islands off Cape Shackleton, at the southern end of Melville Bay. He then crossed Melville Bay, between the 1st and 3rd of July, a most extraordinary piece of good fortune; and, arriving off Cape Dudley Digges, he entered the *North Water*, which "anew revived our hope of a passage".[1] On the 3rd, the explorers anchored off Wolstenholme Sound, but a gale of wind forced them to make sail, and stand out to sea.[2] Their

for about twenty leagues distance (see p. 93). This is the single fact on which Petermann's erroneous theory is based. Baffin or Fotherby never proceeded to 81° N., nor thought they saw land in 82° N., nor is such land marked in any of Purchas's maps.

They were never more than thirty miles from the north coast of Spitzbergen, and their highest latitude was 80° 20′ N. The most distant point they could have seen was the North Cape of North-East Land, or possibly one of the Seven Islands. These furthest points are marked correctly on the map in Purchas as a part of Spitzbergen, called Point Purchas, and the island "Purchas *Plus Ultra*".

[1] Page 144.

[2] Sir John Ross says :—" We found the entrances to this inlet, and the general form and appearance of the land to agree extremely well with the description of it given by Baffin, as well as did bearings and distances from Cape Dudley Digges."—*Voyage of the Isabella and Alexander*, Captain John Ross (1818), p. 156.

foresail was blown away, and the wind blew with such fury that they were unable to show any canvas to it. When it cleared they found themselves embayed in an inlet, which Baffin named Whale Sound. The weather then moderated, and the little *Discovery* sailed past Hakluyt Island, to the entrance of Smith Sound. Next, the explorers sighted the Cary Islands; and in the morning of July 10th, they were off Jones Sound, where a boat was sent on shore. This was the first time they had landed since leaving the Baffin Islands. In 74° 20′ N., they discovered the entrance of Lancaster Sound, but Baffin failed to realize the fact that it was the opening to a strait of which he was in search. Here his hope of a passage began to be less every day, and he ran south along the edge of the ice, trying to reach the west shore. Giving up this attempt when in 65° 40′ N., Baffin stretched across to Greenland, to obtain refreshment for his men, and anchored in Cockin Sound on the 28th of July. This discovery of Baffin Bay was not only very important in itself, but it was achieved by a most remarkable voyage. No other vessel has since been at the entrance of Smith Sound, and recrossed the Arctic Circle within the month of July. The names given by Baffin, during the voyage, were as follows :—

       Women Islands.
       Horne Sound.
       Sir Dudley Digges Cape.
       Wolstenholme Sound.
       Whale Sound.
       Hakluyt Island.

Sir Thomas Smith Sound.
Cary Islands.
Alderman Jones Sound.
Sir James Lancaster Sound.

He thus immortalized the names of his generous patrons.

The omission of Purchas to publish Baffin's tabulated journal and map, led to geographical blunders during the next two centuries, and to such confusion that at length the very existence of Baffin's Bay was doubted. It is interesting to trace the history of these errors respecting Baffin's Bay, and I have, therefore, caused a series of five maps to be prepared, which illustrate the subject.

I. The first is from a very rare circumpolar map, which was drawn to illustrate the narrative of Luke Fox, but is only to be found in one or two copies of his book. The copy in the British Museum has not got it, and a facsimile has been inserted. Here Baffin's Bay is shown correctly, and it seems probable that this part of Fox's map may have been copied from the lost map of Baffin. The date is 1635, less than twenty years after Baffin's discovery.[1]

[1] North-West Fox, or Fox from the North-West Passage (London, 1635).

Luke Fox was a Yorkshire man, an able and intrepid navigator, as well as a quaint and very entertaining writer. In his book he gives a history of discovery in the Arctic Regions down to the time of his own voyage. He then says that he had been itching to start himself ever since 1606, when he was to have gone out as mate to John Knight. Mr. Briggs, the mathematician, encouraged him in

II. But the theoretical map makers, having no
sure guide such as Baffin's own map would have
supplied them with, soon began to delineate the bay
in ways of their own. Hondius first published a
map entirely different from that in Luke Fox's book.
There is a great prolongation westward, and then a
strait leading south into Hudson's Bay. My second
map is reproduced from Hexham's edition of Hondius,
published in 1636. In the *Atlas* of Vischer (Amsterdam, 1651), and in that of De Wit (1680), the
treatment of Hondius is followed. Beyond the
Women Islands there is a long strait ; then Baffin
Bay as a mere indentation, turning north at Cape
Dudley Digges, with an opening due south into
Hudson's Bay. All Baffin's names are given, except
the Cary Islands.

III. My third map is from Moll's *Atlas* (London,
1720), about a century after the discovery. Moll
had before him both the delineation of Luke Fox's
map, and the later developments of Hondius and his
imitators. He, therefore, gives Baffin's Bay, and
Davis Strait, according to Luke Fox ; but also
shows the coast line of Hondius by a shaded line,
adding a legend—"Some will have Baffin's Bay to

the idea, and Sir John Wolstenholme, the younger, became treasurer for the voyage. He sailed in May 1631, went up Hudson
Strait, and discovered the western shore of the channel leading to
Fury and Hecla Strait, which has never been visited since. He
conducted the voyage with judgment and energy, and achieved an
excellent piece of geographical work.

run west, as far as this faint shadow." Van Keulen
(Amsterdam, 1726) was led into still greater confusion. He gives the outline from Hondius and
De Wit, but repeats all the names of Baffin twice ;
first, where the long strait turns to the west, and
again in the westward continuation. D'Anville
(1761) follows De Wit; but opposite Disco is
"James Island", with " Davis Strait" on one side,
and " Baffin Strait" on the other. The *Atlas* of
Bowles (1765) is copied from D'Anville. In the *Atlas*
of Maltebrun (1812) there is a great improvement.
A large bay is given northward, in a line with Davis
Strait ; the Cary Islands are placed close to the
north coast, and there is no Hondius opening to
Hudson's Bay. The *Atlas* of J. Thompson (Edinburgh, 1817) follows Maltebrun.

iv. But all these discrepancies in the Atlases led
to such confusion of ideas that at last the very existence of Baffin's Bay began to be doubted. In the
book entitled *The Possibility of approaching the
North Pole, asserted by the Hon. Daines Barrington*, which was published in 1818, there is a circumpolar map "according to the latest discoveries".
Here the distance between Greenland and Cumberland Land, on the Arctic Circle, is given as about
400 miles. " James Island" is in the centre, with
Davis Strait on the east, and Baffin Strait on the
west side of it. This seems to have been copied
from D'Anville. To the north is a great bay with
an enormous westward extension, and a third strait

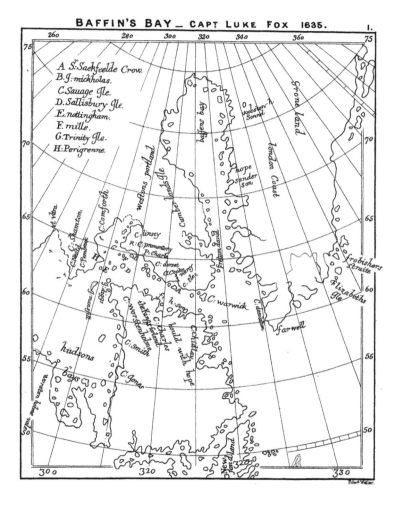

BAFFIN'S BAY _ CAPT LUKE FOX 1635.   I.

A S.: Sackfeelde Crow.
B. J.: mickholas.
C. Sauage Jle.
D. Sallisbury Jle.
E. nottingham.
F. mille.
G. Trinity Jle.
H. Perigrenne.

BAFFIN'S BAY FROM HENRY HEXHAM'S EDITION OF HONDUIS ATLAS PRINTED 1636.

II.

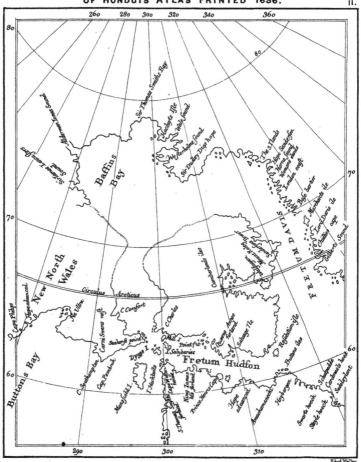

Edw.ᵈ Weller.

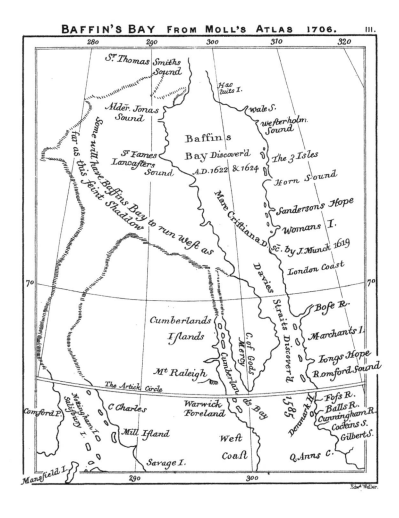

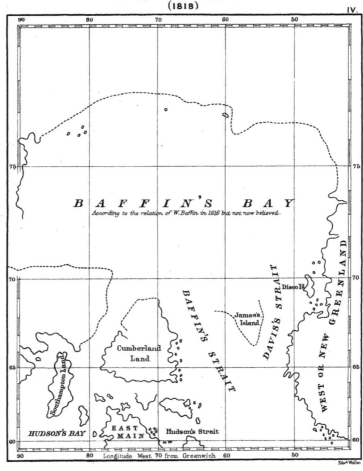

BAFFIN'S BAY
ENLARGED FROM THE CIRCUMPOLAR MAP
IN DAINES BARRINGTON'S "POSSIBILITY OF APPROACHING
THE NORTH POLE ASSERTED."
(1818)

IV.

B A F F I N ' S   B A Y

According to the relation of W. Baffin in 1616 but not now believed.

BAFFIN'S STRAIT

DAVIS'S STRAIT

Disco I?

James's Island

Cumberland Land

WEST OR NEW GREENLAND

Southampton Land

HUDSON'S BAY

EAST MAIN

Hudson's Strait

Longitude West from Greenwich

Edwᵈ Weller.

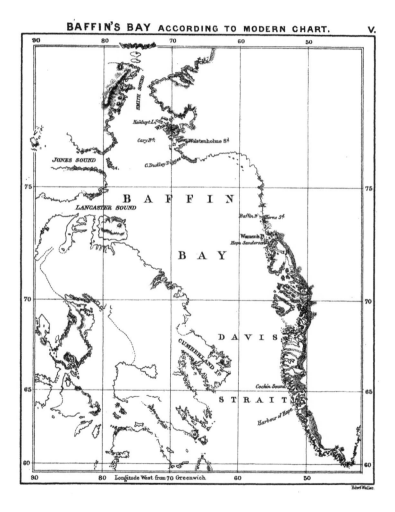

leading into Hudson's Bay. Across the great bay is written, "Baffin's Bay, according to the relation of W. Baffin in 1616, but not now believed".

In the same year Sir John Barrow published a circumpolar map to illustrate his "*Chronological History of the Voyages into the Arctic Regions* (1818) in which Baffin's Bay is entirely expunged. Davis' Strait is made to open northwards on to a blank space. Thus, after many varied methods of treatment, the great discovery of Baffin was at length entirely ignored and discredited.

v. But in the very year of the publication of these incredulous maps, Captain Ross made his voyage in company with Lieutenant Parry, re-discovered Baffin's Bay, and finally cleared away all this mystification. At length the great navigator received full credit for his discovery, and for the admirable way in which he had conducted it. Ross and Parry were as much struck with Baffin's accuracy as an observer, as with his gallantry and skill as a navigator in pushing the little *Discovery* of 55 tons through the middle pack into the "North Water", and bringing her safely back again. My fifth map shows the outline of Baffin's Bay, according to recent charts.

Sir John Ross says, in the narrative of his voyage of 1818, "In re-discovering Baffin's Bay I have derived great additional pleasure from the reflection that I have placed in a fair light before the public the merits of a worthy man and able navigator,

f

whose fate, like that of many others, it has not only been to have lost, by a combination of circumstances, the opportunity of acquiring during his lifetime the fame he deserved, but, could he have lived to this period, to have seen his discoveries expunged from the records of geography, and the bay with which his name is so fairly associated, treated as a phantom of the imagination." Ross identified all the places mentioned and named by Baffin, and bears frequent testimony to his accuracy, especially as regards the latitude of Lancaster Sound.

The main object of Arctic exploration is the extension of scientific knowledge. A secondary, but in many instances an equally fruitful, aim has been the increase of national wealth ; in both these respects the work of Baffin gives him pre-eminence. His geographical discoveries were extensive, and his scientific observations were important and of permanent value. At the same time his voyages, and the information he brought home, pointed the way to a new source of commercial profit, and eventually opened up a lucrative whaling trade. Among the naval worthies of the seventeenth century, side by side with Frobisher, and Davis, and Hudson, the devoted zeal and untiring industry, the gallantry and intrepidity of Willam Baffin, and his great services, have secured for him a permanent and an honourable place.

I have added to Baffin's Voyages a discourse inserted by Purchas on the probability of a North-West Passage, because it contains some remarks on

Baffin and a notice of his death by Purchas, and
because the remarks of Briggs, the mathematician,
show the state of opinion on the subject immedi-
ately after Baffin's last Arctic voyage.   Purchas
adds to his discourse a story heard at Lisbon by a
shipmaster named Cowles ; a report by Michael Lok
on the discoveries of Juan de Fuca ; and a Treatise
by Henry Briggs on the North-West Passage.

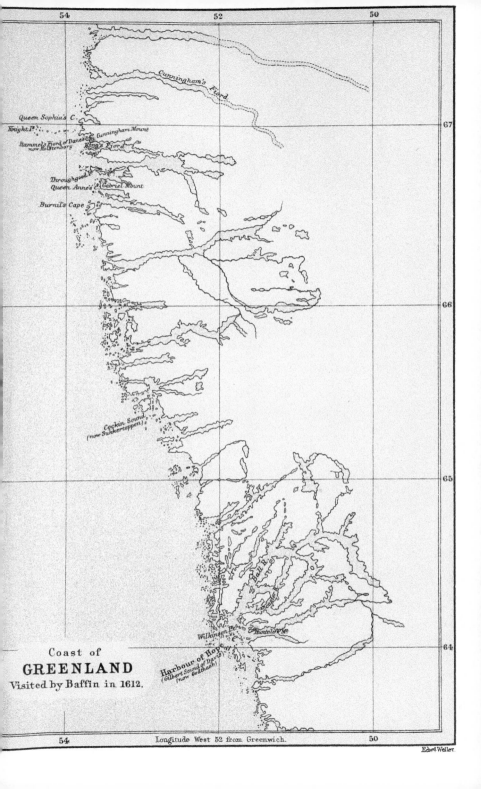

Cunningham's Fiord

Queen Sophia's C.

Knight I.

Rummel's Fiord of Danes   Cunningham Mount

now Holstenborg   King's Fiord

Droughood I.

Queen Anne's C.   Gabriel Mount

Burnil's Cape

67

66

65

Cockin Sound
(now Sukkertoppen)

Ball R.

Wilkonson

Harbour of Hope

(Gilbert Sound of Davis)

(now Goodhaab)

64

Coast of
GREENLAND
Visited by Baffin in 1612.

Edwd Weller.

THE FIRST RECORDED VOYAGE

OF

WILLIAM BAFFIN.

PART I.

Written by JOHN GATONBE[1] (ending 8 July 1612).

To the Right Worshipfull Sir Christopher Hilyeards,[1] Knt.

John Gatonbe wishethe in this life the contynvance of
health and prosperitie, with great increase of worship, and everlasting felicitie in Christ our Saviour.

PURPOSING with myselfe to present this journall, or travis
book, to you, which is ussally kept of seafayringe men and
mariners, in ther navigation of long voyagies and unknowne
countryes; and having been lett thes two yeares, being
travelling upon the sea to mayntayn my poore estat of wife
and children; and this winter being at home, and remem-

[1] From Churchill's *Collection of Voyages and Travels*, vol. vi [1732],
pp. 241-251.

[2] Sir Christopher Hildyard, of an ancient East Riding family, succeeded to his uncle (also Sir Christopher) at Winestead, in Holderness,
in 1602. He was High Sheriff of York in 1613, M.P. for Hedon in
1589, 1593, 1597, and 1601, for Beverley in 1620, for Aldborough in
1621, and again for Hedon from 1624 to 1627. He was also a member
of the High Commission of York. In 1598 Sir Christopher married
Elizabeth, daughter and heir of Henry Welby, of Goxhill, co. Lincoln,
by Alice White, whose mother was Anne Cecil, sister of the great Lord
Burleigh. Sir Christopher was buried at Winestead, on November 23rd,
1634. The Winestead Hildyards also owned the old palace at Hull,
built by the Poles, Dukes of Suffolk. Sir Christopher's son, Henry
Hildyard, let it to the king for a magazine of warlike stores. His
second son, Robert, was a prominent royalist commander at Marston
Moor and elsewhere, and was created a baronet at the restoration.
The baronetcy became extinct on the death of Sir Robert Hildyard, of
Winestead, in 1814.

B

bring the manyfold cortesies shewed by you to my anciente father, Nicholas Gatonbe,[1] I thought good this simple labour, such as it is, to offer vnto you, right worshipful, desiring you to accept it, as a gift that proceedeth from such a one who hartily wisheth you well, and would, if ability served, present you with a better, seeing and knowing your worship and your ancesters have been alwayes well-wishers to this towne and the inhabitants of the same; wherefor I intreat your worship to pervse it over.

And, First, you shall see the setting out of our voyage, what adventures we had with our generall.

Secondly. The tym of our saylling.

Thirdly. Our travis upon the sea, with the windes and weyther we had.

Fourthly. The height of the poll observed.

Fifthly. The ice we saylled by, with the coldness of the aire.

Sixthly. The barrenness of the country, with huge mountayns lying full of snow.

Seventhly. The nature and conditions of the inhabitants and salvages of the same.

Eighthly. The thinges we bought of them for old iron, with that which happened vnto vs in the countrye.

Lastly. Of our returne homeward and our safe arrivall.

Thvs craving both pardon for my boldnes, and also requesting your favorable accepting of my simple travell, I cease from further troubling your worship with my rudnes, praying Gode to inriche you with the plentyfull increase of the gifts of his spirite.

From the poore house of John Gatonbe, this 25th day of Februarie, 1615.

[1] Nicholas Gatonby was five times Warden of the Trinity House at Hull, namely in 1587, 1591, 1596, 1602, and 1609; having been elected Steward in 1577. A John Gatonby was Steward in 1570 and Warden in 1578 and 1586. Another Nicholas Gatonby made voyages to Greenland in the *Patience* in 1616 to 1618, and brought home cargoes of oil.

A Voyage into the North-West Passage, undertaken in the Year 1612.

By the Merchants Adventurers of London, Sir George Lancaster,[1] Sir Thomas Smith,[2] Mr. Ball,[3] Mr. Cocken,[4] and Mr. James Hall, being Venturer with them, and General of both the ships.

The 10th of April, being Good Friday, we haled both our ships into Hull road, the one being of the burden of 140 tons called the *Patience*, we being 40 men and boys in her; the other of 60 tons, called the *Heart's-Ease*, containing 20 men and boys. This day we cross'd both our yards, and entred into pay, making fit to take the first wind to sail withal.

[1] There was no Sir George Lancaster. It is a misprint for Sir James, the commander of the first East Indian voyage. James Lancaster was a native of Bishopstoke, in Hampshire. For his voyages and some account of him see *The Voyages of Sir James Lancaster to the East Indies* (Hakluyt Society's vol., 1877). After his return from his last voyage, which was the first voyage of the East India Company, in 1603, Lancaster was knighted, and he afterwards served as a Director of the East India Company. He was possessed of some wealth, lived in something more than comfort in his house in St. Mary Axe, and actively promoted all voyages of discovery. He died in June 1618, leaving his money in numerous legacies, and a larger sum to found a school at Bishopstoke. He appears to have been unmarried.

[2] For a notice of Sir Thomas Smith see the Introduction.

[3] This was probably Mr. Richard Ball, an eminent London merchant, who embarked in various enterprises having discovery as their object. His name appears in the list of adventurers to whom the charter of incorporation of the East India Company was granted, on December 31st, 1600. He was also a member of the Company for the Discovery of the North-west Passage. In 1618 he is mentioned as having fitted out two ships for the discovery of an island in the West Indies. His brother George was a factor for the East India Company at Bantam, and was prosecuted by the Company, on various counts, before the Star Chamber in 1622. Richard Ball was then dead.

[4] This Mr. Cocken, called by Baffin Alderman Cocken, is a name

Monday, April 20, we set sail in Hull road, the wind at E.S.E. and bore down to Cleeness and anchor'd ; and towards night the wind came to the N.E., and so we return'd into Paul road again this night, being much wind.

21. This day the wind came to S.S.W., and so at night we went over and rode at the Ness, our pinnace being about business at the town.

Set sail. 22. This day, being Wednesday, we weigh'd and set sail, the wind at S.S.W., and came out of Humber at 12 o'clock at noon, going our course N. and by W.

23. This day the wind southerly, we going the same course, being seven leagues off Whitby at noon, and at six o'clock at night we were 9 leagues off Hunclife,[1] it bearing from us S.S.W., we sailing N.N.W.

April 1612. 24. This day the wind at E.S.E. and very fair weather, we being some 12 leagues off Stabs-head, it bearing W.S.W. from us. At noon we observ'd the sun, and found the altitude of the pole to be 56° 12′.

25. This day the wind at S.E., we sailing N.N.W., and at 9 o'clock in the morning we spake with north sea fisher-

mis-spelt. There was no Alderman *Cocken*, but at this time there was a notable Alderman William *Cockayne*, who is no doubt the personage here mentioned. He was son of William Cockayne, and grandson of Roger Cockayne, of Ashborne in Derbyshire. He was Governor of the Eastland Company, and also of the London planters in Ulster ; and it was under his direction that the city of Londonderry was founded. On June 22nd, 1616, King James I dined with him and knighted him, and in 1619-20 he was Lord Mayor of London. He was also an active member of the East India Company, and one of the Farmers of the Customs. His daughter, Martha, with a dowry of £10,000, married that John Ramsay who had the credit of having saved James VI when he was attacked by the Gowries. Ramsay was created Earl of Holderness and Baron Kingston-upon-Thames in 1621, but died childless in 1625. His widow married secondly Montagu Bertie, second Earl of Lindsey, and was mother of the third Earl and other children. She died in 1641. Another daughter, Mary Cockayne, married the second Earl of Nottingham ; and the eldest son Charles was created Viscount Cullen. Sir William Cockayne died in 1626. He was buried in Old St. Paul's.   [1] Huntcliff, near Redcar.

men, and had fresh fish of them, they belonging to Yarmouth, being from Bohomness W.S.W. 9 leagues off, the
pole being rais'd 58° 30′.

26. This day, being Sunday, the wind southerly, we sail'd
betwixt Orkney and Fair Isle and Foullay, leaving the
islands and Shetland off our starboard side at 3 o'clock in
the morning; and at 6 o'clock we sail'd W. and by N. to
the sea, Foullay bearing from us N.E. 5 leagues off; and at
noon the wind came southerly, we sailing then W. This
day at night the wind came contrary, to the S.W., we
sailing to the northward N.W.[1] After we parted from
these two islands, we had sight of no other land till we came
to sight of Greenland.

27. This day we had much wind at N.W., being forc'd
to take in our topsails for our vice-admiral, she being
a-stern of us, we sailing W.N.W., and at four o'clock at
night we tack'd about to the southward, we sailing S.W.
and by S., the wind coming to the W. and by S.

28. This day the wind came to the N.W. with cloudy
weather. This day at 6 o'clock in the morning we tack'd
about to the southward, sailing W.S.W., and at noon we
did observe the sun, and found the altitude of the pole to
be 59° 47′.

29. This day, the wind at N.W., we standing to the
southward W.S.W., being thick hazy weather.

30. This day calm and misty from 12 o'clock to 6 o'clock
in the morning; then the wind came to the S.W., we sailing all the day after W. and by N.

May 1, being Friday, the wind at W.S.W., we sailing to May 1612.
the northward N.W. and by N., being misty and much
wind; and at noon it cleared up, and we did observe the
sun, and found the pole rais'd 61° 31′, we tacking about to
the southward, wending S. and by W., having fair weather;

[1] Two woodcuts: "Fair-Isle showeth thus 2 leagues off"; "Foullay
showeth thus 3 leagues off."

and at 8 o'clock at night we tack'd about and stood to the northward, wending N.N.W.

2. This day stormy weather, with the wind at S.W. and by W., being misty and rain, we standing to the northward N.W. and by W., and at 10 o'clock it fell little wind and calm; and the wind ran to the N.E., we sailing our course W., having a fresh gale of wind at noon.

3. This day we had fair weather, the wind at E.S.E., we sailing W. This day we did observe the sun, and found the pole to be rais'd 61° 46'; and at 4 o'clock at night the wind came contrary, being westerly, we standing to the northward N.N.W.; and at 6 o'clock we stood to the southward again.

4. This day the wind at N.W., we sailing W.S.W., and at 5 o'clock our vice-admiral sprung her fore-mast, whereby she was forc'd to take in her top-sails and fore-sails; and so did we in the admiral, till such time as they had fish'd it and made it strong. This day at noon we did observe the sun, and found the pole rais'd 61° 8', the wind being come to N.N.E., we sailing our course W.

5. This day the wind came to W. and by S., and began to blow, we standing to the northward N.W. and by N.

6. This day the wind at W., and at 6 o'clock in the morning the wind came to N. and by W., and so we steer hence W., the altitude of the pole being 61° 36'.

7. This day the wind at N.W. and by N., we sailing W. and by S., and at 2 o'clock in the afternoon it came up to the N.E., being cloudy and thick, which turn'd to much rain, we sailing our course west.

8. This day much wind and rain at E.N.E., we sailing W., and at noon we had fair weather, the wind being come to the N. This day we hoped to see Friesland,[1] yet did not.

---

[1] The old navigators were always hoping to see this imaginary Friesland, and were always disappointed. It got into the sea-charts from

9. This day the wind at N.N.E. stormy weather, we sailing our course W., and at noon it grew fair, and we observ'd the sun, and found the altitude of the pole to be 59° 51'. This day our master found by his instrument the compass varied 15°. to the westward of the north, the occasion we had no sight of Friesland sailing to the southward some 12 leagues; so that for our west course we kept, we had made but a W. and by S. way; yet I suppose it to be the current which doth set to the southwestward, and so doth set from the westermost part of Friesland into the N.W. Passage.

10. This day the wind northerly, we sailing W. and by N., and at noon we observ'd the sun, and found the altitude of the pole to be 60° 4', being very fair weather.

11. The wind N., and at noon we sounded, and had no ground of 150 fathom, it being little wind and calm, sometimes southerly, and sometimes at S.W., sometimes easterly; thus it did continue variable all the day, being fair weather and smooth sea, we sailing for the most part W. and by S.

12. This day calm, and at 4 o'clock in the morning the wind came to E.N.E., we sailing W. and by N. This day the water changed of a blackish colour; also, we saw many whales and grampus's.

the old "*Carta da navegar de Nicolo et Antonio Zeno*" (A.D. 1380), first published in 1558, and was placed near the east coast of Greenland. Here it remained in every successive sea-chart for many long years. Frobisher assumed that Greenland was Friesland when he first made the coast. But Davis, when he sighted Greenland, at once saw that this was not the Friesland of the Zeno map; hence Friesland retained a separate place on the charts. Mr. Major holds that the Friesland of the Zeni was the Feroë Islands (see *The Voyages of the Venetian Brothers Nicolo and Antonio Zeno, translated, with Notes and an Introduction, by R. H. Major, F.S.A.*, Hakluyt Society's volume, 1873; and a paper in the *R.G.S. Journal*, xlix, p. 412, entitled, "Zeno's Frisland is not Iceland, but the Færoës"), while Admiral Irminger, of Copenhagen, is of opinion that Friesland was Iceland (see *R.G.S. Journal*, xlix, p. 398, "Zeno's Frislanda is Iceland and not the Feroës").

13. The wind at E. we sailing W. and by N. This day being hazy, we met with ice, the wind being come to N.N.E. Much wind and snow at 9 o'clock at night, so that we were forc'd to take in our sails and stand with our foresail to the eastward, wending E. Also, some of our men spied land, yet we could not well discern it, it snowing so fast.

14. We stood in with the land again at 2 o'clock in the morning, wending N.N.W., and had sight of land betwixt 5 and 6 o'clock in the morning ; and our master made it Cape Farewel, so called by Captain Davis at the first finding of the country in anno 1585 because he could not come near the land by 6 or 7 leagues for ice.[1] It bearing from us N.N.W., and we sailing along by the ice W.N.W. all the day.[2]

Cape Farewel.

15. The wind at N.N.W. sailing W., and at 4 o'clock in the morning we tack'd about again to the ice, again sailing N.N.E., and at 10 o'clock in the morning we tack'd about again, being hard aboard the ice, having sight of the land, it stretching more to the northward. The ice lieth

[1] Cape Farewell, the southern extreme of Greenland, is in 59° 48' N. This is an interesting statement that it was named by Captain Davis, in 1585; but in his first voyage in 1585, Davis did not sight Cape Farewell. The first land he made, which he called "Desolation", was on the east coast; and he did not sight land again until he was in 64° 15' N. In his second voyage, in 1586, he did sight Cape Farewell. He says—"And the 15th of June I discovered land in the latitude of 60 degrees mightily pestered with ice and snow, so that there was no hope of landing." But in the narrative written by himself he does not give it any name. On the Molyneux Globe, where the discoveries of Davis are shown, it is called "Reg: Elizabeth Foreland". Still, the tradition mentioned in the text, that Davis originally gave the name of Farewell to the Cape because he could not come near the land, is no doubt true, and is very interesting.

[2] Here there is a woodcut: "The land did rise thus full of snow. The Cape 7 leagues off, N.N.W." "This land is the southermost point in Greenland, the heighth of the Pole there being 59° 15'."

all along it, being as it were a great bay betwixt two head lands.

16. This day a cold hazy wind, it being at N.N.W., we sailing W., and at 7 o'clock in the morning we tack'd about, lying N.E. and by N., and at 2 o'clock we met with ice again; we lying to and fro, hoisted our shallop out; and espying seals lying upon the ice, our shallop rowed to them, and killed one of them; the rest tumbled into the water, being 20 in a company. This day we observ'd the sun, and found the altitude of the pole to be 59° 30', we being some 70 leagues within the streights, it being 115 leagues between the coast of America and Greenland in the entrance of this passage.

17. The wind at S. in the morning, we sailing N.W. This day we run among the ice, and were inclosed with the ice, so that we could get no passage to the northward; and so we were forc'd to stand out again, and were glad that God had deliver'd us from amongst it; it being 4 o'clock in the afternoon before we were clear of the ice, sailing S.W. to the sea. This day, being Sunday, we had ^{May 1612.} sight of the land called Desolation,[1] it being from us 15 _{Land of Desolation.} leagues N. and by E.

18. This day, at one o'clock in the morning, we had much wind and snow, the wind being westerly; and at six o'clock in the morning it prov'd fair weather. We tacking about into the shore, did wend N. and by W., which did near the land of Desolation: and at noon we tack'd about and stood back again, being ten leagues from the land, it bearing N.N.E. of us: the ice hindering of us this day, we did observe the sun, and found the pole 59° 53'.

19. The wind southerly, we sailing for the most part N.W. by N. and N.N.W. Then the land of Desolation did bear off us N.E. and by E. This day we did meet with great islands of ice. This day we did observe the sun, and found

[1] So named by Davis.

the altitude of the pole to be 60° 35′: also we had a force-able current, which we went along the coast with till we came to bring Desolation point E. of us. This current set from Desolation into America side, and into Hudson's streights, being so called by his men, they leaving him behind them in that country, which was his death in the year 1611.[1]

May 1612. 20. This day, the wind at N. and by E., we sailing E. and by N. to the land, which we had no sight of as this day. This day we did observe the sun, and found the altitude of the pole to be 61° 33′, being to the northward of Desolation some 30 leagues. This day we stood to the westward; and at 10 o'clock at night we stood to the east-ward, again meeting ice.

21. The wind at N.E. and by E. This day we had sight of land at 2 o'clock in the morning; and our master's mate, John Hemstay and I called it the land of Comfort.[2] And we call'd up our men, and tack'd about our ships, the ice hindering us from coming near the land, we sailing along the land N., and N. and by W., being distant from it 7 leagues. And at noon, we being near the ice, our men went with the shallop to it, and killed four seals, and

The land of Comfort.

[1] Woodcuts with the following notes: "Cape Desolation rises thus 15 leagues off, N.E. by N." (cut). "The land of Desolation rises thus 12 leagues off, N.E. by E." (cut). "This land so called by Captain Davis, it being so desolate and comfortless, with huge mountains of snow lying upon it, such as he had never seen nor any of his men before him."

[2] The two cones of Umanak, off Arsuk Fiord, are the Cape Comfort of the Admiralty chart. The name appears on the map in the English translation of the description of Greenland, by Hans Egede, published in 1745, and also on the map in Crantz's History of Greenland (1757). On the Admiralty chart it is placed in 61° 49′ N., but Gatonbe, in the text, gives 62° 33′ as the latitude. This is the position of some islets, called Fulluarlalik Islands, between the Danish settlements of Fredrikshaab (62° N.) and Fiskernaes (63° 4′ N.). Of course, the Admiralty chart, and the Danish chart from which it is copied, must be wrong, for Gatonbe's evidence as to the point of land named by himself must surely be conclusive.

brought other two aboard quick, we having good sport
betwixt them and our mastiff dogs.[1]

22. The wind at N. and by E. This day we turn'd
amongst the ice, meeting with many islands of ice, which
were very high, like great mountains : some of them we
judg'd to be 30 yards from the water, fleeting upon the
seas, being 15 leagues off the land. This day we had
sight of the land, yet could not come near it for ice. This
day we did observe the sun, and found the pole rais'd
62° 55.'

23. The wind at N.N.W. This being calm at noon, we May 1612.
sounded with our lead, and had no ground of 180 fathom,
being some 110 leagues within the passage. This day we
found the altitude of the pole to be 63°, sailing N.E. and
by E. in with the land.

24. This day the wind at N. and by E., we sailing N.W.
and by W., being thick cloudy weather; and at 8 o'clock in
the morning we tack'd about to the eastward, it being
little wind, and sometimes calm.

25. This day calm, with little wind and variable; sometimes at N., sometimes at N.W., we sailing for the most
part N.E. and by E. This day we sounded by an island
of ice with our shallop, and found no ground of 150 fathom,
being off the land 21 leagues : and at 10 o'clock at night
it was thick and misty weather, so that one ship could not
see the other.

26. This day the wind at N., we sailing E.N.E., sailing
in with land, being very thick and misty weather; and at
2 o'clock in the afternoon it clear'd up, and we saw the
land, being some three leagues from it, it seeming as
tho' we were hard by it, being a very high land, having

[1] Here another woodcut, with the following note: "Cape Comfort rises
thus, the heighth of the Pole being 62° 33', the smoothest land, and
best to look to of all the country of Greenland ; yet we could not come
near it for ice."

much snow lying upon it. Also two of the savages came rowing to our ships in their boats, we sailing in still with the land, sounding, and having with our lead and line 25 fathom, sometimes 20, 18, 15, 12 fathom, it being rocky ground, coming amongst many dry rocks and islands. This day we look'd for a harbour with our shallops, for the ships to ride in safety, and found one, which our

Harbour of Hope.

general call'd the harbour of Hope; for here we came to land with our ships; the which we could not come near, the time we sail'd along the land, from the sight of Cape Farewel until we came to this place.[1]

27. The 27th day we harboured in the harbour of Hope (the islands we call'd Wilkinson islands; the mountain we call'd Mount Hatclife[2]) at 2 o'clock in the morning; praising our God for our safe arrival in this unknown country, having been from home 5 weeks and 2 days.[3]

Inhabitants of Greenland.

28. The 28th day our general found a convenient place

[1] The southern part of the western side of Greenland is blocked by the stream of ice drifting down the eastern side from the north, and then turning northwards round Cape Farewell. The current sets into Davis Strait, keeping close to the coast, but gradually decreasing in strength as it advances northward and disappears in about 64° N. The pack ice follows the track of this current, pressing upon the coast with southerly winds, and dispersing with those from the north. This belt of ice is often found to be quite impenetrable, though of no great width, and it sometimes locks up the southern coast for the greater part of the summer.

[2] A misprint, I think, for Huntcliff, a point on the coast of Yorkshire, near Redcar ; so named, no doubt, from a fancied resemblance.

[3] This anchorage was the Gilbert Sound discovered by Davis in 1585, and visited in his two subsequent voyages. (See *Voyages of John Davis*, pp. 6, 15, 16, 17, 22, 35, 38, Hakluyt Society's vol., 1880). Davis gives the latitude 64° 15′ N. Here, in this Gilbert Sound, the "Harbour of Hope" is now the modern Danish settlement of Godthaab, in 64° 8′ N., the principal station in South Greenland. The Godthaab-fjord runs in a north-eastern direction for 70 miles, and sends off a branch to the south-east 25 miles long. The greater part of the coast is sheltered by clusters of low islands. Godthaab was founded by Hans Egede in 1728.

to land the quarters of our pinnace for our carpenters to set together, it being an island hard by our ships. This day also our general caused our ship's boat to be mann'd, and our shallop, and went himself to discover the country, and what rivers he could find in the main; the savages rowing to and fro to our ships, holding up their hands to the sun, and clapping them on their breasts, and crying, *Elyot*,[1] which is as much to say, in English, Are we friends? thus saluting us in this manner every time they came to us, and we offering the same courtesy to them, making them the more bold to come to our ships, they bringing with them sealskins, and pieces of unicorn horn, with other trifles, which they did barter with us for old iron.

29, 30, 31. These days our carpenters made haste with our great pinnace to get her down, the weather being fair, and the wind for the most part easterly; for our general was minded to make what speed he could for to sail along the coast further to the northward, being as yet not come to the place where he was at afore by 70 leagues.

June 1. Our general return'd aboard again, having found two rivers in the main, the one he call'd Lancaster river; the other, Ball river;[2] for Greenland is like Norway, having many islands and rocks along the main. June

2. Our master and Mr. Barker,[3] master of the *Vice Admiral*, went in the shallop and rode amongst the islands, and to one of the rivers where they were afore, having their fowling-pieces with them to shoot fowl with, which that country affordeth small store.

---

[1] See the list of Eskimo words given by Davis. (*Voyages*, p. 21). He has *Yliaoute*—"I mean no harm".

[2] These were the two deep branches of Godthaab-fjord, called after two of the merchant adventurers who set forth the voyage—Sir James Lancaster and Mr. Richard Ball. (See notes at p. 3.) The latter name got corrupted into Baal's River, but it is correctly spelt on the Danish chart of 1832.

[3] Andrew Barker, master of the second ship, was a seaman of repute at Hull. (See note further on.)

3. This day we employ'd ourselves in searching the country, which affordeth nothing as yet for the profit of our voyage.

4. At night one of the savages stole a musket from our men which kept the island, where our great pinnace was set up, they keeping a bad watch, and leaving their musket where they kept centry, being at the fire in the coy, the weather being cold, it was taken away by one of the wild men, they could not tell when. The cause of our watching was, for that the salvages will steal all things they can come by, but chiefly iron.[1]

5. This day we launch'd our great pinnace, which our general call'd the Better Hope. This day also James Pullay catching hold of one of the salvages, another did cast a dart at him, and struck him into the body with it, on the left side, which gave him his death's wound. Also the salvage he took we haul'd into the ship, and by him we had our musket again; for two of the salvages being aged men, and rulers of the rest, came with great reverence to know the occasion we had taken one of their men; we with signs and other tokens did shew them the occasion, being the best language we all had amongst us, delivering their man, his boat, oar, and darts. Our general gave unto him a coat, a knife, and a seeing-glass also, to requite the injury we had done; yet he, with a frowning look, desiring to be gone from us, we let him go out of the ship, and helping him into the chains, he leapt over-board, and the other two did help him ashore; and when he was ashore, the salvages cut off the coat our master gave him, from his back, so little did they regard it. It was made of yellow cotton, with red gards of other cotton about it.

[1] Here there is a woodcut of a kayak: "The fashion of the salvages rowing in their boats, the boat being made of seal skins, and clos'd all but the place where he rows in her, and that is clos'd about him when he sits in her, from his waste downward. His oar hath two webs, and he useth both hands to row with. (Wilkinson's Islands, The Harbour of Hope, and Mount Hatcliffe)."

6. James Pulley departed this life to the mercy of God, at three o'clock in the morning, and we bury'd him at noon upon one of the islands we rode by. This day also we carry'd the quarters of Mr. Barker's small shallop to be set together by the carpenters ashore, that we might have our shallops ready to go with us along to the northwards.

7, 8, 9. Rainy weather, otherwise our shallop had been done, and we gone from hence to the northwards.

10. The shallop was done and launched this day. Mr. Hall, being general of both the ships, did hold a parley with all the company of both ships, strictly commanding that none of us should barter for anything, but Mr. Wilkinson, who was merchant for the venturers, and them that were appointed by the merchant, in pain of forfeiting their wages; which articles were wisely answer'd by the officers of the ships.

11. We cross'd our yards, and got an anchor home, but the wind came contrary, spending our time in rowing from island to island, and the salvages came to and fro to our ships, bringing us fresh fish, which we bought for iron nails.

13. One of the salvages brought two young seals, which he had kill'd at sea, and our master bought them, and we haul'd them into the ship, we wondering he could kill them at sea, it blowing so much wind at S.W.

14. This day, being Sunday, we came out with the wind N.N.E., and the salvages rowed to us, being 6 leagues off the land into the sea; and for that our captain gave one of them a knife. This day we observed the sun, and found the pole's altitude to be 64°, being the height of the place we came out of, being the harbour Hope; Wilkinson's islands and mount Hatcliffe we rowed under, they bearing off us E.

15. The wind at E.S.E., we sailing along the land to the northward N. by E., being fair weather.

16. The wind at N. by W., we sailing into the shore
N.E. by E. This day Mr. Hall and Mr. Barker took their
shallops, being well mann'd, and rowed into the land to
discover the country, and to see what traffick they could
have with salvages. This day, lying off and on with our
ships, they being ashore with the shallops, the wind came
out of the sea, and we stood of, sailing N.N.W. The wind
being come to west, and the vice-admiral following of us,
struck on a blind rock, and took no harm, praised be God!
our shallops not coming to us till we were 5 or 6 leagues
off the land.

17. The wind at S.E., we sailing along the land to the
northward N. by E. This day, being Wednesday, we row'd
with both our shallops into the land, and sounded the harbour we anchor'd in, being the second harbour we came in.[1]

18. At 8 o'clock at night we had a sore storm off the
land at S.E., with such mighty whirl-winds, which came
from the mountains, that all our cables we had, being new
ones, we bent to our great anchor, and let it fall to keep us
from the rocks.

19. In the morning we broke one of our cables, and we
rode by our great anchor, having much wind and rain.

20. The weather faired, and our general caused our great
pinnace to be made ready, and to row along the coast, he
going with us himself, we being in her 22 men and boys.
This day we rowed some 4 leagues, and came to a great
island, and anchor'd there 3 hours ; and from thence we
went into a river lying E. by N. up the river.

---

[1] This second anchorage was named Cockin (Cockayne) Sound, after
one of the four merchant adventurers who set forth the voyage—
Alderman Sir William Cockayne. (See note at p. 4). Baffin gives
the latitude 65° 20′ N. This is nearly the latitude of the Danish
settlement of Sukkertoppen, which was founded in 1755. Sukkertoppen
(Sugar-loaf) is in 65° 25′ N., and is situated on an island, the conical
elevations of which present the appearance expressed in its Eskimo
name *Manitsok* (uneven). It is the most populous place in Greenland,
and has a fine stone-built church.

21. We rowed up the river still, and we found nothing in it for any profit, rowing some 3 leagues into it, the ice stopping that we could get no further.

22. We being left by ice, return'd and rowed out again, and the salvages follow'd and row'd after us, and so along with us, intending to do us some harm ; for when we came near any island they did throw stones at us with their slings.

23. The wind at N.N.W., and we row'd amongst the islands to the northward, and so came to a great river, which troubled us to row over, there went such a forceable tide of flood, it being within a league of Queen Anne Cape,[1] and came to an island, and rested us there till the flood was done ; and then we rowed about the cape, and came to an island, whereon was a warlock, and rowed into it, and found it a good harbour for ships. This day we rowed into a river, as we supposed, but found it to be a bay, we being 3 leagues to the northward of the cape. This day our men went ashore and kill'd 6 partridges, and spy'd in a valley 7 wild deer, yet as soon as they did see us, they did run away as fast as their feet could carry them.

24. We row'd out again, and so along the land. This day we came to a mountain, where we rowed to it amongst Gabriel mount. the islands, taking it for a river our master had been at afore, yet it was not : the mount we call'd Gabriel mount.

25. We row'd from thence to an island which lieth two leagues off the land, with many broken rocks about it, that stretch from the main, and so to the sea-board ; and there we rested all that day, the wind blowing very much at N., it being against us. This island our master call'd by the

[1] Cape Anne, so named by Hall during his former voyage with the Danes, after the queen of Christian IV. Hall, on his map accompanying his report to the Danish King, gives the latitude of Cape Anne 66° N. On the modern charts it is in 66° 24′ N., just to the south of Cockin (Cockayne) Sound.

Through-
good island.

name of Throughgood island. Here we got great store of mussels, being of a great bigness. Here one of our men killed a fox with a fowling-piece, being many in this island that run from the main, and feed upon fish they got off the island.

26. It being very fair weather we row'd from thence, amongst many broken rocks, and so along the land; and at noon we came to the river our master had been at afore, he naming it the King's-ford;[1] there is a mount he named Cunningham mount;[2] we had traffick with the salvages; and at night we anchor'd in a haven, on the south-side of

Denmark
haven.

the river, call'd Denmark haven, there being in the entrance 40 fathom deep, and had traffick with the salvages for seal skins, and some salmon trout.[3]

27. We rowed over to the north-side of the river, and sought for a roadstead for our ships, and found one, having 12 fathom deep, meaning to bring our ships thither, with God's help.

28. We rowed to our ships again, having but two days victuals; none could we get, being from our ships, the salvages eating raw meat do kill with their darts, both fowl, fish, and flesh, so that there was little to get but that they brought us.

29. We came to our ships again, being from them nine days, having had much tedious weather, with thicks and snow, as we rowed along the coast, it being some 25 leagues betwixt the ships and the King's-ford. The vice-

---

[1] King Christian's Fiord was discovered and named by Hall during his first voyage with the Danes. He gives the latitude 66° 25′ N., close to Cape Anne.

[2] So named in Hall's first Danish voyage, after the commander of the expedition. This majestic peak is called *Kœrlinghœtten* by the modern Danes, and *Nusasak* by the Eskimo.

[3] " Cunningham Mount; the height of the Pole 66$\frac{1}{2}$°; King's-ford " (this river was the first harbour he anchored in when he was pilot of the King of Denmark's ships); " and Throughgood Islands."

admiral welcomed us to our ships with a volley of small shot, being all in health, God be thanked.

30. We made ready to sail to the river we had been at with our pinnace; fetching home an anchor, and getting our yards across.

1. This day, being the 1st of July, the wind northerly, ^{July.} yet at night it came southerly, and we set sail, hoping to have got to the sea, but the wind came westerly, with rain, and so we came in again.

2. The wind northerly, and rain, we riding in this harbour still.

3, 4, 5, 6, 7, 8. The wind northerly, we rode still, being wind-bound, and much rainy weather; we buying of the salvages such things as they brought us, being fresh fish, namely, salmon-trout, muskfish, codfish, and butfish, a little quantity serving for our victuals.

THE FIRST RECORDED VOYAGE

OF

WILLIAM BAFFIN.

PART II.

Fragment written by BAFFIN himself, beginning 8th July 1612.

The fourth Voyage of James Hall to Groenland, wherein he was
set forth by English Aduenturers, Anno 1612, and slaine
by a Greenlander.[1]

WEDNESDAY, the eighth of July 1612, in the morning I
perceiued the sonne and the moone, both very faire aboue
the horizon, as I had done diuers times before. At which
time I purposed to finde out the longitude of that place,
by the moones coming to the meridian. Most part of this
day I spent about finding of the meridian line; which I
did vpon an Iland neere the sea, hanging at the extreames
of my meridian line two threeds with plummets at them,
instead of an index and sights.

Thursday, the ninth day, very early in the morning, I
went on shoare the iland, being a faire morning, and obserued till the moone came iust vpon the meridian. At
which very instant I obserued the sunne's height, and
found it 8° 51′ north; in the eleuation of the pole
65° 20′. By the which, working by the doctrine of
sphericall triangles, having the three sides giuen, to
wit, the complement of the poles eleuation; the complement of the almecanter;[2] and the complement of

---

[1] From *Purchas*, Part 3, lib. IV, cap. xvii, pp. 831-836.

[2] An almicanter is a circle parallel to the horizon—a circle of altitude.

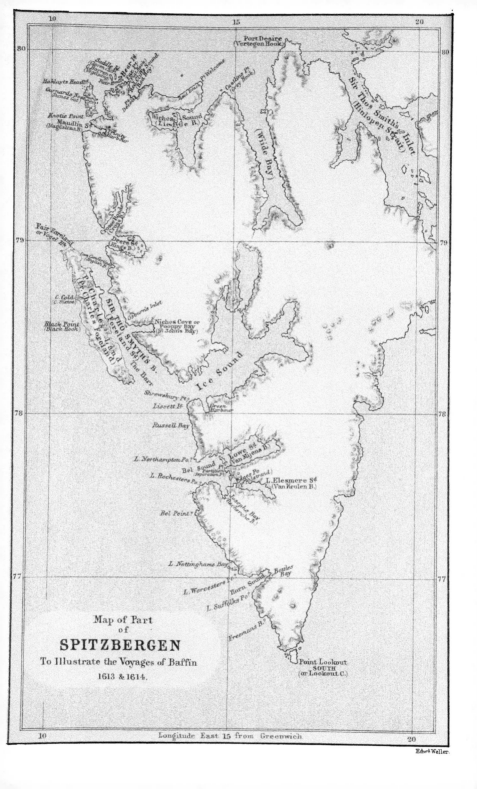

Map of Part
of
SPITZBERGEN
To Illustrate the Voyages of Baffin
1613 & 1614.

Longitude East 15 from Greenwich

Edwd Weller.

the sunne's declination, to find out the quantitie of the angle at the pole. I say, by this working, I found it to be foure of the clocke, 17 minutes and 24 seconds. Which, when I had done, I found by mine ephemerides, that the moone came to the meridian at *London* that morning at foure of the clocke, 25 minutes, 34 seconds : which 17 minutes, 24 seconds, substracted from 25.34, leaveth 8.10 of time, for the difference of longitude betwixt the meridian of *London* (for which the ephemerides was made) and the meridian passing by this place in *Groenland*. Now the moone's motion that day was 12° 7′, which, conuerted into minutes of time, were 48 minutes, 29 seconds; which, working by the rule of proportion, the worke is thus : if 48 minutes, 29 seconds; the time that the moone commeth to the meridian sooner that day then she did the day before, giue 360, the whole circumference of the earth ; what shall 8 minutes 10 seconds giue, to wit, 60 degrees, 30 minutes, or neere there about which is the difference of longitude betweene the meridian of *London* and this place in *Groenland*, called *Cockin's Sound*, lying to the westward of *London*.[1]

60° 30′ difference of longitude betweene the meridian of London and Sound in Groenland.

This finding of the longitude, I confesse, is somewhat difficult and troublesome, and there may be some small errour. But if it be carefully looked vnto, and exactly wrought, there will be no great errour, if your ephemerides be true. But some will say, that this kinde of working is not for marriners, because they are not acquainted to work propositions by the table of signes,[2] and an instrument is not precise enough to find out the houre, minute, and second. For the losse of one minute of time is the losse of 7 degrees of longitude. I answere, that although the most part are not vsed to this worke, yet I

Objection.

Answere.

[1] Baffin's result is a longitude too far to the westward. It is, in fact, nearly the longitude of Cape Walsingham, on the other side of Davis Strait. Cockin Sound is in 52° 50′ W.   [2] Sines.

know some of the better sort, which are able to worke this and the like propositions exactly. And those which yet cannot, and are desirous to learne, may in short space attaine to such knowledge as shall be sufficient for such things. And how necessary it is that the longitude of places should be knowne, I leaue to the iudgement of all skilfull marriners, and others that are learned in the mathematicks.

This afternoone it was agreed by the chiefe of our company, that our master, *James Hall,* should goe in the smaller ship farther to the northward.

The foresaid Thursday, in the evening, he departed out of the *Patience* into the *Harts-ease,*[1] to get forth of the harbor, which our master called *Cockins-ford,* in remembrance of Alderman *Cockin,* one of the aduenturers;

Cockins Ford, in 65° 20'. Variation, 23° 58'. which place is in the latitude of 65° 20'.[2] And the variation of the compasse is 23° 28' to the westward. That evening was very calme, and we towed our shippe forth with the shallops and ship's boat. But within an houre or two after we were got into the offin, the winde being at north, it blew a great storme, which continued all that night.

The fourteenth, our master turned the ship vp to the river againe, toward the riuer where the supposed mine[3] should

---

[1] Gatonbe, the quartermaster, who wrote the preceding account of the voyage, printed in Churchill's collection, says the arrangement was that Hall, with twelve men of the *Patience*, should go on board the *Heart's Ease* to explore to the northward. Baffin and young William Huntriss were of the number. Two masters' mates and two quartermasters were left on board the *Patience*, and she was to follow from Cockayne Sound to King's (or Christian's) Fiord. The boats and shallops towed the vice-admiral (*Heart's Ease*) out to sea.

[2] The Admiralty Chart places Cockin Fiord in 65° 10' N. The Danish settlement of Sukkertoppen is really Cockin Fiord, in 65° 25' N.

[3] The main object of the expedition appears to have been to visit and collect ores from a supposed silver mine which Hall had discovered during his voyage with the Danes. Like Frobisher, he had mistaken the glittering pieces of mica occurring with the granite for silver ore.

be. But the tyde was so farre spent that we could not get to sea, but were constrained to anker in a roade at the south side of the riuer, some three leagues from the *Patience*, in which place are many good rode-steeds to be found.[1]

Many good Rodes.

Thirsday, the sixteenth day, the winde was at north-west, and blew so stiffe a gale that we could not get to sea that day. That night, eighteene of vs went into the ilands to looke for some deere, but found none. But we perceiued the foote-steps of some great beast, which wee supposed to be of some great elke; the foote was as bigge as any oxe foote.

Great footing.

Tuesday, the twentie-one, the weather still continued in such sort that wee could not by any means get to the riuer, where the supposed myne should bee. Wherefore our master bare roome for Ramels-ford,[2] being a river southward of another, called *Cunninghams-ford*,[3] some twelve leagues. And we came to an anchor at the entrance on the south side of the ford, about seuen of the clocke.

Ramels River.

Wednesday, the two and twentieth day, about nine or

[1] According to Gatonbe, there was a quarrel between Hall and William Gordon, the master's mate of the *Patience*, while the two ships were at anchor in King's Fiord. " Our general, being angry, would not come aboard of us, but was in the vice-admiral."

[2] Henrik Rommel's Fiord was discovered by the Danes when Hall was with them in 1605, and so named. Hall, in his report to King Christian IV, places Rommels Fiord in 66° 35′ N. latitude. Further on, in a marginal note, Baffin gives 67° as the latitude. Rommels Fiord is the harbour of Holsteinborg. The settlement on the south side is in 66° 54′ N. The original settlement of Holsteinborg was founded, on the north side of the harbour, in 1759, in a spot now overgrown with willows and overshadowed by the lofty range of the Prœste-fjeld. This is exactly in Baffin's latitude. It was removed to its present site, on the south side, in 1771, and the church was founded by Paul Egede on January 6th, 1775.

[3] North of Rommels Fiord is the promontory named Cape Sophia by Hall, in 1605, after King Christian's mother ; and beyond it is Cunningham's Fiord, which Hall places in 67° 25′ N. The Danish chart of 1832 places its entrance in 67°15′ N.

ten of the clocke, the sauages came to barter with vs, being
about fortie of them, and continued about an houre and an

halfe : at which time our master, *James Hall*, being in the
boate,[1] a sauage with his dart strooke him a deadly wound
vpon the right side, which our surgeon did thinke did
pierce his liuer. We all mused that he should strike him,
and offer no harme to any of the rest; vnlesse it were that
they knew him since he was there with the *Danes ;* for out
of that riuer they carried away fiue of the people, whereof
neuer any returned againe;[2] and in the next riuer they
killed a great number. And it should seeme that he which
killed him was either brother, or some neere kinsman to
some of them that were carried away ; for he did it very
resolutely, and came within foure yards of him. And for
ought we could see, the people are very kinde one to
another, and ready to reuenge any wrong offred to them.
All that day he lay very sore pained, looking for death
euery houre, and resigned all his charge to Master *Andrew
Barker,* master of the *Harts-ease,* willing him to place
another in his room master of the small ship.[3]

[1] Gatonbe says that William Huntriss and two others were in the
boat with Hall, when he was murdered.

[2] There is a sad account of the kidnapping of natives during the
Danish voyages of 1605 and 1606, in which Hall was engaged. In the
first voyage Hall's people seized four Eskimo, but killed one to strike
terror into the rest, who were untractable. Two were seized by the
crew of the other ship. These poor people were brought to Denmark,
but constantly cast an eye northward with sorrowful countenances and
pitiable sighs. At last they took to flight in their kayaks, but were
caught and brought back to Copenhagen, where two of them died of
grief. One of the Eskimo used to weep bitterly whenever he saw a
little child hanging on its mother's neck, from which it was concluded
that he must have had a wife and children. But no one could speak
with them. Two died on the voyage back to Greenland. The last once
more fled in his kayak, and was not overtaken until he was sixty or
seventy leagues from land. On being brought back he also died of
grief. See *Crantz's History of Greenland*, i, p. 277 ; and *Peyrere*, p. 150.

[3] Doubtless Hall named his constant and faithful attendant William
Huntriss to be Master of the *Heart's Ease*.

Thursday, the three and twentieth, about eight of the clocke in the morning he dyed, being very penitent for all his former offences. And after wee had shrowded him wee carried him in the shallop, to burie him in some out iland,[1] according to his owne request while he was liuing. After we had buried him, we went in the shallop to seeke for the mine, which we had expected so long. All that day we rowed along toward the north, passing by a cape called *Queen Sophias cape.* That night we staied at an iland, some three leagues short of the river.

Friday, the four and twentieth, in the morning, wee rowed along and came to the place which is on the south side of the entrance of *Cunningham's* river. And we found diuers places where the Danes had digged; it was a kinde of shining stone, which, when our goldsmith, *James Carlisle,* had tried, it was found of no value, and had no mettall at all in it, but was like vnto *Moscouie fludde,*[2] and of a glittering colour. That day, after we had dyned, wee rowed vp that riuer some foure leagues, where diuers of our company went vp into the mountaines, and found a valley more pleasant than they had seene in the countrey. That euening we returned, and came to the place where the *Danes* had digged their supposed mine, and tooke some of it in our boate to carry with vs, and returned toward our ship. That night we rowed and sailed, and the next morning, about nine of the clocke, we came to our ship.

Saturday, the fiue and twentieth, being Saint *James* his day, in the forenoone, we came to our shippe, lying on the south side of the riuer called *Ramels* river. And as soone as our master found that the people came no more to trade with vs, he determined to depart with the shippe into the Kings Ford to the *Patience;* and rowing about the harbour, where we lay to finde some neerer way out to the sea, we

Margin notes: The death of James Hall. Queene Sophias Cape. Cunningham River. The supposed Mine found to be of no value. A pleasant Valley.

[1] One of the Knight Islands, outside Holsteinborg.
[2] Mica.

Many of their winter houses in Ramels River. The fashion of their greater Boates. found among the Ilands where many of their winter houses had bin, and some of their tents were but lately carried away. In which place wee also found one of their long boates, made of wood, and bound together for the most part with shiuers of whales fins, and covered with seales skinnes, being some two and thirtie foote in length, and some fiue foote broad, having tenne thoughts or seates in it. That day, about twelue of the clocke, we weighed

Ramels ford in the latitude of 67°. The variation is 24° 16'. anchor, and departed out of Ramels Ford, which lieth in the latitude of 67°, and the variation of the compasse is 24° 16', being a very faire riuer, and one of the most principall which we saw in that countrey, stretching in east and east and by south. This night, about one of the clocke, we came to the *Patience,* lying in the Kings Ford.[1]

Sunday, the sixe and twentieth, Master Andrew Barker, and our merchant, Master Wilkinson, with other of the company, were in conference about returning home, because that since our master was slaine, none of the sauages would trade with us as they were wont.

Wednesday, the nine and twentieth, we were likewise occupied about taking in of ballast, for our shippe was very light; and that evening it was agreed that *Andrew Barker,*[2] master of the *Harts-ease,* should goe master of the *Patience,* which was sore against the minde of *William*

---

[1] Gatonbe says: "This day at night came our vice-admiral, with our great pinnace at her stern, her flag hanging down, and her ancient hanging down over the poop, which was a sign of death."

[2] The appointment of Andrew Barker, to succeed Hall, appears to have been unpopular with the two master's mates, William Gordon and John Hemsley, and with some of the men. There was a display of mutinous feeling. Several called out for Hemsley to be general; but the quartermasters, boatswains, gunner, and other officers declared for Barker. Gatonbe says that Barker was an old and experienced seaman, having before been ruler and overseer of many good men in ships in Hull, besides other places, and having been one of the chief masters and wardens of the Trinity House. The officers

Gourdon ;[3] and *William Huntrice*[4] was appointed master of
the *Harts-ease ;* and *John Gatenby,*[5] one of the quartermasters of the *Patience,* was masters-mate of the *Harts-
ease.*

William
Huntrice
Master of
the Hearts-
ease.

eventually succeeded in persuading the two crews to accept Barker as
general of the expedition and the arrangements made by him.

Through the kindness of Mr. Wilson, of the Trinity House, at Hull,
I am able to give the following additional particulars respecting Andrew
Barker. He was admitted a younger brother of the Trinity House of
Hull in the year 1594, and was three times Warden, namely, in 1606,
1613, and 1618. In 1611 Barker made a voyage to the northern seas,
and brought back a cargo from Wardhous (Vardö in Norway).

Among the Lansdowne Manuscripts in the British Museum (923),
there is a collection of pencil-notes on Hull and the neighbourhood by
Warburton, made in the summer of 1724. From one of these notes it
appears that Andrew Barker presented one of the compartments of
painted glass in the east window of the old chapel of the Hull Trinity
House. The figure was that of St. James-the-less. This has disappeared ; but there still hangs in the Hall of the Trinity House the

---

[3] William Gordon was afterwards employed in Spitzbergen voyages.
He cannot have been the same William Gordon whom the Muscovy
Company sent to reside at Pustozera on the Pechora river in 1611 as
one of their traders. This William Gordon wrote an interesting report,
in 1615, on the Samoyeds, their dress, sledges, tents, customs, etc.,
which is published in *Purchas,* iii, p. 553.

[4] William Huntriss, or Huntrice, was a Yorkshire lad. Purchas says
he came from " Stoneborough". But there is no such place in York-
shire. It is probably a misprint for Scarborough. Huntriss is a Scar-
borough name, and there is Huntriss Row in the old town. Young
William Huntriss went the first voyage to Greenland with James
Hall. This expedition, under Captain Cunningham, was sent by the
King of Denmark, and sailed from Copenhagen on May 2nd, 1605.
Hall was master of the *Troost,* Cunningham's ship, and Huntriss was
Hall's boy. The ship anchored off the Greenland coast, and Hall went
to explore in the pinnace, attended by his boy. On this occasion young
Huntriss, when in the boat, was shot through both buttocks by an
Eskimo arrow.

He went with Hall in his second and third voyages, and was allowed
£30 a year by the King of Denmark for his skill in navigation.

When Hall left the Danish service his faithful boy accompanied him,
and went out in this Greenland voyage from Hull, of which Baffin is
the historian. Now we find him promoted to be Master of the second

Tuesday, the fourth of August, in the morning, the winde
They come
out of
harbour. being northerly, a very small gale, we got to sea, where the
winde came to the southward, and we tacked sometime on
the one boord, and sometime on the other, making small
way on our course.

Munday (*sic*), the tenth, was raine and foule weather,
as it had continued euery day since wee came from harbour,
sauing the seuenth day, which was somewhat faire; for
Thick and
foggie
weather,
the winde
being south. commonly, while the winde is south, it is very thick and
foule weather. We tacked sometimes on one boord, and
sometimes on the other, making a south-by-west way, at
noone six leagues.

Wednesday, the twelfth, it waxed calme, we being some-
Burnils
Cape. what southward of a cape, called *Burnils Cape*;[1] and about

model of a *kayak*, with an Eskimo in it, which was presented by
Andrew Barker. It has the following inscription:—
   "*Andrew Barker, one of the Masters of this House, on his voyage from
Greenland, anno domini 1613, took up this boat and a man in it, of which
this is the effigy.*"
In the accounts for the second quarter of Andrew Barker's third
Wardenship, A.D. 1619, are the following entries:—
         " Item to Edward Ffewlis for carving the Greynlander   .   vs
         " Item to the paynter for the Greynlander   .   . iiij."
And in the succeeding Warden's accounts (A.D. 1620) is the following
entry:—" Item to Andrewe Barker, wch he paid about the Gren-
         landman more than he accompted for at the auditt .   viijs."
Kayaks from Greenland were also brought home by Frobisher and
Davis, and there was one hanging in the hall of Sir Thomas Smith's
house. In the curious old *Schiffer-gesellschaft*, at Lubeck, there is an
old *kayak* hanging from the beams, which appears, from the inscription, to have been brought to Europe by the Danish Expedition of 1607.
   [1] Burnil's Cape is the Cape Burnitt of the Admiralty Chart, which is
copied from the Danish Chart of 1832. The name was given by Hall

---

ship, the *Heart's Ease*. Further on we shall find that Baffin's ship, the
Patience, lost sight of the *Heart's Ease* in a gale on September 2nd. She
arrived safely in the Thames on September 19th, and I have not been
able to find any further trace of young Huntriss.
   [5] Or Gatonbe, writer of the other account of the voyage in Churchill.
See note at page 2.

three or foure of the clocke in the afternoone, the winde
came to the north and by west, an easie gale, with faire
weather.

The eighteenth, at noon, we were in 58° 50'. The seventeenth day I tooke the variation of the compasse, finding
it to be 13° 22', contrary to the obseruations of others in
this place. And if any doe doubt of the truth thereof,
they may with a little paines prove it. The eighteenth of
August, the declination of the sunne was 9° 58', for the
meridian of London. But we being almost foure houres of
time to the westward thereof, there are three minutes to be
abated from the rest: and so the declination was 9° 55';
and his height aboue the horizon was 24° 40' in the latitude
of 59° 0'; and his distance from the south to the westward,
by the compasse, was 81°. And for truth of the first obseruation, I tooke another shortly after, finding them not
to differ aboue 4'.

Wednesday, the nineteenth, the winde still continued
with thick and hasie weather, we being at noone in the
latitude of 58° 30', or thereabout, making a south south-
east way, about ten leagues.

Thursday, the twentieth, was faire weather, the wind at
east north-east, wee steered away south-east and south-
east and by east, making at noone a south-east and by
south way, about thirtie leagues, being at noone in the
latitude of 57° 20'. This day, in the afternoone, I tooke
the variation of the compasse, and found it about 11° 10'.

Friday, the one and twentieth, faire weather, with the
winde at north and north by east, and we made an east

Variation 13° 22'.

Variation 11° 10'.

in the voyage of 1605, and I think it probable that it should be Cape
Brunel, after Oliver Brunel, the Dutch explorer, who was for some time
in the Danish service. For a full account of Brunel, and of the difficult questions connected with his history, see Lieut. Kooleman Beynen's
Introduction to the *Barents' Voyages* (Hakluyt Society's vol. 1876). See
also the note at the end of the Voyage of Knight (Hakluyt Society's
vol. *Voyages of Lancaster*).

south-east way, half southerly, some twentie-foure leagues, being at noone, by obseruation, in the latitude of 56° 50'.

Saturday, the two and twentieth, faire weather, the wind at north and north by east, wee made an east way half southerly, some twentie-two leagues, being at noone in the latitude of 56° 47'.

Sunday, the three and twentieth, faire weather, the wind at west north-west, we making an east and east by north way, about twenty-four leagues. This day I tooke the variation of the compasse, and found it to be 7° 23', being at noone in the latitude of 57° 26'.

Munday, the foure and twentieth, being *S. Bartholomewes* day, faire weather with a north north-west, wee making an east north-east way, halfe northerly, about twenty-seven leagues, and were at noon, by observation, in the latitude of 58° 4'. This day I obserued and found the compasse to be varied 7° 20'.

Tuesday, the fiue and twentieth, faire weather and calme; the winde at north, wee made a north-east and by east way, seuenteene leagues, being at noone in the latitude of 58° 30'. This day I found the common compasse to be varied one point, and the true variation to be 6° 4'.

Wednesday, the sixe and twentieth, faire weather also, with the wind north north-west, wee made a north-east and by east way halfe, about twentie two leagues, being in the height of 59° 10'.

Thursday, the seven and twentieth, indifferent faire weather, with a stiffe gale of wind at the north north-west, we making a north-east way about thirty-one leagues, being at noone in the latitude of 60° 10'.

Friday, the eight and twentieth, the wind at south-east, with a stiffe gale, wee made good about noone a north-east and by east way, about twenty-nine leagues. This day, in the afternoon it blew so greate a storme that we were in great distresse, the winde at east south-east. But about

Variation 7° 23'.

Variation 7° 20'.

The true variation 6° 4'.

eleuen of the clocke it came to the north-west, and north-west by north. And we ranne some twentie leagues.

Saturday, the nine and twentieth, it blew so stiffe that wee could beare none but our foresaile, making an east and by south way, halfe southerly, about thirtie leagues.

Sunday, the thirtieth, all the forenoone it blew a very stiffe gale, and about noone the winde came southerly ; and it blew a very great storme, which continued all that day and that night, in such sort that we could not saile at all, but all that night lay at hull.

Monday, the one and thirtieth, in the morning about foure of the clocke, the winde came to the south-west a very stiffe gale, at which time we set our fore-saile. The wind continued all this day and night; we steered away east and by south, making at noon an east north-east way, about thirtie foure leagues.

Tuesday, the first of September, the wind still continued at south-west, blowing a very stiffe gale; we steered away east and by south, making an east way about fiftie leagues. This day, at noon, we were in the latitude of 60° 45'.

Wednesday, the second, faire weather, with the wind at south-west; wee made an east and by south way, half a point southerly, about fortie-two leagues, being at noone in the latitude of 60° 10'. This day I obserued, and found the compasse to be varied three degrees to the westward.

Thursday, the third day, faire weather, the wind at south-west; wee made an east by north way at noone, about twentie leagues. This day, in the after-noone, the winde being at north north-west, it blew a very stiffe gale for two watches; and toward seuen or eight of the clocke the storme so increased that our shippe was not able to beare any saile. And all that night wee lay at hull.[1]

Friday, the fourth, the storme still continued, and we

---

[1] Lying-to.

could beare no saile all that day till about foure of the clocke in the afternoone, at which time we set our fore course and our maine course. The night before, in the storme we lost the *Harts-ease*.[1] This day wee made some twelue leagues east and by north, and we fell to lee-ward, lying at hull some fiue leagues south by west.

The lose company of their con- sort, the Hartsease.

Saturday, the fift, calme weather, but very thicke and close all the fore-noone : the wind continued still at north north-west; we making, from the time wee set our courses the day before, about twentie leagues east half southerly, beeing at noone in the latitude of 59° 53′.

Sunday, the sixt, faire weather, the wind at north north-west, we steering away east north-east, and east and by north, made an east by north way, half northerly some 29 leagues, being at noone in 60° 10′. This day the compasse was varied to the east sixe degrees. This afternoone it was almost calme, and wee sounded, and found ground at sixtie eight fathomes. This evening, about ten of the clock, the wind came to the south-east.

Variation 6 degrees to the East. Ground found.

Munday, the seventh, very faire weather, the wind south-east and south-east by east ; wee tacked in the morning to the northward, and ranne east north-east and east by north vntill seuen or eight in the afternoone, at which time we tacked vp to the southward, and went away south-west till toward twelve a clocke that night, twentie leagues.

Tuesday, the eight, in our morning watch I found our selues to be in 59° 20′, and about fiue of the clock I espied land, which wee supposed to bee the Isles of *Orkney*, as

[1] The *Heart's Ease*, under command of young William Huntriss, with John Gatonbe on board, diligently writing his journal, lost sight of the *Patience* on the 4th of September, as here recorded by Baffin. On the 8th she sighted Fair Isle, and on the 15th arrived in Yarmouth Roads, proceeding to London instead of going to Hull, as the *Patience* did. The *Heart's Ease* entered the Thames on the 19th of September, and Huntriss caused the flags to be hoisted half mast, in token of the death of his beloved commander, James Hall. He brought the ship up to St. Katherine's Pool.

afterward we found them to be the same; and toward three The Iles of Orkney. of the clocke we came to an anchor in a channell running betweene the Ilands, where the people came to vs, and brought vs hennes, geese, and sheepe, and sold them to vs for old clothes and shoes, desiring rather them then money. There are about eighteene of these Ilands, which are called by the name of the Orkneis.

Wednesday, the ninth, it was thicke weather, and the wind so easterly that wee could not weigh anchor.

Thursday, the tenth, faire weather, and the wind came to the north-west, and about noone we weighed anchor; and towarde fiue of the clocke we were cleere off the Iles. The channel, for the most part, lyeth north-west and south-east. The lying of the Channel in Orkney. All that night we stood away south-east.

Friday, the eleuenth, faire weather, with the wind at north north-west; and about nine of the clocke in the morning we steered away south south-east, at which time wee had sight of Buguham-nesse,[1] and about two of the Buguham-ness. clocke we were thwart of it. The seuenteenth, we came to an anchor in Hull Road, for which the Lord bee praysed. They arrive at Hull.

Here I thinke it not amisse briefly to relate the state and manner of the people of Groenland, forasmuch as I could learne; as also what likelihood there is of a passe into the sea, which lyeth vpon Tartarie and China.

The north-west part of Gronland is an exceeding high land to the sea-ward, and almost nothing but mountaynes, which are wonderfull high all within the land, as farre as wee could perceiue; and they are all of stone, some of one colour, and some of another, and all glistering, as though they were of rich value, but indeed they are not worth No profitable Vre. anything; for our gold-smith, James Carlisle, tryed very much of the Vre, and found it to bee nothing worth.[2] If there bee any mettall, it lyeth so low in the mountaynes

---

[1] Buchan Ness, the east point of Aberdeenshire.

[2] The mica, often found in masses in clefts of the gneiss, was mistaken for silver ore.

that it cannot bee well come by. There are some rocks in these mountaynes, which are exceeding pure stone, finer, and whiter then alabaster.[1] The sides of these mountaynes continually are covered with snow for the most part, and especially the north sides, and the No[r]th sides of the valleyes hauing a kind of mosse, and in some places grasse, with a little branch running all along the ground, bearing a little black berrie; it runneth along the ground like three-leaued grasse heere in England. There are few or no trees growing, as farre as wee could perceiue; but in one place, some fortie miles within the land, in a river, which wee called *Balls* River. There I saw, on the south side of an high mountayne, which we went vp, and found (as it were) a yong groue of small wood, some of it sixe or seuen foot high, like a coppice in England that had beene some two or three yeers cut; and this was the most wood that wee saw growing in this country, being some of it a kind of willow, juniper, and such like.[2]

We found in many places much angelica. We suppose the people eate the roots thereof, for some causes, for we haue seene them have many of them in their boats.[3]

Left margin notes:
Continuall snow.
Grasse.
No trees.
Balls River.
A grove of small wood.

---

[1] Quartz.

[2] The largest tree ever seen by Dr. Rink, in Greenland, was a birch fourteen feet high, in the Tasermiut fjord, in 60° N. lat. This *Betula alpestris* is only found south of 62° N. South of 65° N. the alder (*Alnus repens*) grows scantily.

[3] The *Quan* (*Archangelica officinalis*) is found in the fjords of South Greenland, and more rarely in Disco. The word *Quan*, now used by the Eskimo, is Norse, and hence it is supposed that angelica was introduced by the Normans. The young stalks are eaten raw, being brittle and sweet. In sheltered spots the plant will grow to a height of six feet. Angelica was well known in the kitchen gardens of England in the days of Baffin. Gervase Markham, in his "*Country Farm*" (published in 1616), includes it among the physic herbs, which should, he recommends, be grown in certain borders below the kitchen garden, near the wall of the orchard. The root was believed to be sovereign against the plague and all sorts of poisons, and Englishmen then used the leaves and stalks in sauce with their meats, because it was supposed to help digestion

There are a great store of foxes in the Ilands, and in the *Foxes.*
Mayne, of sundry colours; and there are a kind of hares, *White hares*
as white as snow, with their furre or haire very long.

Also there be deere, but they are most commonly vp *Deere.*
within the Mayne very farre; because the people doe so
much hunt them that come neere the sea. I saw at one
time seuen of them together, which were all that wee did
see in the country. But our men have bought diuers coates
of the people, made of deeres skinnes, and have bought of
their hornes also. Besides, we have diuers times seene the
footsteps of some beast, whose foote was bigger than the *These seeme to be*
foot of a great oxe. Furthermore, the inhabitants haue a *elkes, or Loshes.*
kinde of dogges, which they keepe at their houses and *Dogges like Wolues.*
tents, which dogges are almost like vnto wolues, liuing by
fish, as the foxes doe. But one thing is very strange, as I
thought; for the pizzles of both dogges and foxes are bone. *The pizzles of Dogges*
The people, all the summer time, vse nothing but fishing, *and foxes are bone; so*
drying their fish and seales flesh vpon the rockes, for their *also is the Morses piz-*
winter prouision. Euery one, both man and woman, haue *zle, of which I*
each of them a boate, made with long small pieces of firre- *have by me one of stone.*
wood, couered with seales skinnes very well drest, and
sewed so well with sinewes or guts that no water can
pierce them through, being some of them aboue twentie
foot long, and not past two foot, or two foot and an halfe
broad, in forme of a weauers shittle (*sic*), and so light, that
a man may carrie many of them at once for the weight.
In these boates they will row so swiftly, that it is almost *The great swiftnesse*
incredible; for no ship in the world is able to keepe way *of their Boats.*
with them, although shee haue neuer so good a gale of
wind; and yet they vse but one oare, who, sitting in the
middle (*sic*) of their boate, and holding their oare in the *Their Oares broad at both ends.*

very much. The leaues were held to be good against sorcery and en-
chantment. For notices of angelica in Greenland, see *Crantz*, i, p. 61 ;
and *Egede*, p. 45.

middle, being broad at each end like our oares, will at an
instant goe backward and forward as they please.[1]

In these boates they catch the most part of their food,
being seales and salmons, morses, and other kinds of fishes.
Some they kill with their darts, and other some with
angles, hauing a line made of small shiuers of whales
finnes, and an hooke of some fishes bones, with which lines
and hookes we also have caught very much fish.

Salmons
and Morses,
etc. Angles
and Lines.

Also they haue another kinde of boate, which is very
long; for wee haue seene one of them thirty-two foot in
length, open in the toppe like our boates, hauing tenne
seats in it; in which, when they remooue their dwellings,
they carrie their goods or house-hold stuffe; for they remooue their dwellings very often, as their fishing doth
serue, liuing in the summer-time in tents made of seales
skinnes, and in winter in houses somewhat in the ground.

Their great
Boats 32
foot long.

Wee could not particularly learn their rites or cere-
monies; but generally they worship the sunne, as chiefe
authour of their felicitie. At their first approach vnto vs,
they vsed with their hands to point vp to the sunne, and
to strike their hands vpon ther brests *Ilyout*[2]; as who would
say, I meane no harme; which they will doe very often,
and will not come neer you vntil you do the like, and then
they will come without any feare at all.

They wor-
ship the
Sunne.

Their salu-
tation.

They burie their dead in the out-Ilands neere the sea-
side. Their manner of buriall is this :—vpon the tops of
the hils they gather a company of stones together, and
make thereof an hollow caue or graue, of the length and
breadth of the bodie which they intend to burie, laying the
stones somewhat close like a wall, that neyther foxes nor
other such beasts may deuoure the bodies, couering them

Their
burials.

---

[1] Both Frobisher and Davis brought home kayaks, and one was hanging in the hall of Sir Thomas Smith's house.

[2] Davis, in his list, gives the same word with the same meaning—
"*Yliaoute*", "I mean no harm" (Hakluyt Society's ed., p. 21).

with broad stones, shewing afar off like a pile of stones. And neere vnto this graue where the bodie lyeth is another, wherein they burie his bow and arrowes, with his darts and all his other prouision which hee vsed while hee was liuing. Hee is buried in all his apparell ; and the coldnesse of the climate doth keepe the bodie from smelling and stinking, although it lye aboue ground.

They burie the weapons and all other furniture of the dead.

They eat all their food raw, and vse no fire to dress their victuals, as farre as wee could perceiue. Also wee haue seene them drinke the salt-water at our shippes side ; but whether it be vsuall or no, I cannot tell. Although they dresse not their meate with fire, yet they vse fire for other things, as to warme them, etc.

They vse fire.

Diuers of our men were of opinion that they were man-eaters, and would haue deuoured vs, if they could haue caught vs. But I do not thinke they would ; for if they had bin so minded, they might at one time haue caught our cooke, and two other with him, as they were filling of water at an Iland a great way from ovr ship. These three, I say, were in the ships boate, without eyther musket or any other weapon ; when, as a great company of the sauages came rowing vnto them with their darts and other furniture, which they neuer goe without, and stood looking into the boate for nayles, or any old iron, which they so greatly desire, while our men were in such a feare that they knew not what to doe. At length our cooke remembered that hee had some old iron in his pocket, and gaue each of them some, as farre as it would goe, with his key of his chest. And presently they all departed, without offering any harme at all : but this I speake not that I would haue men to trust them, or to goe among them vnprouided of weapons.

They are not Man-eaters.

Nailes and old Iron greatly desired of the Sauages.

SECOND RECORDED VOYAGE

OF

WILLIAM BAFFIN.

I.

A Journall of the Voyage made to Greenland[1] with sixe English
ships and a Pinasse, in the yeere 1613.

Written by MASTER WILLIAM BAFFIN.[2]

Ascension
day.

By the prouidence of Almightie God wee departed from
Queenborough the thirteenth day of May with sixe good
ships, viz., the *Tigre*, admirall; the *Matthew*, vice-admirall:
the *Sea-horse*, called the *Gamaliel*, the reare-admirall; the
Desire, the *Annula*, and the *Richard and Barnard*, with
the *John and Francis* shortly to follow.[3]

---

[1] Spitzbergen.

[2] From *Purchas*, Part III, lib. IV, cap. v, pp. 716 to 720. There is
another account of this voyage, believed to have been written by
Fotherby, which follows this journal.

[3] The Fotherby Narrative tells us that Mr. Benjamin Joseph, of
London, was chief captain—"a man very sufficient and worthy of his
place". There were twenty-four Biscayners, the most expert whale
fishers of those days, in the fleet. The *Tiger*, of 260 tons, was admiral;
the *Matthew*, of 250 tons, vice-admiral; and the *Gamaliel*, 200 tons,
rear-admiral. The other vessels were the *John and Francis*, 180 tons;
Desire, 180 tons; and *Annula*, 140 tons. The *Richard and Barnard*
was a pinnace of 60 tons, intended for further discovery. The fleet
dropped down to Gravesend on April 30th, and on the 4th of May
"wee entered into the Swaile at Quinborowe". On the 7th, the Royal
Fleet, returning from landing the Count Palatine and the Princess
Elizabeth, passed them, and there was an exchange of salutes. On the

The one and twentieth day, faire weather, the winde southwarde, wee still making to the northwards. This morning wee had sight of land on the coast of Norway, it lying east and by north off about twelue or fourteene leagues. This day, at noone, we were in the latitude of 61° 30′, the variation of the compasse at Scoutes-nes is eight degrees east, it being about ten or twelue leagues off; wee hauing made a north way halfe east, about thirtie leagues.

The three and twentieth, at noone, in the latitude of 65° 45′, in which place the needle of declination doth dippe vnder the horizon 63° 30′ by that instrument, which declineth 54 at London.

The thirtieth day, about three of the clock,[1] wee espied the land of Greenland,[2] being about eight or nine leagues off. The southwardest part of it bare south-east and by east off it, which shortly wee perceiued to bee the land lying in 76° 55′, which is called Horne-sound.[3] This land

Greenland attayned in eighteen dayes.

13th of May the exploring fleet sailed from the Swale. Benjamin Joseph, the general of the voyage, was a man in high repute for skill and conduct. After his return from Spitzbergen he commanded a small ship of Bristol, and brought timely relief to Waterford, when Captain Downton arrived there from the East Indies in October 1613, in sore need of provisions. At that very time the Court of Directors was recognising his claim to command one of their fleets. He appears to have made demands at first which were considered unreasonable ; but an agreement was arrived at, and in December 1613, Benjamin Joseph was appointed to command the East India Company's fleet. He himself was in the *Charles*, on board of which a journal was kept by Henry Crosby, master's mate *(preserved at the India Office—No. 23)*, and his vice-admiral was the *Unicorn*. In 1617 Captain Joseph was slain in a fight with a Portuguese karrack. His widow Isabell petitioned the Company for a gratuity, and a sum of £40 was granted, and thankfully accepted by her son-in-law, Mr. Maddocks.

[1] The Fotherby Narrative says four o'clock in the morning, all the ships being in company.

[2] Spitzbergen.

[3] Discovered and so named by Jonas Poole in his voyage in the *Amity* for the Muscovy Company, in 1610.

lyeth, by our common compasse, north north-west. Within two houres after we had sight of land, it began to snowe, and was very cold. This euening the compasse was varied thirteene degrees west.

The one and thirtieth day, variable weather with snowe, and very cold, and the winde also variable; and in the afternoone the winde was at the north-east. In the morning wee espied a ship, and about noone wee spoke with her, and their master and pilot came aboord of vs; and wee knew them to bee that ship of Saint John de Luys, which had leaue of the Companie to fish ; and they told vs that there were eight Spaniards on the coast. Also wee espied another ship, which we supposed to be a Frenchman, and had one Allan Sallas to their pilot.

A ship of Saint John de Luz.

Eight Spaniards on the Coast.

The Generall was Captain Beniamin Joseph, after slaine in a fight with a Carrike.

The second of June, in the morning, about fiue of the clocke, our generall sent our shallop to a small pinke, that all this night we saw along the shoare, to bid their master and pilot come aboord vs, which presently they did. The masters name was Clais Martin of Horne, and his ship was for Dunkerke, and he told vs that he was consorted with another ship that was his admirall; the captaines name was Fopp of Dunkerke, and that he was on the coast. Wee kept the master and pilot aboord of vs, and sent some of our men aboord of her, and brought her vnder our lee; and then wee sent their master aboord againe, charging them to follow vs. This afternoone we took their shallop, with fiue or sixe men, whereof two were English men, and one Scot, at the Faire foreland.[1]

Dutch ship.

No night the 23 May.

The fourth day, also faire weather. This morning was the first whale killed.[2] We had no night since the three

[1] The northern point of Prince Charles Island, so named by Jonas Poole in 1610.

[2] Fotherby, who was in the *Matthew*, says that they ran before a fresh gale to the north end of Prince Charles Island, and then beat up into Sir Thomas Smith's Bay, where the fleet anchored. Then the Bis-

and twentieth of May. The fift day, faire weather, but very cold, the winde north.[1] We sayled along the Iland, being about eighteene or twentie leagues in length, lying for the most part, by the common compasse, north and by west half westward. About nine of the clocke in the afternoone we saw our other three ships, viz., the *Gamaliel,* the *Desire,* and the *Richard and Barnard,* which lay there to and fro, because they could not goe into their harbour by reason of the ice ; and also because there were foure other ships in a bay or coue, called Pooppy Bay, or Nickes Coue ; and also other ships on the other side in Greene Harbour. We sailed along the drift ice vntill about one or two of the clocke·in the morning, at which time we came to an anchor in the entrance of the sound, because the ice came driuing out so fast.

The sixt day, faire weather, the wind variable till the afternoone, at which time it came to the northwards. About three in the afternoone we weighed anchor, and about ten of the clocke we came to the foure ships lying in Pooppy Bay, two of them being Hollanders, and one a Rocheller, and the other a ship of Burdeaux. The masters of the Hollanders came aboord of our ship to speake with the generall, both of them being of Amsterdam, and

Divers strangers.

cayners, " our whale stickers", went away in their boats to look out for whales off the Foreland. The rest of the men took the coppers for melting blubber, and the casks on shore, and got everything ready for boiling down. Then came the news that the Biscayners had killed a whale, and from that time the work of boiling down went briskly forward.

[1] On the 5th, word was brought from Green Harbour that five ships, Spanish and French, were come into Ice Sound, intending to fish for the whale. So the *Tiger* weighed anchor and made sail for Ice Sound. " Then did our Admiral continue as a *wafter* alongst the coast, till the 27th of June, and then he came to us againe into Sir Thomas Smyth's Baye." A "*wafter*" was a term applied to ships of war, probably from their carrying flags or *wafts*.

brought a commission granted by the Graue Maurice, for to fish in this country. But, when they saw our Kings Maiestys Commission granted to the worshipful companie, they told our generall that they would depart this coast, hauing our general's ticket to shew to their aduenturers that they were there, and had made their port, and how he would not suffer them to fish. We anchored close by the French ship, wherein was Allane Sallis,[1] being ready to fight if they refused to come aboord vs. So when we sent our shallop, the master came presently, and their surgeon, who could speake English. At the first, they denyed that Sallas was aboord of them; but, being hardly urged, they confessed that hee and one Thomas Fisher, an English man, was aboord, who were both presently sent for. This Sallas was their pilot, and Fisher was their gunner.

The seuenth day, faire weather, we road still at anchor. This day I obserued the latitude of the place, and found it in 78° 24'. The variation of the compasse is, in this place, 15° 21' west. About a north sunne, a small ship of Biscay came into the harbour where we roade.

The eight day, for the most part snow, the winde southward. This day the master of the French ship, being a ship of nine score, or two hundred, called the *Jaques* of Burdeaux, agreed with our generall that he might fish on the coast: our generall was to have halfe the whales he could kill. Also, this day the master of the ship of Rochel, and the master of the small ship of Biscay, were agreed to depart from the coast.

The ninth day, faire weather. This morning the *Gumaliel*, our rear-admirall, and the *Desire*, weighed anchor to goe for Greene-harbour, where two ships lay, one of Dunkerke, and the other of Saint Sebastian in Biscay. The captaine of the Dunkirke, called Fopp, had beene with our generall, and told him that he would depart from this coast. Our generall gaue him leaue to take the pilot of the small

Marginal notes:
Lat. 78° 24'.
Ship of Biscay.
Snowe.

---

[1] Allen Sallowes, an English pilot.

pinke, and the other Dutch men he had taken of his, keeping only the English men and the Scots; also the two ships of Holland, with the ship of Biscay, and that of *Rochel* weighed anchor, and departed from this harbour. About sixe of the clocke in the afternoone came the master of the ship of Saint Sebastian aboord of vs, being brought by one of the masters mates of the *Desire* (they hauing taken two of his shallops) to know our generals pleasure, whether he should haue them againe or no. Our generall gaue them him againe, vpon condition that he would depart the coast. About a north north-west sunne, we weighed anchor to goe for Horne-Sound, where we heard that there were diuers ships; the wind northward; a small gale.

The tenth day, faire weather, the winde at north, being very close weather. About a north sunne, we came to an anchor, in the entrance of Low Sound, where we saw two ships ride at anchor. Our generall sent our shallop to see what ships they were, who found them to bee the two ships of Holland. Also our long boate went on shoare, to set vp the Kings Maiesties armes vpon a low point of land, lying a great way off, called Low-nesse. We set vp a crosse of wood, and nayled the armes vpon it.

Low Sound.

His Maiesties Armes and a Crosse set up at Lownesse.

The thirteenth day, in the morning, it snowed very fast, being very thicke weather, the winde variable, we standing off from the land. About seuen of the clock it began to cleere vp, at which time we espied three ships; and making toward them, at length we perceiued them to be the three ships which came from the bay where we road; the winde also was at east and by south, and blew a very stiffe gale. Then we stood in for the shoare, and spent most of this day in turn vp Horne-Sound. And about a north north-west sunne, at ten a clock, wee espied six ships lying at anchor on the south side of the Sound, in a small bay. The one of them was Captaine Fopp, the Dunkerker, who came in before vs, and was appointed by our generall to

come into this harbour, and there to stay for vs, and to
goe to the Foreland, to haue his other ship which we kept
there. Foure of them were Biscaines of Saint Sebastian;
and one of them was in the harbour where we road and
found the French ship. The sixt was a ship of Amsterdam

wherein Thomas Bonner was master and pilot, and aboue
twentie English men more. All the Biscaines came aboord
of vs, as soone as we were at an anchor; but Thomas
Bonner refused to come, being sent for by our generall.
Our generall commanded our gunner to shoot at him, he
himself discharging the second ordnance. Then presently
he began to set saile, and cut his cable, thinking to get
from vs; but wee hauing shot him through three or foure
times, they began to weaue vs, so we sent our shallop and
he came aboord. There were fiue or sixe more of the
English men fetched aboord, and some of our men sent to
bring her to an anchor, where she might ride safe, for shee
was almost run ashoare. This was about a north sunne, or
eleuen a clocke. The Biscaines were charged presently to
depart, so soone as they had filled fresh water, which they
said they wanted; and to bring what whale finnes they had
found, or had taken, or other things.

The fourteenth day, faire weather, the winde at east
north-east. This morning, one of the Biscaines brought a
few whale finnes aboord of vs, and the skin of a beare,
which they had killed. Then was our boate-swaine sent
aboord of them to search their ships, and to bid them depart.
Our generall kept the Holland ship, wherein was Thomas
Bonner, to the vse of the Companie. This day I obserued
the latitude of this place by a quadrant of foure foote semi-

diameter, and found it to stand in 76° 55': the declination
of the needle vnder the horizon is 67° 30', pointing to the
northwards; but pointing to the southwards, it is 80°.
The variation of the compasse is 12° 14' west, from the
true meridian; but from our common sayling compass it is

17°, because the compasse is touched five degrees and a halfe to the eastward, and the variation is to the westward. This day, in the afternoone, the foure ships of Biscay departed from this harbour, which is called Horne-sound; and about a north sunne, I, with the master, Thomas Sherin, went ashore with other, to set vp another crosse with the Kings Maiesties arms, cast in lead, nayled vpon it. Then I obserued the sunne vpon his north meridian, by my foresaid quadrant, and found it eleuated aboue the horizon 10° 30'; but because his height at the south meridian, and his height at the north, did not agree in finding of the latitude, I did abate fiue minutes from each, as the meane betwixt both; for his altitude at the south meridian was 36° 40', the declination 23° 29'.

The fifteenth day, faire weather; the winde in the morning south, but almost calme. This day, about noone, we weighed anchor with the ship of Amsterdam, and diuers of her men were fetched aboord vs with their shipper, and some of our men were sent aboord her with one of our masters mates, called Master Spencer. All this day it was so calme, that wee were faine to towe our ship. Our carpenter did trim vp two of the Biscaine shallops, which they did leaue behind them, and they did leaue diuers hoopes and caske [s?] staued ashore.

The eighteenth day, faire weather; the winde variable, we stearing away northward. This afternoone wee met with another ship of Biscay, being a ship of two or three hundred tunnes. Our generall, as he did to the rest, caused her master and pilot to come aboord vs, to whom he shewed his commission, charging them to depart this countrey. They, seeing no remedie, were content, so soone as they had filled fresh water. We met with them off the southward part of the Iland. Our generall being so neere Greene Harbour, where the *Gamaliel* and the *Desire* road, wee went into the Sound to see them, with this great ship of Biscay, and the ship of Amsterdam. We found that the

Abundance of Ice. entrance of Greene Harbour was quite stopped with ice, and ran our ship into it, thinking to get through, but wee could not. Then wee got her out againe and came to the bay, where we roade on the other side of the sound in Pooppy Bay, or Nickes Coue.

The nineteenth day, faire weather, the winde northward. This day, about twelue of the clock, we came to an anchor in the foresaid bay. This afternoone there came another ship of Saint Sebastian into the bay where wee roade ; and about seuen of the clock the captain came aboord of vs, who told us that he had lost six of his men and a shallop

An Iland in 72° on the Coast of Groinland. vpon the coast of Groineland, vpon an Iland in the latitude of 72°, or thereabouts. This was the master which had beene here last yeere, and made a great voyage, Master Woodcocke being their pilot. His making so great a voyage was the cause that so many ships were here this yeere.

The twentieth in the morning we had news that the *John and Francis* was come about two days agoe, and that they had killed one and twentie whales at the Foreland, and had also killed two at Greene harbour. This day it was very close weather with some snowe ; the winde north-west. This afternoone the captains of the two Biscay ships were commanded to depart this coast.

The one and twentieth wee perceiued another ship standing toward vs. Wee lessened our sailes, and stayed for her to see what she was. At length we perceiued her to bee another Biscaine. About a north sunne we came to an anchor in Greene harbour, by the *Gamaliel* and the *Desire*, and the ship of Burdeaux, and the Biscaine followed vs. So soone as they were come to an anchor, their captaine came aboord of vs, to whom our generall shewed his commission, as he had done to the rest, charging him to depart those coasts, and told him that hee would take away some

of their shallops. They earnestly intreated him not to take
them away, and they would depart; the captaine offering
his bond to our generall, that if he stayed either in Greenland, Groineland, or Cherie Iland, he would willingly forfeit
all he was worth. There was another whale killed in Greene-
harbour, in the killing whereof there was a man slaine, and A man slaine.
a boate ouerwhelmed by too much haste of following him,
after the harping iron was in him.

The three and twentieth day, faire weather, the winde
northward. This day and the last night I obserued the
latitude of the place where we roade, and found it by both
to bee in the latitude of 78° 7'; the skie at both obserua- Lat. 78° 7'. Note.
tions being very cleere, where I find that there is no
sensible error betweene a south obseruation and a north,
the skie being cleare. But if the skie be hasie, there will
be some difference as of eight or ten miuutes, being obserued on shore by some large quadrant or other instru-
ment for the purpose; also a south south-west moone, by A South South west Moone
the common compasse, maketh a fulle sea in this place.[1] maketh a full Sea here.

The ninth of July, faire weather, the winde at north.
This day wee stood to the southward along the Iland; but
toward night it fell calme, and then the winde came to the
west. The tenth day, faire weather, but thicke and close,
the winde south south-west. All this day we stood for
Bel-sound.[2] Our generall went on shoare this afternoone,
and killed foure deere, and brought a young morse aliue
with him aboord.

The eleuenth day, faire weather, but calme. This afternoone wee perceiued fiue shippes in a bay in Bel-sound.

[1] On the 27th of June the *Tiger* returned to Sir Thomas Smyth's
Bay, rejoining the *Matthew*. During her cruise as a *wafter*, she had
met seventeen ships,—four from Holland, two from Dunkirk, four from
St. Jean de Luz, and seven from San Sebastian. All their commanders
had submitted to the English commander, and had agreed either to leave
the coast or to remain upon such conditions as he proposed to them.

[2] So named by Jonas Poole in 1610.

The winde was so calme that wee were faine to towe in our shippes, and about a north north-west sunne we came to an anchor by them, with our three ships, *viz.*, the *Tigre*, admirall; the *Matthew*, vice-admirall; and the *Richard and Barnard*, hauing made all things readie for to fight. These fiue shippes which rid here, the one was a great shippe of Biscay, of seuen hundred tunnes,[1] and two Hollanders, which we found the sixt of June in Pooppy-bay, and one small pinke of Amsterdam, and another smal shippe of Rochelle. This great shippe of Biscay, which we expected would have fought with vs, sent their captaine aboord of vs before we came to an anchor, and submitted themselues vnto the generall. The two ships of Amsterdam, whose masters names were these, *viz.*, Cornelius Calias, William Vermogan, admirall, and John Jacob, vice-admirall; these two would gladly haue stood out with vs, if the Biscaine would haue assisted them.

A Biscayan ship of 700 tuns.

The twelfth day, faire weather. This day the ship of *John Jacobs* was vnderladen of such goods as shee had in her; as oyle, blubber, and morses skinnes. The thirteenth day I was sent in a shallop to Greene Harborough.

The foureteenth day, thicke close weather, the winde northward; but towarde noone it began to cleare vp, and then it blew more winde. About a west sunne, we came to a small Iland, or rather a rock, where morses vse to come; where we found seauen which we killed, and knocked out their teeth, and let them lye. In this place are many of these rockes, where are great multitudes of foule, and they are called Lizets Ilands. The land all along is so full of rockes, that it is vnpossible for any shippe to come neere the maine, but in the sands, which are very deepe and good to come in. All this euening and night wee rowed betweene this Iland and Ice-sound.[2]

Many rockes full of Fowle.

Lisets Islands.

---

[1] She was a ship of St. Jean de Luz, of 800 tons, called the *Michael de Aristega*.   [2] So named by Jonas Poole in 1612.

The fifteenth day, about nine or tenne o'clock, we came to the shippes in Greene Harborough, where we found that they had killed eighteene whales in all. Foure of these Eighteen Whales killed. ships were French-men, which had killed eight whales for the Companie, according to the agreement which the generall had made with them; which was, that they should kill eight for vs, and after, what they could kill should be for themselues. Our English men had killed three in this Three Whales killed by the English. place, and the Baskes in the *Desire* also three. The *Desire* had taken in an hundred tunnes of oyle when wee came there, and she was to be laden so soone as she could.

The seauenteenth day, also faire weather, the winde northward. This day, toward a west sunne, the master of the French shippe came from Sea-horse Bay, who went thither to speak with our generall; because Master Mason and Master Cooper had stayed his shallops from going to sea, in regard they would not obserue the orders which the generall had appointed them; which were, that those whales which our Englishmen did chase, they should not follow; nor our men should not follow the whales they chased. For the order of the Biscaines is, that whoso doth strike the first harping iron into him, it is his whale, if his iron hold. This euening, I say, he returned from Sea-horse Bay, hauing lost his labour; for the generall and Master Edge were in Bell-sound. We vnderstood by him, that they had killed some eight and thirtie whales in all; Eight and thirty Whales killed. and that there was one hundred and sixtie tunnes of oyle ready made. The fiue and twentieth day in the morning, the *Desire* weighed anchor to go to the generall, and the master of the French ship also this morning went from thence to speake with the generall, because of a whale which was in strife betweene his Biscaines and ours; when, for pilfering, and for some peremptorie speeches, two of the *Rochellers* were ducked at our yard arme, the one on the one side, and the other on the other. This day I also

E

August 1.
Latitude 77° 40'.

Variation, 13° 11'.

observed the latitude of this place, and found it to be 77° 40'. Also, the variation of the compasse is 13° 11' west. This variation was observed the third of August, in the morning; the height of the sun above the horizon was 17° 24', and the declination was 14° 41' north in the latitude of 77° 40', and his magnetical azimuth was 63 from south to east. The ninth day we had sight of Master Bonners ship, wherein was Master Marmaduke,[1] who had beene to the northward as farre as Faire-hauen; and now, as he said, he was bound to the southward, to discouer beyond Point Looke-out, hauing his direction from Master Edge, as he said. Our generall told him that hee had hindered the voyage more by his absence then his discouerie would profit; and that it were best that he went back with him to the Foreland, and that he would giue no licence to go now for discouerie, because the yeare was far spent; but bad him, according to his commission, so to proceede. The twelfth day I obserued, and found the latitude of this place, by an exact obseruation, to be in 79° 14'. They in the Pooppy Bay had seen a ship of Eng-

Latitude 79° 14'.

This was Ma. Cudners ship of London.

[1] Fotherby says that Thomas Marmaduke was Captain of the Vice-Admiral. He was a Hull man, and Jonas Poole mentions that in the previous year, 1612, he had gone as far north as 82°, in a ship called the *Hopewell*. In 1611 he was in the Spitzbergen Sea, in command of a Hull vessel, and gave the shipwrecked crew of Poole's ship, the *Elizabeth*, a passage home.

Captain Markham (*Northward Ho!* pp. 42, 43) thinks that there is a mistake with regard to Marmaduke having reached 82°; arising from his commanding the *Hopewell*, the same vessel in which Hudson, in 1606, nearly reached that latitude.

In 1617 Thomas Marmaduke of Hull presented a petition to King James. He represented that he could prove the shortest way to Cathay to be by the north-east, which for six months in the year is navigable, without impediment. He asked to be set out to make the passage at the king's charge, or for leave for himself and friends to undertake it. I cannot find what was the fate of this petition, or the subsequent history of Marmaduke.

land off Black-point, and had spoken with her, who told them that they were come from Kildeene.

The foureteenth day, faire weather, the wind at north north-east. This day, about tenne a clocke in the fore-noone, we waied anchor to goe homeward, being sixe ships in company, viz., the *Tigre* admirall, the *Gamaliel* vice-admirall, the *John and Frances*, the *Annula*, the ship of Burdeaux, which the generall agreed to fish in Greene-harborough, and the Biscay ship which fished in Sir Thomas Smith's Bay.[1]

The fifteenth day very faire weather, all the forenoone almost calme; in the afternoone an easie gale at north-east. This day, about twelue a clocke at noone, wee were against Faire-Foreland, which is in the latitude of 79° 8'. This night was very cleere and faire weather, and also calme, by which meanes I had very good opportunitie to finde the sunnes refraction. For, beholding it about a north north-east sunne, by the common compasse, at which time the sunne was at the lowest, it was but one fifth part of his body aboue the horizon, hauing about foure fifth parts below, so neere as I could gesse. His declination for that instant was 10° 35' north, being at noone in the 2° 7' of Virgo, his daily motion was 58', whose halfe beeing nine-teen[2] to bee added to the former, because it was at twelue houres afore noone. I say his place at that instant was 2° 26' of Virgo, whose declination was as before, 10° 35'; the latitude of the place was 78° 47', whose complement was 11° 13', the declination being subtracted from the complement of the poles eleuation, leaueth 38', foure fiue part of which 12'; which, being subtracted from 38, leaueth 26' for the refraction. But I suppose the refraction is more or lesse according as the ayre is thicke or cleare, which I

Latitude 79° 8'.

Sunnes refraction.

Note.

[1] The *Matthew*, *Desire*, and *Richard and Barnard*, had previously sailed for England on the 31st of July, and arrived safely at Blackwall on the 23rd of August, well laden with oil and skins.

[2] Twenty-nine?

leaue for better schollers to discusse : but this I thought
good to note, for the better helpe of such as doe professe
this studie.

The sixteenth day also very faire weather, and for the
most part calme ; the winde that was, was at north-west.
This morning we espied a ship out in the offen, ouer
against Cold cape, which we stood with, and she also stood
with vs ; and when we came to her, wee found her to be
the *Desire*, a shippe of Alborough. Our generall sent for
the master and merchant aboord of vs, who certified him
that they came from Killedeene, and that they had made
but a bad voyage of fish ; and they were come to see if we
could fraight them home. The merchant was of London,

Mr. Cudner
of London. whose name was Master Cudner ; the masters name was
Fletcher, who also brought sixe men, which Thomas Bonner
had left at Cherie Iland. These sixe men had killed but
one morse all this yeere at the Iland ; who also told vs that

William
Gourdon. William Gourdon was gone to the northwards. At noone,
the three and twentieth day, I obserued the variation of

Variation,
1° 5′. the compasse, and found it to be 1° 5′ east.

The three and twentieth day faire weather, with a fine
gale at north and by east, we stearing away south and by
west halfe south, being at noone, by supposition, in the
latitude of 69°, no minutes, hauing sailed, since yesterday
noone, some thirty leagues south, true.

The foure and twentieth day, very faire weather and
cleere, the winde all the fore-noone northwards, but about
noone it came to the south-east. This morning I obserued
the middle starre in the great beares tayle, and found it to
be in the latitude of 68° 24′ about two a clocke, at which
time that starre was on the meridian vnder the pole. Also
I obserued the starre in the beares rump about one a clock,
and found the like latitude. Also all this day we had sight

Rost Ilands
or Rosten. of Rost Ilands,[1] being about ten or eleuen leagues off vs.

---

[1] Roost, the most southern of the Lofoden Islands.

Also at noone I obserued the latitude by the sunne, and found vs to be in the latitude of 68°, no minutes, which 68° no min. did agree with the former obseruations by the starres. Also the variation of this place is 4° 8' east from the true Variation, meridian, wee hauing ranne, since yesterday noone, some 5° 3' East. two and twentie leagues south and by west. Almost all the afternoon it was almost calme.

The fiue and twentieth day also very faire weather, the winde this morning came to the east south-east a fine easie gale. We steered away south and by west half west ten leagues, being at noone in the latitude of 67° 5'. The variation of this place is 5° 3' east, neere to the set of our Variation, compasse. This euening the winde came to the south 5° 3' East. south-west, which continued about two watches.

The nine and twentieth day faire weather, with a good gale of winde at north north-east. From two this last night to sixe we stood away south-west and by south; and at sixe we steered away south south-west, being at noone, The lying by obseruation, in 62°, no minutes. The land about Scoutes- of the land about nesse lyeth in this sort : from sixtie three toward sixtie two, Scouts-nesse. it is nineteen leagues south south-west halfe westward; from thence ten leagues south and by west, which is two or three Ilands, which are the westwardest land in Norway, lying in the latitude of 62° 44'. But whether these Islands, or a point of land which lyeth about three or foure leagues more to the north, be called Scoutesnesse, I know not. The sixt of September we entered the Thames.

SECOND RECORDED VOYAGE

OF

WILLIAM BAFFIN.

II.

Another account, probably written by ROBERT FOTHERBY.[1]

A Short Discourse of a Voyage made in the Yeare of Our Lord
1613, to the Late Discouered Countrye of Greenland; and
a Briefe Discription of the same Countrie, and the
Comodities ther raised to the Adventurers.

In the month of May 1613, seaven good ships bound for
Greenland,[2] were sett forth from the port of London,
beeing furnished with victualls and other prouision necessarie for the killing of the whale, and twenty-four Basks,
who ar men best experienced in that facultie, at the chardge
and aduenture of the right worshipfull Sir Thomas Smith,
knight, and of the rest of the companie of merchants
tradeing into Moscouia, called the Merchants of Newe
Trades and Discoveries.

---

[1] The manuscript of this journal was formerly in possession of Deacon
James Green, a merchant of Boston, who died about the beginning of
the present century. His daughter, Mrs. Nabby Richmond, gave it to
Benjamin R. Howland in 1808. From him it passed to the Honourable
John Howland, the late President of the Rhode Island Historical Society,
who transferred it to the American Antiquarian Society in 1814. The
manuscript is a folio, with wide margins, neatly written and illustrated
with a map of Spitzbergen (mutilated), and sketches in water-colour.
The leaves are stitched into a thick parchment cover. It was first
printed in the *Transactions and Collections of the American Antiquarian
Society* (1860), vol. iv, p. 285, and edited by Mr. Samuel F. Haven, who
gives reasons for the belief that Robert Fotherby was the author.

[2] Spitzbergen.

In this fleet, Mr. Beniamin Joseph, of London, was chiefe captaine and commissioner, a man very sufficient and worthy of his place. A shippe called the *Tiger*, of burthen 260 tonnes, was admirall; the *Mathew*, of 250 tonnes, vice admirall; and the *Gamaliel*, of 200 tonnes, rere admirall; the fourth, the *John* and *Francis*, of 180 tonnes; the sixth, the *Anula*, of 140 tonnes; and the seuenth, the *Richard and Barnard*, a piniace of 60 tonnes, intended for further dis- couerye.

Wee came to Grauesend the 30th of April, where we staied but one tide, and then weyed anchor about 6 a'clock at the euening, and plied to Tilberry Hope, remaining there all night. The next morneing, beeing the first of Maye, wee anchored againe in Lee Roade, where we continued till the 4th of Maye, the wind keeping contrarie to us, blew betwixt north and north-east.

The 4th daie, about 3 a'clock afternoone, wee entered into the swaile at Quinborowe,[1] and rid at anchor there till the 13th of Maye. In which time, namelie, on the 7th of Maye, the kings ships came by us on their retourne out of Holland, from transporting the Count Palatine, and the Ladie Elizabeth, the kings onely daughter. Before they came neere us wee caused our flaggs to be furl'd up, and when they passed by us, our admirall shott off 7 peeces of ordnance, our vice admirall 5, and our rere admirall 3; and the rest of our fleet, ech of them, one. The Great Admirall of England, called the *Prince*, gaue us 3 peeces, and the rest of the kings ships each of them one.[2]

The 13th of Maye, about 9 a clock in the morneing,

[1] Queenborough.
[2] The Princess Elizabeth, who was destined to experience so much misfortune, was married to the Count Palatine, Frederic V, on St. Valentine's Day, with an expense and magnificence before unknown in England. They were conveyed to Flanders in great state by the Lord Admiral, the Earl of Nottingham, with eight of the king's ships, besides transports for baggage.

wee came forthe of the Swaile, and passed by the Sandes
called the Spitts, holdeing our course north-east and north
north-east.

Our depar-
ture from
England. The 14th daie, about noone, wee lost sight of the Cro-
mershield, which is a cape on the coast of Norfolke, and
was the last land of England that we sawe, being outward
bound. Then wee stear'd awaie north, maintaineing that
course till the 22nd of Maye.

On the 21st daie wee had lost sight of land againe upon
the coast of Norwaye, before wee came to the bay of Rosse,
beareing from us east and by north, and distant about nine
leagues, in the latitude of 61° 20′, found by obseruation.
Then, on the 22nd wee directed our course more easterlie,
as north-and-by-east, and north north-east.

The 24th, wee were in the latitude of 67° 36′, while
the sunne was in the horison, at the time of midnight, and
after that time wee had continuall dailight dureing our
voyage; till, in our retourne homeward, wee had the sunne
againe in the circle of the horison, when he came to the
north of our meridian, in the latitude of 75°, on the 2nd
of August.

Wee ariued
on the
coast of
Greenland. The 30th of Maye, about 4 a clock in the morneing, wee
descried our wisht-for coast of Greenland,[1] being all our
ships in company; and wee had bene but 17 daies at sea,
viz., from the 13th till the 30th of Maye, haueing sailed,
according to the difference of latitude and longitude, by
an arch of a great circle 500 leagues, and according to
the ship's way, by our account on dead reckoning, 514
leagues.

Then we plied nearer to the shoare, and discerned the
mountains to be couered with snowe; notwithstanding,
wee had no trouble with ice all this while, as wee expected;
for it was almost all voided er wee came ther. Nowe wee
coasted along towards Sr. Thomas Smyth's Baye, passing

[1] Spitzbergen.

on the west side of Prince Charles his Iland, by reason of a barre that is betwixt the iland and the maine continent of the land, which hinders us to passe with our ships that waie.

The 1st of June, wee were becalm'd on the south-west side of the iland, about fiue leagues from the shoare, where I obserued the north sunne, at the time of midnight, to be 11° 15′ high; so, concludeing the latitude in that place to be 78° 5′ (the sunne's declination for that daie being 23° 10′).

The 2nd of June, haueing gotten a little more northward, and beeing on the best side of the iland, againe becalm'd, about three leagues distant from the shoare, I and Joh. Wilmote, one of the master's mates, with 6 more of our sailors, went ashore in a Biska shallop, purposeing to kill some deare and some wild fowle; and to that end wee took with us such dogs as wee had in our ship,[1] viz., a grewhownd, a mastiffe, and a water spaniell, and two fowleing-pieces, with shott and powder.

We landed upon a hard shingle, comeing close to the shore with our boat, there being no ice to keep us off; notwithstanding, upon fiue or six rocks, near the shore side, there laie a great quantitie of ice, which couered them in such sorte, that the hollowness or distances betwixt one rock and another, appeared under the ice like vaulted caues. After that wee were landed upon the shingle, the ice or congealed snowe was so high upon the shoare, that it withstood vs like a strong wall, to pass anie further; wherefore wee wer faine one to help up another, it beeing mor than a man's height in thickness, and haueing manie long isicles hanging in diuers places.

When wee were up, and had gone about two roods, wee might perceaue that wee were upon the ground or sand; yett could not see it by reason of the snowe. Then wee

[1] The *Mathew*.

did look about if we could see any deere; and presentlie espied one buck, whereupon we dispersed ourselues seuerall waies, to gett betwixt him and the mountaines, slipping sometimes to the mid leg into the snowe, which, for the most part, did beare vs above. In our waie wee went ouer two or three bare spots that were full of flatt stones, whereon ther grew a certaine white mosse, which, it seems, the deare doe feed upon at the first beginning of their somer; for theise spotts were full of their ordure; and besides, wee then sawe not any other thing for them to liue on.

Before that wee came near the buck which wee first espied, wee sawe four more not farre from him, and two in another place, and therefore we hounded at the fairest heard; but then they came all one waie together, and (avoideing all circumstances) we kill'd three of them, being all bucks, which we found then to be but pore rascals, yet verie good meat, as we presentlie made tryall and tasted. For, finding ther (as ther is in all places of the countreye) great store of drift wood, which the sea bestowes on the barren land, and being also well prouided of hunter's sauce, wee made a fier and broiled some of our venison, and did eat thereof with very good appetites; much like to that in Virgil, of Æneas and his companions :—

> " Ac primum silici scintillam exaudit *Achates*[1]
> Susceptiq. ignem *lignis*[2]
> Pars in frusta secant *verubusque*[3] trementia figunt
>
> . . . .
>
> Tum victu reuocamus vires."

Beeing thus well refreshed, wee were willing to have killed more venison, because wee needed not to use much labour in hunteing for our game; for the deare that had latelie escaped us were not gon farre from us. But the

---

[1] Master's mate.
[2] " Folia enim nulla cadunt ubi est neq flos nec arbos."
[3] Wooden spit.

aire began to be so thicke and foggie, that wee aduised better to goe presentlie a-board with that which wee had alreadie gotten, least that the fog, increasing, might haue made vs lose sight of our ship; therefore wee made speedie waie towards her, and came aboord about 11 o'clock, before the time of midnight.

Then wee continued still becalm'd till the next morning, and then were so befriended with a fresh gale of winde that wee sailed to the north end of the iland with a flowen sheat; and makeing manie boards, wee plied into Sir Tho. Smyth's Baye, where we anchored about 8 a clock that euening.

When we came to an anchor, then the Basks, our whale strikers, went presentlie back againe to the Foreland[3] with their shallops, ther to attend the coming-in of the whales; and when our men had taken some rest, they carried ashoare our coppers cask, and other prouisions for makeing of oile, and prepared all things ready for ·use as speedilie as we could. For newes was brought us in the morneing, that the Basks had kil'd a whale; therefore we hasted to sett up our fournaces and coppers, and presentlie began work, which we continued (God be thanked) without any want of whales, till our voyage was made; not receaueing anie intermission of rest, but onlie on the Saboth daie. For when some slept, others wrought; and haueing a con-tinual daie, wee alowed no time of night for all men to sleepe at once, but maintained work from Sundaie about 5 a clock afternoone, till Saturdaie at 12 o'clock, in time of midnight, dureing which time our men receaued no other recreation from work and sleep, but onlie the time of eateing their meat, whereof they had sufficient, thrice in every twenty-four howers; and besides, some of them had alowed aquauitæ at ech four hower's end.

The next daie after that we came into harbour, word was brought our general from Green Harbour (a place where

Wee har-boured in Sr. Tho. Smyths Baye.

---

[1] The northern extremity of Prince Charles's Island.

three ships of our fleet put in to make this voyage) that
fiue ships, French and Spanish, wer come into Ice Sound,
and intended there to fish for the whale; upon which occasion the *Tiger*, our admirall, weyed anchor the 5th of June,
and being well man'd with sixty sufficient men, went out
of harbour from us towards Ice Sound, where, when he
came, he found the aforesaid ships, according to the information, and anchored close by them. Then he hailed
the captains and masters of theise ships to come presentlie
aboord him, which they performeing accordinglie, he
shewed them the King's Majesties patent, graunted to the
Merchants of Newe Trades and Discoueries, and therwithall
his comission, forbidding them, by the authoritie thereof,
to make anie longer aboad ther, or in anie parte of the
countrey, at their perills. Whereupon they, not knowing
how to remedie themselues, did all promise to departe,
desireing a note from our general, wherby they might
certefie their setters-forth, that they had bene in the countrye, except one ship of Burdeux, called the *Jaques*, wherof
was Maister Peirce de Siluator, who was permitted to staie,
upon condition that he should first kill 8 whales for us,
and then to kill more what he could for himself, and by this
conclusion he made a good voyage; for he kil'd 12 whales
in all, wherof we had eight, and he had 4.

Then did our admirall continue as a wafter alongst the
coast till the 27th of June, and then he came to us againe
into Sir Thomas Smyth's Baye. In which time of his
absence he had mett with 17 ships, viz., 4 of Holland,
2 of Dunkirk, 4 of St. John de Luz, and 7 of San Sebastian's. The commanders of all those ships had submitted to our general; and were content either to departe
out of the country, or els to staie upon such condicons
as he propounded unto them.

On the 8th of June, about 11 a clock, before the time of
midnight, Mr. Marmaduke, who was captaine of our vice

admirall, and I, with 6 or 7 sailors, went in a shallop to the beach at the barre, marked with a^9,[1] to cause our men gather drift wood together, and laie it readie at the waters side, to lade a small Flemish flie boat, that was to come hither to fetch it. Upon this beach, wee saw lieing ther, by our estimacion, neare 300 morses, at the verie point or end of it; but wee could not go too near them, for disturbing them. When the flie boat came to take in the wood, Mr. Marmaduke and I came awaie in the shallop; and haueing present occasion to use a peece of straight timber about our crane, before the flie boat could be loaded, wee caused the men that rowed the shallop to towe a tree after them. Nowe, when wee had put off a little from the shoare, there came fiue or six morses swimming hard by us and about us; some of them coming so near the sterne of the bote that we called for our launces, purposeing to strike them. They would, diuers times, laie their teeth upon the tree which we towed (as it were scratching the wood with their teeth), but wee still rowed awaie, and at length they left us. Then we passed through a great deale of small ice, and sawe, upon some peices, two morses, and upon some, one; and also diuers seales, layeing upon peices of ice.

The 19th of June wee had a verie great storme, the winde *A storme in harbour.* beeing at south south-west, which was like to haue driuen our ships upon the shoare; and haueing three dead whales floating at the sternes of our ships, wee were glad to cut the hawsers that they were tyed in, and to lett them driue a shoare; because we feared that otherwise they would haue caused our ships either to break their cables, or to haile home their anchors, and to be driuen upon the shoare. When the storm ceast, haueing continued about 6 howers, the water fell from the shoare, and wee saw two of the whales lie cast upon the shoare, and the water faln from

[1] The bar may be see on the map, but the " a " is wanting.

them againe. The third whale was driuen further off, but wee found him againe cast upon the shoare, hauing lost all his finnes[1] out of his mouth. Ther was also, at the same time, 5 whale's heads driuen ashoare, with toungs and finnes in them, wherby some labour was saued, which should otherwise haue been bestowed about hailing them ashoare, for the cutting out of the fins.

The 21st of June, there came a white beare down from the mountaines, and took into Fresh-water Baye, which is the water you see marked with _e_, within Sr. Thomas Smith's Baye,[2] and Thomas Wilkinson, one of the master's mates in the _Matthew_, vice-admirall, went forth in a shallop, and shott him with a peece as he was swimming, and kil'd him, and brought him to the shoare.

In this harbour ther haue been killed mor whales than in anie other, but verie fewe deare; notwithstanding ther haue been slaine in this country, this voyage, about four hundred deare. Wee kil'd very few morses, by reason the whales came so fast, that wee could not have a fitt opportunitie to goe about that buisines; although ther was said to be at one time about 500 morses upon the beach before mencioned; to which place wee went, prepared for their slaughter, the sixt of Julie, and found ther but about 40, wherof wee killed 32, and wee took their hides, their fat, and their teeth.

We killed also good store of wild fowle, as wild geese, culuerdumes, willocks, and such like, and some white land partridges. Wee caught manie young foxes, which wee made as tame and familiar as spaniell-whelpes. I brought one of them out of the country, till we came to the coast of England, and ther he died.

[1] Whale-bone they called whale's fins.

[2] The position here referred to, belonged to a part of the map that was mutilated; and, although the outline has been restored, the locality above-mentioned cannot be precisely indicated.

On the 24th of June, the *Mathew* began to take in hir ladeing, and was fully freighted the 6th of July with 184 tonnes of oyle, and 5,000 finnes, which wer in 100 bundles, each containeing 50.

On the 8th of July the *Mathew*, and the *Richard and* We wayed anchor out *Barnard* (which was laded with oile and finnes), weighed of Sr. Tho. Sm. Baye. anchor forth of Sir Thomas Smyth's Baye, with purpose to come presentlie for England; and the *Tiger*, our admirall, came also forth with us to waft us alongst the coast of Greenland.[1] But, putting into Bel Sound the 11th of July, expecting to find some strangers there, wee espied accordinglie 5 ships at anchor on the west side of Joseph's Baye. One of them seemed unto us to be a verie great ship, as indeed she was; and other two of them seemed also to be good stowt ships. And therefore wee, supposing them to be such as would withstand vs, resolued to feight with them, and made spedie preparation accordinglie, hanging our waist-cloths and clearing our decks, that the ordnance might have room to plaie; and made readie all our munition, ech one addressing himself with a forward resolucion to perform a man's parte so well as he could.

This was about 9 o'clock, before the time of midnight, the sunne shining very bright, and the aire being very cleare, and so calme that wee caused ye saylers with boats and shallops to rowe ahead of our ships, and towe them into the harbour. When wee came neare them, the captain of the great ship, whose name was Michael de Aristega (his ship being of St. John de Luz, of burthen 800 tonnes), came in a shallop abord our admirall, submitting himself and his gcods unto our generall, and tould him that ther were two ships of the Hollanders, who had insulted over him, and would not suffer him to fish for the whale but upon such condicons as they propounded unto him, namely, that the Hollanders, hauing but 3 shal-

[1] By Greenland, in this narrative, is always meant Spitzbergen.

lops, and he 7 furnished with whale strikers, they
should all joine together; and the Hollanders not onlie
to haue the one-half of all the whales that should be
kil'd, but also to haue the first whale that was stricken
wholie to themselves, ouer and besides the half of the rest.
And he further tould the general that the Hollanders would
haue persuaded him to combine with them against us, and
to beate us out of the countrye. Then the generall willed
him to goe aboard againe of his own ship, and keepe his
men in quietnes, and he would deale well enough with the
Hollanders. So, passing further on, they were knowen to
be 2 ships of Amsterdam, which our admirall had formelie
mett withall, and dischardged to staie in ye country. Then,

Wee an-
chored
againe in
Joseph's
Baye.

comeing by close to them, our admirall anchored on one side of
them and our vice-admirall on the other; but they, as men
unwilling to be depriued of the ritches they had gotten,
allthough unable by force to hold them, kept out their flags
—the one in the maine-top, and the other in the fore-top,
as admirall and vice-admirall. Then our generall comanded
the maisters to come aboard his ship, which they, doeing,
he chardged them with the breach of their promise formerlie made unto him—viz., that they would departe out
of the country. Then, after some other speeches, he, not
finding them willing to resigne the goods they had gotten—
as whale oil and finnes—tould them that they must not think
to carrie anie of it awaie, seeing that they did so sleightlie
esteeme the King's ma'ties grant formerlie shewed them;
therefore, he bad them go againe to their owne ships, and
they should have half an hower's space to consider and
aduise with themselues what to doe; and if they thought
fitt to give him further answer before the glasse were runne
out, then good it were; otherwise, if they would not then
yield their goods, he would feight with them for them.
So ech of them went aboard his own ship, and, without anie
long deliberation caused their flags to be taken in; and

retourning to our generall, yeilded their goods to our disposing. Nowe, although it was intended that our two laded ships should go presentlie for England notwithstanding, it was thought fitting not to leave our admirall alone amongst his offended neighbours ; and, therefore, wee staied till the two Hollanders were gon, who (being dispossessed of some oile and finnes they had alreadie stowed in their ships, and also of some dead whales that were floateing at their ship's side) went forth of harbour, one of them the 15th, and the other the 18th of July.

The great ship of St. John de Luz staied still, the captaine of hir being content that his men should hould on their work, and his whale-strikers to continue fishing, upon condiĉon granted that he should onelie haue one-half the oile he should make. There were also in the same harbour 2 small ships, the one of Biska, and the other a Flemish flie boat ; besides another little pinace of St. John de Luz which was on the east side of the iland, within L. Elesmere Baye, marked with *b*.

On the 23rd of July, about 9 o'clock in the euening, wee sent forth two shallops with men, to goe kill some venison, who retourned againe with 17 bucks and does slaine ; yet had they no dog with them, onelie peeces ; and they brought also aboard the skinne of a white bear, which they had kil'd.

The 25th July, the *Desire* came to us in to Joseph's Bay, out of Green Harbour, and tooke in thirty tonnes of blubber, to make up hir full ladeing ; for shee was to come with us, one of the first, for England.

The 29th of July wee had some trouble with great ice ; the waters being verie rough, and the winde bloweing hard at east south east, which brought some ilands of ice towards our ships, wherof some fell 'thwart our hauses, so that wee were faine, with pikes and oares, to keepe it cleare of our

Wee were troubled with ice.

F

ships; and also glad to lett fall our sheat-anchor, to keep us from being driuen upon the lee shoare.

In this harbour, ther was killed a great store of venison, 3 or 4 white beares, and some sea morses, which the Hollanders had slaine and flayed before wee came thither; for ther laie their bodies, without either fatt, skinnes, or teeth.

One thing more I obserued in this harbour, which I haue thought good also to sett down. Purposeing, on a time, to walk towards the mountaines, I, and two more of my companie, ascended up a long plaine hill, as wee supposed it to be; but hauing gon a while upon it, wee perceued it to be ice. Notwithstanding, we proceeded higher up, about the length of half a mile, and as we went, sawe manie deepe rifts or gutters on the land of ice, which were crackt downe thorowe to the ground, or, at the least, an exceeding great depth; as we might well perceiue by heareing the snowe water run belowe, as it does oftentimes, in a brook whose current is somewhat opposed with little stones. But for better satisfaĉon, I brake down some peeces of ice with a staffe I had in my hand, which, in their falling made a noise on ech side, much like to a peice of glasse throwen downe the well within Douer Castle, wherby wee did aestimate the thicknes or height of this ice to be thirty fathomes. This huge ice, in my opinion, is nothing but snowe, which from time to time has, for the most parte, bene driuen of the mountaines; and so continueing and increasing all the time of winter (which may be counted three quarters of the yeare), cannot possiblie be consumed with the thawe of so short a soṁer, but is onelie a little dissolued to moisture, wherby it becomes more compact, and with the quick succeeding frost is congealed to a firme ice. And thus it is like still to encrease, as (I think) it hath done since the world's creation.

On Saturday, the 31st of Julye, about 5 o'clock in the

afternoone, wee weyed anchor out of Joseph's Bay to come for England, namelie, the *Matthew*, the *Desire*, and the Wee came for England.
for England, namelie, the *Matthew*, the *Desire*, and the
Richard and Barnard; leauing ther our admirall the *Tiger*,
and the great ship of St. John de Luz. At 9 o'clock that
euening wee weare at sea, about 6 leagues from the land,
and then directed our course for Cherrie Iland, south and
by east. The next daie, being the 1st of August, about
8 a clock before noone, there came a shallop aboard the
Desire, with 11 Dutchmen that belonged to one of the
Hollander's ships that we had latelie sent forth of Bel
Sound. The reason of their so comeing was this : sixe of
these men had gon ashoare from their ship to kill some
venison, and landeing at the time of a high water, they
made fast their shallop, and so left her, safe enough, as they
supposed, and went up into the land ; but when the water
fell againe, the shallop was splitt upon a rock, and by that
meanes they were forced to staie ther ; nowe, they that
were in the ship, considering that their fellowes staied verie
long, began to doubt of some unwelcome euent, that
hindered their retourne ; and therfore they sent 5 men
more, in another shallop, to knowe the cause of their so
long absence. When these men last sent forth came
ashoare, they found the other men, who tould them the
occasion of their staie. Then went they all aboard the
shallop, and rowed towards their ship ; but the aire was
growen to be verie mistie, and such a thick fog increased,
that they could not by anie meanes find their ship, wherfore
they were faine to row to the shoare againe.

Then followed stormie weather, the winde bloweing of the
shoare, which caused the ship to haile further of to sea ; so
that when the aire was cleeare, notwithstanding, they could
not see her ; wherby they were much discouraged, being
in a place that could yeild them but little comforte. And
there they contynued 8 daies, in which time they lieued
with the flesh of 2 bucks and a beare, which they had

killed, being eleuen men; and mor they could not kill, because their powder was spent. Then seeing our ships come by, they rowed fast and came aboard of us; and so wee brought them into England, wher they had some monie alowed them for their work at sea, by the Company of Moscouy Merchants, although (God be praised) wee neuer stood any need of their helpe; and so they were free to departe homeward, when they could gett shipping.

On the 3rd of August wee were about 10 leagues distant from Cherry Iland, but could not see it by reason of ill weather; the winde being contrarie, not suffering us to touch ther, as wee intended; therfore wee steered awaie, south-and-by-west and south-south-west, for England. After this daie the sunne began to sett, and to be depressed under the horizon at midnight; the nights began to lengthen, and starres to beare vewe. On the 16th of August, Mr. Greene, one of the master's mates, died in the Matthewe, about 10 a clock before noone; and, about 4 a clock in the afternoone he was cast ouerboard, and a peice of ordnance shott of.

Wee arrived on the Coast of England.

The 18th of August, about 5 aclock in the morneing, wee fell in with the coast of England, and descried land about Huntcliff Foot, which is northward from Scarborough, on the coast of Yeorkshire, and was the first land that wee sawe after wee lost sight of Greenland.

We anchored in Winterton Road.

The next daie, about 3 a clock afternoone, wee anchored in Winterton Roade, which is six miles from Yarmouth. Then I caused the shallop to be taken out, and 6 sailors to sett me ashoare, within 2 miles of Yarmouth, wher I lodged that night; and having prouided a horse, I rid out of the towne the next morneing at 9 o'clock, being Friday, and came to London at 3 a clock afternoone, on Saturday, not haueing receaued anie sleepe at all betwixt Yarmouth and London. Our ships came up to Blackwall on the Tuesday next after; and, so soone as they had deliuered their goods, the other 4 ships of our fleet came also safe home with their ladeings; and thus, by the mercie of God, we ended our voyage with good successe. To God, ther-fore, be praise and glory for euer. Amen.

A Briefe Description of the Country of Greenland, otherwise called King James his New Land.

Greenland is a countrie beareing from England north-ward, nearest upon the pointe of the compasse north-and-by-east. The south-most parte of it is distant from the Arcticque Circle 10° northwards namelie, in the latitude of 76° 30'. This country hath bene discouered by the English almost to the parallel of 83°, which is but 7° eleuation distant from the North Pole, and therefore but 140 leagues from that point, upon the superficies of the earth or water (whither it be), where the Pole shal be our zenith, and the æquinoctiall our horizon.

In the latitude of 76° (which wee made the greatest parte of our voyage this yeare), the sunne, when he entereth into the 1° of Cancer, makeing the longest daie and shortest night to all places betweene the Equator and the Polar Circle, is in his meridinal altitude, or greatest distance from the horizon, 34° 30' high; and at the time of his comeing to the north, is still apparent aboue the horizon 12° 30'.

The compasse varieth on this place, from the true meri-dian, or line of north and south, neare 20°, the north end of the needle inclineing so much towards the west. *Variation of the Com-passe W.*

The nature and condiĉon of this country of Greenland is verie much different from the name it hath; for I think ther is no place in the world, yett known and discouered, is lesse green than it. For when wee first arriued ther, which was on the 30th of Maye, the ground was all couered with snowe, both the mountaines and the lowe lands, saue onelie some few spotts that were full of flatt stones, wheron

ther grewe a certaine white mosse which, it seems, the
deere doe feed upon at the first beginning of their sommer;
for theise bare spotts wer verie full of their ordure; and
besides, wee could not see anie other thing for them to
feed upon.

The thawe began this yeare about the 10th of June, at
which time there began to spring up, in some places where
the snow was melted, a certaine stragling grasse, with a
blewish flower, much like to young heath or ling, which
grows upon moreish grounds in the north parts of England.
And this is that wher with all the deare, in a short time,
become exceeding fatt; but how they liue in the time of
extreame winter, when al is couered with snowe, I cannot
imagine. Yet the meanes of their preseruačon is not more
strange to man's capacitie than is their creation; and therfore we must knowe that He who made the creature, hath
also ordained that he shal be fed; although, to our under-
standings, ther is not any food to sustaine them.

In the moneths of June, Julye, and the beginning of
August, ther is often times warme and pleasant weather;
but, in the other moneths, certainlie uery uncomfortable.
For the temperature of the winter time maie be iudged, by
the qualitie of the place, to be extreame could, especiallie
dureing that time wherein the sunne shal be altogether
depressed under the horizon, which, in the former latitude
of 79°, continues from the 11th of October till the 10th of
Februarye, and contrarilie it is eleuated altogether aboue
the horizon from the 9th of April till the 14th of August;
the rest of the time is an intercourse of long daie and short
night, and contrarilie of short daies and long nights.

The country afoardeth great plentie of fresh water in all
places, which proceeds from the snowe, and therfore there
can be no want thereof at anie time, for ther is alwaies
snowe, and (I think) euer hath bene since snowe first fell
upon the earth. Besides, I found ther, within Sr. Thomas

Smyth's Baye, a very pleasant spring, neare the water side, boiling (as it were) and workeing up sand, euen as our springs doe in England; being as pleasant water as anie I euer tasted in England.

The comodities of the countrie, hitherto knowen, are chieflie whales and sea morses. The whale yeilds oyl and finnes; and the morse yeilds oyl, hydes, and teeth of good valewe, whereof he hath but two, and they growe in his uppermost jawe. Ther be also white whales and seales, which were thought not to be worthy of time and labor to kill them, seeing that wee wer imploied about the aboue mentioned comodities. Wee sawe very fewe fishes ther, or rather none at all; saue onelie one cod, which was caught with a baited hook in Green Harbour. But the Basks, our whale strikers, doe saie that they haue sundrie times seene good store of salmon.

Upon this land ther be manie white beares, graie foxes, and great plentie of deare; and also white partridges, and great store of white fowle, as cueluerduns, wilde geese, sea pigeons, sea parots, willocks, stint, guls, and diuers others, wherof some are unworthy of nameing as tasteing. The land also doth yeild much drift wood, whales finnes, morses teeth, and some times unicorn hornes, which are supposed to be rather of some sea creature, than of anie land beast. And theise things the sea casteth forth vpon the shoare, to supplie the barrenes of the fruitles land, which, by the Diuine Prouidence, hath sufficient to maintaine these un-reasonable creatures which ther wee found, but by all like-lihood was never yet inhabited by anie natiues that beare the shape of man, the country being altogether destitute of necessaries, wherewithall a man might be preserued in the time of winter.

I haue thought good but to sett downe what was written concerning this country by one of Amsterdam, that was this yeare in Greenland (with whom I thus sometimes conuersed) as it is sett forth in printe by some of Holland, and (with other things concerning this present voyage) is inserted in a late edition of *Hudson's Discoueries* :—" Hæc pessima et frigidissima est regio mundi, undique rupes, montes, lapides ; tanta ibi aquarum terram inundantium copia, ut vestigia hominum non admittat ; maxima glaciei ibi copia, tantaque montium glacialium multitudo, ut ab ipsa natiuitate Christi, concreuisse videantur ; tanta enim niuium abundantia, ut fidem superet. Ceruis abundat et vrsis, et vulpibus ; cerui planè sunt albi coloris. Admiror tantos ceruorum greges, vnde viuant, cum regio niuibus tegatur, et planè sit sterilis. Auibus luxuriat, maximè annseribus minoribus qui turmatim conueniunt."[1]

The manner of killing the whale, and of the whole proceedings for performing of the voyage.

The whale is a fish, or sea beast, of a huge bignesse, about 60 feet long, and 18 feet thick. His head seems to be one-third parte of his whole quantitie. His finnes (which wee call whale bone in England) doe growe, and are wholie included within his spacious mouth, being fastened, and, as it were, rooted in his uppermost jawe, spreading on both sides of his toung, in nomber more than 260 on one, side, and as manie on the other side. The

---

[1] The following note is by Mr. Haven, the American editor :— "The title of the book here referred to is ' Descriptio ac Delineatio geographica Detectionis Freti, sive Transitus ad Occasum, supra Terras Americanas, in Chinam et Japonem'. Amst., 1613, 4to. In it the above passage occurs as a quotation, in italics, preceded by the following remark : Hæc vera esse, fidem faciunt testes oculati reduces, etiam literæ Navarchi Thomae Bonaert et Semmij, cujus hæc verba, sub finem, in literis ad patrem de qualitate hujus regionis.' "

This Thomas Bonaert may be no other than Thomas Bonner, who commanded a Dutch ship at Spitzbergen, which was captured by the English, and sent northward for discovery under Master Marmaduke. ("Baffin's Narrative" in *Purchas*, vol. iii, pp. 717, 719).

longest finnes are placed in the midest of his mouth,[1] and
the rest doe orderlie shorten, more and more, both back-
wards and forwards, from 12 feet to less than 3 ynches
in length. His eies are not much bigger then the eyes
of an oxe, and his bodie in fashion round, with a very
broad spreading taile, which is of a rough and solid substance, and therefore it is used for to make chopping blocks,
to chop the whales fatt upon (which we call blubber) ; and
of other like matter, are also his two swimming finnes,
which serue, at some times, for the same use.

The whale comes often aboue water, and will comonlie
spowte 8 or 9 times before he goe under againe, by
which spowteing of water wee maie discerne him when he
is 2 or 3 leagues distant from us. When he entres into
the sounds, our whal killers doe presentlie sallie forth to
meet him, either from our ships, or els from some other
place more conuenient for that purpose, where to expect
him, makeing very speedie waie towards him with their
shallops. But, most comonlie, before they come near him,
he will be gon downe under water, and continue, perhaps, a
good while er he rise againe ; so that some times they rowe
past him, and therfore are they alwaies very circumspect,

---

[1] The description given by Purchas begins as follows: "The whale is a
fish or sea-beast of a huge bignesse—about sixty-fiue feet long and
thirty-fiue feet thicke. His head is a third part of all his bodie's
quantitie; his spacious mouth contayning a very great tongue and all
his finnes, which we call whale finnes. These finnes are fastened or
rooted in his upper chap, and spread over his tongue on both sides of
his mouth ; being in number about two hundred and fifty on one side,
and as many on the other side. The largest finnes are placed in the
midst of his mouth", etc.

Mr. Haven, the American editor, observes :—" The above extract will
suffice to show the resemblance between the description of Purchas
relating to this subject and those of this narrative. The inference
appears to be a reasonable one, that, if Fotherby was the author of the
notes used by Purchas in compiling his account, he was also the author
of this narrative, as the similarity of it, in the two, is too great to be
accidental. Purchas has not improved the accuracy of the statement
by altering the figures.

lookeing if they can discerne his waie under the water
(which they call his wake), or els see him further off by his
spowteing, being risen.   Then, comeing neare him, they
rowe resolutlie towards him, as though they intended to
force the shallop vpon him.   But so soone as they come
within stroak of him, the harponier, (who stands up readie
in the head of the boat,) darts his harping iron at him out
of both his hands, wherwith the whale being stricken, he
presentlie discends to the bottom of the water, and therfor
the men in the shallop doe weire out 40, 50, or 60 fathoms
of rope—yea, sometimes 100, or more, according as the
depth requireth.   For vpon the sockett of harping iron
ther is made fast a rope, which lies orderlie coiled up in the
sterne of the boat, which, I saie, they do weire forth untill
they perceaue him to be riseing againe, and then they haile
in some of it, both to giue him the lesse scope, and also
that it maie be the stronger, being shorter.   For when he
riseth from the bottom, he comes not directlie up aboue the
water, but swimmes awaie with an uncontrowled force and
swiftnes, hurrying the shallop after him, with hir head so
close drawen downe to the water, that shee seemes ever
readie to be hailed under it.   When he hath thus drawn
hir perhaps a mile or more—which is done in a verie short
time, considering her swiftnes—then will he come spowteing
aboue the water; and the men rowe up to him, and strike
him with their long launces, which are made purposelie for
that use.   In lancing of the whale, they strike him as near
his swimming finne, and as lowe under water, as they can
conuentlie, to peirce into his intralls.   But when he is
wounded, he is like to wrest the launce out of the strikers
hand; so that sometimes two men are faine to pluck it out,
although but one man did easilie thrust it in.   And now
will he frisk and strike with his tail very forceablie, sometimes hitting the shallop, and splitting hir asunder, sometimes, also, maihmeing or killing some of the men.   And

for that cause, ther is alwaies two or 3 shallops about
the killing of one whale, that one of them maie relieue and
take in the men out of another, being splitt. When he
hath receaued his deadlie wound, then casteth he forth
blood where formerlie he spowted water; and before he
dies he will sometimes drawe the shallops 3 or 4 miles from
the place wher he was first stricken with the harping iron.
When he is dyeing, he most comonlie tourneth his bellie
uppermost, and then do the men fasten a rope, or small
hauser, to the hinder parte of his bodie, and with their
shallops (made fast one to another) they towe him to the
ships with his taile foremost; and then they fasten him to
the sterne of some ship apointed for that purpose, while
he is cutt up in manner as followeth. Two or three men
come in a boat, or shallop, to the side of the whale, one
man holdeing the boat close to the whale with a boat-hook,
and another, who stands either in the boat or upon the
whale, cutts and scores the fatt, which we call blubber, in
square-like peices, 3 or 4 feet long, with a great cutting
knife. Then, to raise it from the flesh, ther is a crab, or
capstowe, sett purposelie upon the poop of the ship, from
which ther discends a rope with an iron hook at the end of
it, and this hook is made to take fast hould of a peice of the
fatt, or blubber, and as, by tourning the capstowe, it is
raised and lifted up, the cutter, with his long knife, loosest
it from the flesh, even as if the larde of a swine were, by
peece and peece, cut off from the leane. When it is in this
manner cleane cutt off, then doe they lower the capstowe,
and lett it downe to float vpon the water, makeing a hole in
some side or corner of it, wherby they fasten it vpon a rope.
And so they proceed to cutt off more peeces, making fast
together 10 or twelue of them at once, to be towed ashoare
at the sterne of a boat or shallop. Theise peices, being
brought to the shoare side, ar, one by one, drawen vpon the
shoare by the helpe of a high crane ther placed, and at

length are hoised up from the ground over a vessell which
is sett to receaue the oile that runnes from it as it is cutt
into smaller peices; for whilest it hangeth thus in the crane,
two men doe cutt it into little peices, about a foot long and
half a foot thick, and putt them into the forsaid vessel
from which it is carried to the choppers by two boies, who,
with little flesh-hooks, take in ech hand a peice, and so
convey it into tubbs, or ould casks, which stand behinde the
choppers, out of which tubbs it is taken againe, and is laid
for them, as they ar readie to use it, vpon the same board
they stand on.

The choppers stand at the side of a shallop, which is
raised from the ground and sett vp of an equal height with
the coppers, and stands about two yards distant from the
fournaces. Then a fir-deale is laid alongst the one side of
the shallop within board, and vpon it doe they sett their
chopping blocks, which ar made of the whale's taile, or els
of his swimming finne. Nowe the blubber is laid readie
for them by some apointed for that purpose as before is sett
downe, in such small peices as the boies doe bring from the
crane; and so they take it vp with little hand-hooks, laie-
ing it vpon their blocks, where, with chopping knives, they
chop it into verye small peices, about an ynch and a halfe
square. Then, with a short thing of wood, made in fashion
like a cole rake, they put the chopt blubber off from the
block downe into the shallop, out of which it is taken
againe with a copper ladle, and filled into a great tubb which
hangs vpon the arme of a gibbet, that is made to tourne to
and again between the blubber boat and the coppers. This
tubb containeth as much blubber as will serue one of the
coppers at one boiling, and therfore, so soon as it is emptied,
it is presentlie filled againe, that it maie be readie to be
putt into the copper when the frittires ar taken out. Theise
frittires, as we call them, are the small peices of chopt
blubber, which, when the oile is sufficientlie boiled, will

look browne, as if they were fried; and they are taken
out of the coppers, together with some of the oile, by
copper ladles, and put into a wicker basket that stands over
another shallop, which is placed on the other side of the
fournaces, and serues as a cooler to receaue the oile being
drayned throwe the said baskets. And this shallop, because
it receaues the oile hott out of the two coppers, is kept
continuallie half full of water, which is not onlie a meanes
to coole the oile befor it runnes into cask, but also to
cleanse it from soot and drosse, which discends to the
bottome of the boat. And out of this shallop the oile
runneth into a long trough, or gutter of wood, and therby
is conveyed into butts and hogsheads, which, being filled,
are bung'd up, marked, and rowl'd by, and others sett in
their place. Then is the bung taken out againe, that the
oile maie coole; for, not with standing the shallop is halfe
fulle of water, yet, the coppers being continuallie plied, the
oile keeps very hott in the boat, and runs also hott into the
cask, which sometimes is an occasion of great leakage.
Now concerning the finnes.

When the whale lies floating at the sterne of the ship,
where he is cutt up, they cut off his head, containing his
toung and finnes, comonlie called whalbone; and by a boat
or shallop they towe it so neare the shoare, as it can come,
and ther lett it lie till the water flowe againe; for at high
waters it is drawn further and further upon the shoare, by
crabs and capstowes ther placed for that purpose, untill,
at a lowe water, men maie come to cutt out the finnes,
which thing they doe with hatchets, by 5 or 6 finnes at
once. And theise are trailed further vp from the shoare
side, and then are seuered ech from another with hatchetts,
and by one, at once, are laid upon a fir deale, or other
board, raised up a convenient height for a man to stand at,
who scrapeth off the white pithie substance that is upon
the roots or great ends of the finnes, with such scraping

irons as coopers use, being instruments very fitting for the purpose. Then are they rubbed in the sand, to cleanse them from grease, which they receauve when the heads are brought to the shoare side; for whilst the whale is in cutting up, his head is under the water, and his finnes remaine cleane; but being brought near the shoare and grounded, then does the grease cleaue vnto them at the ebbing or falling of the water, which is alwaies fattie with blubber that floats upon it continuallie. When the finnes are thus made cleane, they are sorted into 5 seuerall kindes, and are made up into bundells of 50, contayneing of ech sort 10 finnes. These bundles are bound vp with coards, and upon ech of them ther is tied a stick whereon is written some number, and the Companies mark sett, and so they are made readie to be shipped.

Nowe a little concerning the sea morse (of manie called the sea horse), which, indeed, maie seeme to be rather a beast than a fish, and partakes both of the sea and the land. He is in quantitie about the bignesse of a oxe.

Theise morses used to goe ashoare upon some beach or pointe of lowe land, which the snowe doth soonest melt or dissolue; and there will they lie upon the sand close together, grunteing much like hoggs, and sometimes creeping and tumbling one ouer the other. They neuer goe farre up from the water side, and therfore the men that goe to kill theise strike the first that are next the water, that their dead bodies maie be a hinderance to barre the rest from escapeing, for they all make towards the water, with out anie feare, either of man or weapon that opposeth them.

Theise also are killed with launces, which are verie broad headed to the end, so that they maie make the more mortal wound, for the speedie killing of them, because they are so neare the water, and also many in nombers; for in some places there will be 400 or 500 morses all together.

This sea beast being dead, his teeth are taken out of his

upper jawe ; and his skin, or hide, is fleyed of him, first on
the one side, and his fat or blubber, which lies next to his
skinne, aboue his flesh, is also taken off; and then is his
other side tourned up, and ye like againe done with it.
Then is the blubber put into a cask, and carried to the
choppers, and by them it is chopped and put into the
coppers, and then it is tryed and reduced to oile.

THE THIRD RECORDED VOYAGE

OF

WILLIAM BAFFIN.

A Voyage of Discouerie to Greenland,[1] etc., Anno 1614.[2]

Written by RO. FOTHERBYE.[3]

THE ship *Thomasine* went downe from Black-wall to Woolwich the sixteenth of April, and from thence to Grauesend,
the three and twentieth, where shee remayned vntill the
eight and twentieth of the same; and, weighing from
thence, she anchored againe in Tilberie Hope, with ten

---

[1] Spitzbergen.

[2] *Purchas*, Part III, lib. ii, cap. iv, pp. 720 to 725.

[3] There was a family of Fotherbys at Grimsby in Lincolnshire.
Martin Fotherby of Grimsby had a brother Robert, and two sons—
Charles, Dean and Archdeacon of Canterbury, who died in 1619 ; and
Martin, Bishop of Salisbury. Archbishop Whitgift was also a native
of Grimsby, which accounts for Dr. Fotherby's Kent preferment.
There is a very elaborate altar tomb to Archdeacon Fotherby's memory
in Canterbury Cathedral—the marble sides being carved with skulls
and bones in high relief. Our Robert Fotherby probably belonged
to the Grimsby stock. He was in the Spitzbergen Voyages of 1613,
1614, and 1615, and wrote narratives of them all, the first in manuscript
until it was printed in 1860 in the *Archæologia Americana*, the two others
in *Purchas*. These narratives afford evidence that their author was a
man of classical, as well as of mathematical culture. After his return
in 1615, a Court's Minute of the East India Company, dated in the
October of that year, records the opinion that Robert Fotherby is " a
very fit person to be employed upon a discovery for the south side of
the Cape". He probably went on a voyage to the Indies, but in November 1618 he was appointed the East India Company's overseer for making
cordage, to reside at Deptford. In 1621 he was confirmed in his place
and salary, and in August of that year he was removed to Blackwall, to
act as the Company's Agent there. In October 1624 his wages were
increased.

ships more of good burthen, and two pinnasses, all of the
Greenland fleet, set forth also at the charge of the said
Company, vnder the command of Master Beniamin Joseph,
chiefe captayne and generall of the said fleet.

We set sayle out of Tilberie Hope the fourth of May, and
came to an anchor the same day in Lee Road, where we stayed
till the next morning, then wee set sayle againe, and went
forth to sea before night. We proceeded in company of the
fleet, and met with stragling ice the fiue and twentieth of
May, in lat. 75° 10′, thro' which wee passed without danger,
holding on our course all that day, till time of midnight; then
we found the ice so close packt together, that we were forced
to tacke about and stand to the westward, till wee found
more open passage; wee plyed through it without any great
danger, till the eight and twentieth day; but then, being
in sight of land, we passed amongst very much ice all the
fore-noone, which lay in great abundance on both sides of
vs; but a desire (as it seems) to get through it drew vs on
to be the more intangled with it, for about noone we could
neither find a passage to goe forward, nor way to retyre
backe againe, but being nine ships and two pinnasses (for
the *Prosperous* and the *Desire* lost company through foule
weather, the one and twentieth of May, otherwise we had
beene thirteene sayle), we began very suddenly to bee inclosed, and shut vp with ice. Now euery one wrought the Eleven
best meanes he could for the saftie of his ship; our master, in the Ice.
in the *Thomasine*, caused a hauser and a grapnell to be M. Th.
carried forth, and laid vpon a great iland of ice, and so we Sherwin.
rid as at an anchor, and by that meanes wee stayed from
forceable rushing against other peeces; afterward we laid
forth an anchor for surer hold, and made fenders of an old
cable, which was hung ouer the ships sides to keepe the
ice from piercing of her plankes. Wee rid thus from the
eight and twentieth of May till the second of June, still
floating as the wind droue vs, with our anchor holding iland,

which now we accounted as the shoare, and made vse thereof accordingly, for vpon it our carpenter sealed and trimmed our lesser shallop.

On the second of June we had a great homeming[1] sea, the wind being at north-west, whereby we iudged we were not farre from an open sea to windward of vs; there wee resolued to make tryall what we might doe to free our selues out of the ice. In the afternoone, about three a'clock, we got aboard our anchor, letting fall our fore top-sayle, and putting forth our mizen; and so droue a sterne for a while, till the floating iland gaue way; then wee filled our top-sayle, and attempted diuers places where to passe, but had repulse, and fell asterne againe; notwithstanding, at the length we preuayled, and with much adoe we attayned an open sea at a north and by west sunne, parting very gladly

from these ill neighbouring ilands; which, at our parting from them, gaue vs, or rather receiued from vs some knockes; but whilest we remayned amongst them, they seemed much more perillous than they proued hurtfull, so wee prayed God for our safe deliuerance, wishing that the rest of the ships which we left in the ice were as cleere out of it as was the *Thomasine.*

Hauing attayned the open sea to the westwards, we proceeded to the northwards, keeping the ice still on our starboord side, and met with the *Mary An-Sarah,* that got also

free of the ice the same day that we came forth of it; we kept company together till the next day, when being as high as Prince Charles Iland, we both stood in for the shoare, the *Mary An-Sarah* going for Bel-sound, her assigned harbour; but we proceeded to the Fore-land, where,

when wee came the sixt of June, wee met with two shallops that belonged to the *Desire,* wherein was Cuthbert Appleyard and William Sunmes, harponiers; by whom we vnderstood that the *Prosperous* and the *Desire* had more desiredly prospered then all the rest of the fleet; they es-

---

[1] A misprint. Perhaps " hummocking".

caped the danger that all the rest fell into, and came to
the Foreland the third of June, finding the harbour open.

Here was yet no worke begunne, for they had not seene
one whale since their comming into the harbour; so that
for vs there was no cause of stay to bee helpfull vnto them;
and therefore we proceeded to the northward, hoping to Wee pro-
ceeded to
find the shoare still as free from ice as it was at this place; the North-
wards.
but it fel out contrary to our expectations, for being come
as farre as Maudlen Sound, in the latitude of 79° 34′, we Maudlen
Sound.
met with some stragling ice, and from the mayne top we
saw much ice lye betwixt vs and Hackluyts Headland, Hackluyts
Headland.
which seemed to bee close to the shoare, therefore we sent
some men in a shallop to Maudlen Sound, to see if it were
open, that wee might harbour our ship there, and search
for a leake which wee found her subject vnto in foule weather.

The Sound was open, and we anchored in a good har- We an-
chored in
bour, but the ice was not gone cleere from the shoare, Maudlen
Sound.
therefore we could not hale our ship aground, but we carined
her, and set vp our *Biscaine* shallop, which we carried with
vs out of England in pieces.

The next day after our comming hither, I went forth I went forth
in a shallop.
in a little shallop (the other being then vnset together),
to see how the ice lay at Hackluyts Headland, and whether
we might passe with our ship that way or no. Being come
forth of the harbour, we perceiued that it was very foule
weather at sea; notwithstanding, I proceeded into Faire
Hauen, where the south harbour was then open, but much
ice lay then in the Sound, vnbroken from shoare to shoare;
otherwise wee might haue passed that way to Hackluyts
Head-land, betwixt the iland and the mayne land; we
stayed here till the next morning, then the weather beganne to cleere vp, and we put forth to sea againe, intending to goe without the Ilands; but being out of the harbour,
wee found the foule weather to be such as our little weake
shallop was not able to endure; therefore we returned

againe to our ship into Maudlen Sound, where we killed two female morses, and took their teeth, hides, and blubber.

We set sayle out of Maudlen Sound, and followed the Ice.

On the tenth of June we set sayle out of Maudlen Sound, and coasted along to the northward till we were past Hackluyts Headland, but then we saw the ice lye before vs, extending close to the shoare, so that for us to passe further that way it was not possible; therefore wee turned to the westward, to see if wee could finde passage further from the shoare. Wee sayled as the ice trended, west and south-west, till the thirteenth day, and, keeping still alongst it, we found it to trend neerest south and south south-west. We proceeded well thus far, till we came vnder the latitude

Prince Charles Iland in 78° 40'.

of Prince Charles his Iland in 78° 40', being eight and twentie leagues from shoare; but then we altered our

Wee stood againe for shoare.

course, and stood in for the foreland, to goe and be helpfull to the other ships there, for the furthering of their voyage, according to our instructions (as some did vnderstand them), but contrary, I am sure, to some of our desires. When we

Eleuen Holland ships.

came neere the Foreland, we saw eleuen ships of Hollanders vnder sayle, plying to the southwards. One of them came roome, and struck her top-sayles twice, whereby we supposed they took vs for some of their fleete which they wanted, but wee held on our course still into Sir Thomas

We anchored in Sir T. Smiths Bay.

Smiths Bay, where we came to an anchor the fifteeuth of June by the *John-Anne-Francis* and the *Desire*, the *Mary Margaret* being then vnder sayle to go to the Foreland.

Here was yet no need of any helpe that we could make them, for they had hitherto neyther killed one whale since their first comming in hither; therefore we thought it best not to stay here, but rather goe to Faire Hauen, where wee should bee more readie to proceed on our discouerie when the ice would giue vs leaue, and in the meane-time wee might bee helpfull to the two ships thither assigned for the making of their voyage; and so much the rather wee hasted, because we vnderstood that the Hollanders also set forth a ship on discouerie.

We set sayle the seuenth of June, and met with the We went
forth of
Sir T.
Smiths Bay
Prosperous, that came from Cross-road, and was going into
Sir Thomas Smith Bay, there to get some bricke and lime
to mend their fornace, as Nicholas Woodcocke,[1] the
master, told vs. Then we went forth to sea, and, being
about foure leagues from the shoare, the winde began to
blow so hard from the north-west, that wee were forced
back againe to seek harbour, and came to an anchor the We were
driven back
againe into
Crosse-
road.
nineteenth of June in Crosse-road. Here we stayed two
dayes, much wind blowing at the north north-east, till the
one and twentieth of June, and then, in the after-noone,
the wind came to the east and by south, and the weather
was faire; therefore, at a north north-west sunne, we We set
sayle out of
Crosse-
road.
weighed and set sayle againe, and so did the *Thomas*
Bonauenture, that came to an' anchor by vs this morning,
beeing also bound for Faire Hauen.

This next day, in the afternoone, we were thwart of
Maudlen Sound, and, the weather being faire and calme,
we sent a shallop to the northward, to see what alteration One shallop
to the North
ward.
there was amongst the ice, and to seeke out some good
harbour for a ship, and also to set vp the kings armes at
Hackluyts Headland, or some other conuenient place.

When Master Baffin was gone from the ship in the fore-
said shallop, I went presently into the other shallop into The other
into Maud-
len Sound.
Maudlen Sound, there to set vp the kings armes, and also
to see if there were any morses come ashoare. When I was
within the Sound, I found no beeches bare for morses to
come vpon, for ice and snow lay yet vndissolued from the The Kings
Armes set
vp in Trini-
tie Harbour
shoare side; but I went to the harbour, and there caused a

---

[1] There was a seaman of this name, which is not a common one, sent
out by the Muscovy Company in 1568, on a voyage to reach the river
Ob, but the particulars have not been preserved. Nicholas Woodcock
may have been a grandson of this earlier namesake. He was pilot in
Jonas Poole's voyage of 1610, but in 1612 he piloted a Spanish ship,
and is said to have been the cause of so many Dutch ships having gone
to Spitzbergen in 1613. For that offence he was arrested and suffered
imprisonment. (*Purchas*, iii, p. 466.)

crosse to be set vp, and the kings armes to be nayled thereon, vnder which also I nayled a piece of sheet lead, whereon I set the Moscouie Companies marke, with the day of the moneth and yeare of our Lord. Then, cutting vp a piece of earth, which afterward I carried aboard our ship, I took it into my hand and said, in the hearing of the men there present, to this effect :

I take this piece of earth, as a signe of lawfull possession of this countrey of King James his New-land, and of this particular place, which I name Trinitie Harbour, taken on the behalfe of the company of merchants called the Merchants of New Trades and Discoueries, for the vse of our Souereigne Lord James, by the grace of God King of Great Brittaine, France, and Ireland, whose royall armes are here set vp, to the end that all people who shall here arriue may take notice of his Maiesties right and title to this countrey, and to euery part thereof. God saue King James.

Trinitie Harbor is vnder the parallel of 79° 34'.

This is a good safe harbour, and is vnder the latitude of 79° 34', as I haue found by good obseruation, and haue of westerly variation 25°. When I had here set vp the kings armes, I returned toward our ship, which was come to an anchor at the entrance of Faire hauen, staying the floud came, because that at the tide of ebbe there runnes a great current out of the Sound; so, at the next floud, we came into Faire hauen, and anchored by the *Gamaliel* and the *Thomas Bonauenture* the three and twentieth day of June.

We came to an anchor in Faire Hauen.

Then John Mason, master of the *Gamaliel*, came aboord of our ship, and I asked him if he had any worke for our men, for I would cause them to come a shoare. He told me that hitherto he had not seene a whale come in ; but his furnaces and coppers were already set vp, and therefore as yet he had no neede of helpe, but when occasion serued he would imploy them. This day, about eleuen a clocke, Master Baffin returned in the shallop from the northwards. He said that he had beene at Cape Barren, which is the point of an iland three or foure leagues from Hackluits

No Whales were yet come in.

The shallop returned from the Northwards.

Cape Barren.

headland; but further than that he could not passe for ice
which lay close to the shore, and he had not set vp the
kings armes in any place.

On Munday, the seuen and twentieth of June, I went
forth againe in the shallop to the northward, partly to see
what alteration there might be in the ice with the easterly
windes, which had blowne hard since the shallop last returned, but chiefely to set vp the kings armes in some
place conuenient, because there was none set vp to the
northwards of Maudlen Sound.

We rowed to Cape Barren, where formerly Master Baffin
had bin, and, finding the ice there gone from the shore, we
proceeded further, to an iland which now we call the Saddle, ^{Saddle Iland.}
in respect of the forme thereof, more than a league distant
from Cape Barren. In our way thither it began to snow,
and grew to be a great and vehement storme from the A Storme.
west north-west; therefore we hasted and got to the lee
side of the aforesaid iland, and there made fast our shallop
with a grapnell laid vpon the icie shore, vsing the best meanes
we could with our shallops saile to keepe vs from the ex-
tremitie of so cold an harbour. We staid here eight houres,
and the storme continued driuing the ice still eastward in
great abundance, and with wonderfull swiftnesse. When
the weather began to cleere, I caused the men to rowe to
leewards to another iland, a league distant, which seemed
then to be a cape of the maine land, purposing there to set
vp the kings armes; but afterwards wee found it to be an
iland, and to the maine wee could not come for broken ice.

This stormie weather continued from Munday night till
Friday morning, during which time we had beene but
eleauen leagues at the furthest from our ship; yet went we
so farre as we could haue gone had the weather beene
neuer so faire, for at foure leagues distance from Cape
Barren the ice lay firme and vnbroken two or three miles
from the shore, and close againe to it lay the shattered ice,

Julii.

thronged together with this present storme. On Friday
morning we came backe againe to Hackluit's Headland,
and there I set [up?] the kings armes in the like manner
as at Trinitie Harbour. From thence we rowed towards
our ship; and as we entred into Faire-hauen, there came a
whale that accompanied vs into the harbour, leaping and
aduancing himselfe almost quite out of the water, falling
headlong downe againe with greate noise. We hasted
aboord our ship, and I sent forth both our shallops to
strike this whale, if they could, and told Master Mason of
her comming in, who also went forth in his shallop; but it
seemes the whale past vnder the ice which lay yet vnbroken
betwixt the north harbour and the south harbour, for they
could not see her againe.

The next day there came more whales in, and Robert
Hambleton, our masters mate, strucke two, which vnluckily
escaped, the first for want of helpe, the *Gamaliel's* shallop
being in chase of another whale, and our owne little shallop
not able to row against a head sea to assist the other; so
that at length, the whale hauing towed the shallop forth to
sea, the harping iron came out; the second was also strucken
within the sound, and ranne vnder the ice, which lay yet
vnbroken at the east end of the Sound, and drew the
shallop vpon it cleane out of the water, by which meanes
the harping iron came forth. Here we remained till the
sixt of Julie, our men and boates being helpefull at all
times to further the voyage.

The sixt of Julie we set saile forth of Faire-hauen, intending to make triall if we could to get to westwards of the
ice, and so proceede to the northwards, hauing sent away
one of our shallops the day before, prouided with twentie
dayes bread, to coast along the shoare, search the beach
for commodities, and set vp the Kings armes at places
conuenient, hoping thereby to preuent the Hollanders, who
now rid in the north harbour of Faire-hauen, and were

The Whales
began now
to come in.

Two
Whales
escaped.

We came
forth of
Faire-
hauen.

ready for the first opportunitie to discouer and take possession of other harbours, hauing two ships to goe forth
onely vpon discouery.

We sailed westwards from Faire-hauen seuen leagues, *We met with ice and stood to the northward.* and then met with a maine banke of ice, which trended
north and south, the sea appeared to the northwards to be
open, so far as we could see, therefore we plied that way.
When we had run seuen or eight leagues more, the ice lay
so thick on euery side, that we were bard from proceeding
any further; then we stood in toward the shore, and being
a little to the northwards of Cape Barren, our shallop had *Our shallop came to vs.*
sight of vs, and came rowing to vs through the broken
ice. Master Baffin told vs the shore to the eastward was
much pestered with ice, and he had set vp the Kings armes
at the entrance of a faire sound, about four leagues distant
from Cape Barren.

Now the weather being faire and calme, Master Sherwin,
Master Baffin, and I, went in the shallop to the place where
the Kings armes were set vp, purposing (because the ayre
was very cleere) to goe vpon some high mountaine, from
whence we might see how the sea was pestered with ice,
and what likelihood there was of further proceeding. According to this our intent, we ascended a very high hill,
and from thence we saw the ice lye vpon the sea so farre as
we could discerne, so that the sea seemed to be wholly
toured with ice, saue onely to the eastwards; we thought
that we saw the water beyond the ice, which put vs in
some hope that we should ere long get passage with
our shallops along the shore, if we could not passe with
our shippe. Being thus satisfied, we returned abord our
ship and plyed towards Faire-hauen, aduising amongst our- *We re-turned towards Faire hauen.*
selues of the best course we could to further the businesse
committed to vs.

We resolued to make our discouery along the shore with *We in-tended to discouer with our shallops.*
both our shallops, and to carry with vs our prouision for

the whale-killing, conceiuing good hopes besides, of profit
which the beaches would afford vs ; therefore we intended,
when our ship was brought safe into harbour againe, to goe
from her with both our shallops, and to put in practice this
our late resolution.   But the weather falling calme, and a
fogge succeeding, which continued three dayes, so that our
ship came not into harbour till the twelfth of July.   I went
from her the eleuenth day, intending to search the beaches,

I went forth
in the one
shallop. till Master Baffin came to me with the other shallop, and
then we to proceede both together ; but before he came, I
had gone so farre as that the ice would not suffer mee to
passe a boates length further, and I had also searched a very
faire beach, which was altogether fruitlesse.

Master
Baffin came
to me in the
other
shallop. Master Baffin came to me at a place appointed, the fourteenth of Julie, in the other shallop, and we proceeded
both together to the eastwards againe, and found passage
amongst the ice, that lay almost two miles from the shoare
Red-beach. of Red-beach, vnbroken vp this yeare.   Here wee haled vp
We hailed
our shallop
upon the
ice. our shallops out of the water, lest the broken ice, which is
carried to and fro with the winde, might split them or
bruise them.   Then Master Baffin and I, with foure men
more, walked ouer the firme ice, and went ashore on Red-
beach, where we trauelled about the space of three miles
by the shore side, but found no commodities, as we expected
to haue done ; for here had the Hull-men[1] been in 1612,
as we might know, by the fires that they had made, and
gathered the fruites that many yeares before had brought
forth.   Thus, as we could not finde that which wee desired
to see, so did we behold that which we wished had not
beene there to be seene, which was great abundance of ice,
that lay close to the shore, and also off at sea, so farre as
we could discerne ; wherefore, being thus satisfied, and
more wearie to know that we could passe no further then
We re-
turned to
our shallop. with trauelling so farre, we returned to our shallops, and

---

[1] Hull men, under the command of Captain Marmaduke.

went aboord of our ship in Faire hauen on Sunday, the seuenteenth of July, passing the neerest way betwixt the islands and the maine land, for now the ice was broken betwixt the south harbour, where we rid, and the north harbour, where the Hollanders rid.

The next day we sent our shallop to the north-east side of Faire-hauen, there to lye for the comming of the whales ouer against the *Gamaliels* two shallops that lye on the other side for the same purpose.

The twentieth of July, wee were vnder saile to goe forth of Faire-hauen with the *Gamaliel*, purposing to haue taken two ships that rid at the entrance of Maudlen-Sound with John Mason, who first descried them, supposed to be one a Bask, and the other an English man ; but the winde blew right into the harbour, so that we could not get forth, and therefore we came to an anchor againe where we rid before. *We were vnder saile and came to an anchor againe.*

On the one and twentieth of July our harponiers killed a whale, which split óne of our shallops, and strucke the harponier that was in her ouerboord ; but both hee and the rest of the men were relieued, and taken into another shallop ; then we sent our carpenter to mend the shallop that was split ; and on the fiue and twentieth day they helpt to kill another whale. *We killed a Whale.*

On the sixe and twentieth of July I drew the plat of Faire-hauen, as it is here proiected (but here too costly to insert).

When this scoale of whales were past, we went out of Faire-hauen the first of August with both our shallops, Master Baffin in one, and I in the other, with fiue men more in each shallop, thinking that now we should find the ice broken, and cleere gone from the shore, conceiuing some good hope to proceede, and make some new dis-couery, which was the chiefe occasion of our imployment. Wee passed ouer Red-cliff Sound, which we found cleare of ice ; and from thence we proceeded to Red-beach, where *August.*

We went to
the north-
ward with
our shal-
lops.
we also found great alteration since our last being there,
notwithstanding the ice was not clearely voided from the
shoare; for in some places it was firm and vnbroken off,
for the space of almost halfe a mile; so we rowed alongst it,
We got to
the shoare
of Red
Beach with
our shal-
lops.
till wee came neere the north end of the beach, which lyeth
furthest into the sea, and there we found an open way to
the shore with our shallops, and went on land; but seeing
in all places great abundance of broken ice, we lay close to
the shoare; and doubting that although perhaps with much
adoe we might get about the point of the beach, yet should
we still be pestered with ice from proceeding any further,
We walked
ouer Red-
beach.
we resolued to walke ouer land to the other side of the
beach, where we saw a hill about foure miles distant, from
which we thought we should be satisfied how much further
it was possible for vs to proceede; so thither we trauailed,
where, when we came, wee saw a very faire sound on the
east side of the beach which was open within; but there
lay very much ice at the entrance of it, which, although it
was extended more than halfe ouer [the] sound, yet we
doubted not but if we could get our shallops about the
beach, we should finde either one way or other to passe
ouer the said sound, and from the high land on the other
side we should receiue very good satisfaction, if the weather
continued faire and cleare as now it was, therefore we intended to make triall what we might do; but before we
returned we went down to the point of the beach, at the
entrance of the sound, and there set vp a crosse, and nailed
The Kings
armes are
set vp at
Wiches
Sound.
a sixepence thereon with the Kings armes. This being
done, we returned to our shallops, and according to our
late determination, we rowed about the point of Red-beach,
We passed
ouer Wiches
Sound.
and with many crooked windings amongst the ice, at
length we got ouer Wiches Sound (for so it is now termed).
As soone as we were ouer on the other side, about two
leagues from Red-beach, Master Baffin and I clambered vp
a very high hill, from whence we saw a point of land,

bearing east north-east by the ordinary compasse, eighteene
or twentie leagues distant, as I supposed. We likewise
saw another faire sound to the southwards of vs, which was
much pestered with ice, but we could not see the end of it.
Here, vpon the mountaine, wee set vp a warelocke, and
then came downe againe with lesse labour but more danger
then we had in getting vp, by reason of the steepinesse
thereof. Then we walked to the shoare side, and there
found many beach finnes, whereby I coniectured that We found beach Fins.
Master Marmadukes men, in his first discouery, made in
Anno 1612, had not beene vpon this land to search the
beaches, for in all other places where we had beene heretofore we could finde nothing at all. Now, therefore, we
resolued to make further search alongst this shoare, and to
proceede with our shallops so farre as we possibly could;
wherevpon wee returned to our men againe, whom we left
with our shallops where we first landed.

Hauing stayed here a while, and obserued the latitude,
which I found to be 79° 54′, we saw a shallop come rowing We met with the <i>Harts-ease</i> shallop.
towards the extreamest point of this shoare; therefore we
hastened towards them, to see who were therein, and found
them to be Master Marmadukes men, lately come from their
ship, the <i>Harts-ease</i>, which they said they left at sea amongst
the ice, about a league from Red Beach. Here they were
setting vp a crosse, which they said that they found there
fallen downe, and had beene formerly set vp, in the time of
Master Marmadukes first discouery, by one Laurence Prest- Note.
wood, whose name I saw thereon engrauen, with two or
three names more, and it had the date of the seuenteenth
of August 1612. Vpon this crosse they nailed the Kings
armes.

Here we parted from them, and, according to our former
determination, we proceeded, some in the shallops amongst
the ice, and others on shoare, till wee went about foure
leagues further, in which space we found many more finnes,

and one pair of morses teeth; but now we found the ice so close packt together, that wee could not proceede any further with our shallops; wherefore Master Baffin and I intended to walke ouer land vntill we should be better satisfied how farre this sound went in, for wee could as yet see no end of it, and it seemed to make a separation of the land; so, leauing our men here with the shallops, wee trauailed almost a league further, till we came to the point of a sandie beach that shot into the sound, which was wonderfully stored with drift wood in great abundance. From this point we receiued such satisfaction as we looked for, because we saw the end of the sound, which lies south in about ten leagues. It hath in it harbour that is landlockt; and, doubtlesse, it is a good place for the whale killing, if it be not euery yeare, as now it is, pestered with ice. Here I saw a more naturall earth and clay then any that I haue seene in all the countrie, but nothing growing thereupon more then in other places. This sound is that which formerly had, and still retaineth, the name of Sir Thomas Smiths Inlet.[1]

The end of Sir Thomas Smiths Inlet discouered.

Being thus satisfied, we came backe againe to our shallops, and, seeing no way but one, we returned to our ship; but before we could get to Red-beach, there arose a very great storme from the east north-east after we had entered among the ice in Wiches Sound, so that we were separated the one shallop from the other, whereby our danger was the greater; for whiles wee were both in company together, the one might have beene helpefull to the other when neede required, and more easie it seemed to saue them both then, being separated, to keepe either of them from wracke. But God (who, in his wonted mercie, is euer ready to relieue the faithfull distressed) did not onely so prouide that we met together againe—and, indeede, were helpefull the one to the other (otherwise, I doubt the one shallop had mis-

We returned towards our ship. A storme began when we were amongst the ice.

---

[1] Called Hinlopen Strait on the modern charts.

carried, for she was in great danger)—but also deliuered vs
safely out from amongst these perillous rockes of ice, which
it was very hard to shun, and at the length brought vs into
an open sea, where, with as scant a saile as we could make,
we past swiftly before the winde, the sea comming diuers
times ouer the sternes of our shallops, which wet our skinnes,
that had scarse any dry cloathes on before to keepe them
warme, by reason of a drizeling snow which fell with the
storme. Then we went aboord our ship, into the south har- We came
bour of Faire hauen, the fift of August, with one hundred ship.
and fiftie beach finnes, and one pair of morses teeth, giuing
thanks to God for his blessing and mercifull deliuerance.

The ninth of August, two ships of the Hollanders, that TheHolland
were appointed for Northern Discouery, were seene thwart go home-
of Faire Hauen, sayling to the southwards.

The eleuenth of August we set sayle forth of Faire
Hauen, the winde at south south-west, intending to make
tryall if yet the ice would admit vs to haue passage to the
northwards or the north-eastwards. We held our course Our ship
from Cape Barren, north-east and by east, till seuen a clocke to sea.
at night, at which time, hauing runne eight leagues from
the shoare, wee met with the ice which lay east and by We meet
south, and west and by north, and bore vp alongst it to the leagues
eastwards, for the winde was now come to the north north- shore.
west; then wee tackt about to the westwards, and plyed We plyed
off and on close by the ice till the thirteenth day at mid- the ice two
night, still expecting a change of the weather, that we
might haue made some aduenture amongst the shatterd
ice, for both on the twelfth and thirteenth day the winde
blew hard at north, and the weather was cold, thicke, and
very winter-like, with fall of snow ; this winde being so contrarie, droue both the ice and our ship to leewards towards
the shoare, so that wee were forced to put into harbour Wee an-
againe, and came to an anchor the fourteenth day in the againe in
north harbour of Faire Hauen, where the fleet of Hollanders Harbour.

lately rid, at which time the *Hartsease* was there at an anchor.

Now was the land, both mountaynes and plaines, wholly couered with snow, so that almost all mens mindes were possessed with a desire of returning for England. But to preuent a sudden resolution for a homeward voyage, without further satisfaction, I made mention that once againe we might goe forth with our shallops, to see what alteration there might bee found alongst the shoare. It fell out that I was to goe in one shallop for this purpose, so I tooke with me eight men, and went from our ship the fifteenth day of August.

I went to the east-wards in a shallop.

We rowed to Red-cliffe Sound, where we passed through much ice that was newly congealed, being thicker than an halfe crowne piece of siluer, notwithstanding we broke way through it, and being ouer the sound, we had a cleere sea againe; then we proceeded to Red-beach, where, finding the shoare cleere of ice (which, at my last being there, was wonderfully pestered), I conceiued good hope to finde passage to the furthest land from thence in sight, bearing east halfe a point southerly, nine or ten leaages distant; to this end we put off from the shoare of Red-beach, and rowed a league and more in an open sea, and then we met with ice, which lay dispersed abroad, and was no hinderance to our proceeding, so that we continued rowing the space of sixe houres, in which time we had gotten more then halfe way ouer; but then we found the ice to lye very thicke thronged together, so that it caused vs much to alter our course, sometimes southward, and sometimes northward; and euen in this time, when we thought wee stood in most need of cleere weather, it pleased God to send vs the contrary, for it beganne to snow very fast, which made the ayre so thicke that we could not see to make choice of the most likely way for vs to passe; therefore I thought good to stay here awhile, hoping that ere long the weather would

Ice was newly frozen in Red-cliffe Sound.

I intended to goe once to Port Desire.

A great snow began.

bee more agreeable to our purpose; so a grapnell being
laid forth vpon an Iland off, to hold fast our shallop, a
tent was made of the shallops sayle, to keepe the weather
from vs, and we remayned here fiue houres; but finding
no alteration in the constant weather, I willed the men to
take downe the tent, and with faire tearmes perswaded
them, that notwithstanding the wet weather it were good
to be doing something, to get ouer to the desired shoare,
where we might refresh our selues, and haue fire to dry our
wet clothes: they seemed well content with this motion, and
so we rowed the space of foure houres more, the ice still
causing vs to hold a south and south south-east course,
which carried vs further into Sir Thomas Smith's Inlet, ^{I could not passe for ice.}
and put vs from the place where we wished to be.

The thicke snowie weather continued all this time, which
was very vncomfortable to vs all, but especially to the men
that rowed; and as the snow was noysome to their bodies,
so did it also begin to astonish their mindes, as I well perceiued by their speeches which proceeded vpon this occa-
sion. The snow hauing continued thus long, and falling ^{The originall cause of ice at sea.}
vpon the smooth water, lay in some places an inch thicke,
being alreadie in the nature of an ice compact, though not
congealed, and hindred sometimes our shallops way; this,
I say, caused some of them, not altogether without reason,
to say that if it should now freeze as it did that night when
we came ouer Red-cliffe Sound, we should be in danger
here to be frozen vp. Howsoeuer, this search might bee a
meanes to discourage the rest, that considered not of such
a thing till they heard it spoken of: yet true it is, that I
saw no likelihood, by reason of the ice, how to attayne my
desire at this time, and therefore I bade them row
toward the shoare of Red-beach againe, where I intended ^{I went back to Red-beach.}
to stay till the weather might happily be more conuenient.
So holding a west north-west course, so neere as the ice
would suffer vs, wee came to the east side of Red-beach,

hauing been eighteene houres amongst the ice, during all
which time the snow fell, and as yet ceased not. When
we had been here about an houre it began to cleere vp,
and the wind to blow hard at east, which rather packt the
ice close together in this place then disperst it, so that I
was now out of hope to get any than I had done alreadie ;

wherefore I returned toward our ship, intending as I went
to make a more particular discouery of Broad-bay and
Red-cliffe Sound, hoping that one place or other would
afford some thing worthy of the time and labour. When we
were come to the west side of Red-beach it began to blow
much wind, where withall the sea growing to be great, all
men aduised to passe ouer Broad-bay, whilst the winde
and weather would serue vs to sayle, for they said it was
like to be very foule weather : so seeing that it was no
conuenient time for coasting, we came ouer the bay to

Point Welcome (which I so named because it is a place
where wee oftentimes rested when wee went forth in our
shallops), it is about foure leagues distant from the north
end of Red-beach.

At this point the Hollanders had set vp Prince Maurice
his armes, neere vnto a crosse which I had caused to bee
set vp aboue a month before, and had nayled a six pence
thereon with the Kings armes, but the men that were with
me went (without any such direction from mee) and pulled
downe the said Princes armes, whilst I was gone vp a
mountayne to looke into the sea, if I could see any ice ;
and when I came downe againe they told me that the sixe
pence was taken from the crosse I had set vp, and there
was another post set by it, with the Hollanders armes made
fast thereon, which they had pulled downe ; so, because the

sixe pence was taken away, I caused one to nayle the Kings
armes, cast in lead, vpon the crosse ; which, being done, we
rowed to the bottome of Red-cliffe Sound, and as we
coasted along the shoare, we searched two little beaches

which had some wood on them, but nothing we found of better value.

About two leagues within the sound, on the east side, there is an harbour, where shippes may ride in good ground land-lockt; but if other yeeres be like this, I cannot say that this is an harbour fitting for ships, because it is late ere the Sound breake vp; for euen now there lay much ice at the bottome of it, insomuch that I was forced to leaue the shallop, because I could not passe with her for ice, and walke two miles ouer stonie mountaynes, with another man in my company, to bee satisfied concerning a point of land that shot into the Sound, whether it were an Iland or no, as by all likelihood it seemed to bee : but when I came to the farthest part of it, I saw it joyne to the mayne land, wherefore I called it Point Deceit, because it deceiued mee so much. From hence wee proceeded toward our shippe, and came aboord of her in the north harbour of Faire Hauen, on Friday night, being the nineteenth of August, where she rid alone, for Master Marmaduke was gone forth to sea that day.

Point Deceit.

I come aboord our ship.

The two and twentieth of August, John Mason, master of the *Gamaliell*, came ouer from the south harbour for helpe to hayle vp a whale which had beene sunke fourteene dayes, in one hundred and twentie fathome depth, or else to pull the wharpe and harping iron out of her, for now it was time to take her or forsake her. Master Sherwin, our master, caused our long boate to be manned, and went with him; when they came where the whale was sunke they haled, and shee presently rose, bolting suddenly vp with a thundring cracke, made with the bursting of her bodie ; and notwithstanding she had layen so long, yet had shee all her finnes fast. Whilst this was in doing, the *Hartsease* was comming into the harbour from the northward, and anchored by our ship an houre after.

A whale lay sunken fourteene dayes.

Here wee stayed till the seuen and twentieth of August,

and since my last returne hither in the shallop from the
eastwards, the weather hath beene commonly warme, and
the mountaynes were now more cleere of snow then they
had beene any time this yeere, notwithstanding there had
much snowe fallen since the beginning of this moneth, but
it was quite consumed, and a greater signe of warmth and
thaw was now to bee obserued then any time of the yeere
heretofore; namely, by the often falling of the ice into the
sea from the huge snowie bankes, making a noyse like
thunder, so that the time was very hopefull, but thus wee
made vse of occasion offered.

The seuen and twentieth of August, it was faire and
warme weather, calme till noone, then had wee a gale of
winde from the south south west, wherewithall wee set
sayle out of Faire-hauen in the company of the *Hartsease*,
with whom wee had beene in termes of consortship, but
nothing was concluded. About sixe a clocke at night wee
were sixe leagues from Cape Barren, which bore from vs
south-west and by south.

Wee proceeded still to the north-eastward, and on the
eight and twentieth day in the morning wee had runne
about twentie leagues from Cape Barren, in an east north-
east way by the ordinary compasse, being open of Sir
Thomas Smith's Inlet nine or tenne leagues from the
shoare, at which time wee were come to the ice that trended
east south-east, and west north-west, but the sea being
very rough, wee stood off againe from the ice; in the afternoone it fell calme, and at night we had a gale of winde
at east, and the ship was steered west, and then south-west
homewards.

The nine and twentieth day, the winde easterly, an easie
gale. At foure a clocke in the afternoone, Hackluyts Headland bore from vs, south-east by east, foure leagues distant.
This euening was very warme.

The thirtieth day, the winde at north-east, an easie gale.

Warme weather in the end of August.

We set sayle to the East-ward.

The Thomasine returnes for England.

At foure a clocke in the afternoone, Maudlen Point bore
east north-east, halfe a point easterly, about three leagues
distant. Towards the euening it fell calme ; the weather
not cold.

The thirtieth (?) day, faire sunne-shine weather, and
calme till noone, and then we had a good gale of winde
from the north-east, being fiue leagues distant from the
foreland, which bore south-east. Now we altered our course,
and stood to the west-ward ; therefore, to keepe vs still in
the parallel that now wee were in, which was 79° 8′, a west
north-west course was directed, in respect of the variation,
to make good a true west way.

This course wee held till wee had runne about twentie
leagues, and then wee ranne twentie leagues more in a west
and by north course till one a clocke on Friday morning, at
which time it fell calme ; and wee heard the sea make a
great noyse, as if wee had beene neere land, but wee rather
iudged it to bee ice, as, indeed, it proued to bee ; for in the
morning, when it was light and cleere, wee saw the ice,
about a league from vs, which trended southerly. Hauing
now a gale at east north-east, wee steered away south and
south-east, but in the afternoone we were embayed with a
long banke of ice, which wee could not weather ; therefore
wee were faine to tacke about, and, the winde having come
more southerly then it was in the morning, wee stood off
from the ice north-east and north-east and by north, and
then to the southwards againe, making sundrie boardes to
get forth to wind-wards of the ice.

The third day, befoore noone, wee had sight againe of
ice to westwards of vs, and at noone were vnder the parallel
of 78° 27′, according to my obseruation. Then wee stood
away south, to keepe cleere of ice ; for wee had a great
homing sea, although but little winde, and therefore durst
not be to bold to edge too neere it, especially the winde
being easterly, as then it was.

We stood
to the west-
wards.

Wee met
with ice.

On the fourth day our men saw the ice againe from the mayne top-mast head, and therefore wee still maintayned a southerly course. The next day it began to be foggie, and continued close weather and hazie for three dayes, so *We left the ice and came for England.* that we had no more sight of the ice, neyther could we at this time receiue any further satisfaction concerning the same; therefroe [*sic*—therefore?] wee kept a southerly course, so neere as wee could, although wee had but little winde, and the same very variable, till the ninth day, but then wee had a good gale of winde at west north-west.

On the tenth, beeing Saturday, we were, by my reckoning, fiftie leagues distant from Low-foot, which bore from vs east south-east, halfe a point southerly. This day the wind shifted to the south-west, and at night came to the south with much raine, then came backe againe to the west *A storme beganne.* north-west, and began a great storme.

This night the master and others saw a light vpon the *A Corpo Santo. It is often seen at the end of stormes.* fore-bonnet, which the saylers call a Corpo Santo. It appeared like the flame of a candle, and (as sea-men obserue) it always presageth an ensuing storme; which to verifie, this foule weather continued the next day, and grew to be so vehement on Sunday night that the sea oftentimes ouer-raked our ship, and wee were faine to lye atry with our fore course onely, and our mayne top-mast also strucke, which last thing (as sea-men say) is seldome done at sea; then, about one a clocke, we were forced to take in our fore course, and to lye a-hull for fiue houres.

The fourth of October the shippe came to Wapping, with the whole number of men she carried forth (my selfe excepted, that was come before), being six and twentie, all in perfect health.

[AUTOGRAPH MAP OF BAFFIN'S FOURTH VOYAGE

mill ile

salisbury iland

nottyngam ile

diggs ile

cape wolstenholme

resolatyon ile

salisge iles

buttons ile

60

61

62

63

64

65

66

61

60

70

75

0

59

58

57

56

55

THE FOURTH RECORDED VOYAGE

OF

WILLIAM BAFFIN.

1615.

TO THE

RIGHT WORSHIPFVL AND TRVLYE HONORABLE *Sir* THOMAS SMITH:
knight. Sir DUDLY DIGGES: *kt. Mr.* JOHN WOLSTENHOLME:[1]
esquire. and the rest of the worthy ADUANCERS *and*
ADUENTURERS *for the* FINDINGE OF A PASSAGE
by the NORTH WEST.

THE AUNTIENTE (*Right Worshipfull*) had so much regard to
the worthies of those tymes, that any waye sought the good
and preferment of theare countrye and common wealth
wheare they lyued, That ingratytude was so far from them,
they honoured, yea with diuine honoure, those to whome
theire countrye was in any way obleeged. But wee which
liue in an age, whome the poets tearme an jron age, are so
far from honouringe our worthies with due prayse, that many
had rather seek occation of slander then otherwise, although
not agaynst theare persons, yet agaynst theare acctions.

You are the worthyes of our tyme, whose many fould ad-
uentures are such, but espetiall this of the north-west, which
are not discouraged with spendinge and loss of many hun-
dreth poundes, ney rather many thousand pounds; reapinge
no other profitt butt onlye bare reports, and those little
auaylable to the purpose. But I feare if I should take on
me to sett forth your due prayse, I should come so far short
of the marke I aymed at; that it weare better for me to

---

[1] See the Introduction for notices of Sir Thomas Smith, Sir Dudley
Digges, and Sir John Wolstenholme.

leaue it undoone, then badlye doone : knowinge that who so
seeketh to amend APELLES pictture had need be some good
artist, and who so seeketh to sett forth the worthie prayse
of our LONDON MARCHANTS, had need bee more than a good
rethoritian.   But what neede I spende tyme hearin, when
neuer dyinge fame hath, and will, enroule your names in
TYMES CHEEFEST CHRONICLE OF ETERNYTIE : where no ENUIOUS
MOMUS shall have power to rase out the smallest tythe thereof.

And seinge I haue beene imployed, and haue reaped
some profitt from your purses, I might be counted a uery
bad seruant if I gaue not in some accounte howe we spent
our tyme.   Such as it is, I present it to your worshipps
vewe : whearin I haue indeuoured to set doune our pro-
ceedinges in so short a methode as conueniently I coulde,
referringe our pertyculer courses, latytudes, longitudes,
windes, leagues we run, and variatyon of the compas, to
the breefe table or Jurnall in the beginninge of the booke,
wheare euery of these is sett in their seuerall collombes,
with the tytles at the heade.

And whereas in the collombe tytle TRUCOURSE, in many
places is sett a number betweene the letters, as on the last
day of *Aprill*, is N. 20 E, which is north 20 degrees eastward, or allmost north north east : the tru waye that the
shipp had room that 24 houers, the variatyon of the compas, and other accidentes alowed.   Also there is a collombe
wheare is sett downe the longitude, wheare we weare ech
day at noone (although not usual in Jarnales) that theareby
ech seuerall uariatyon of the compas, and any other acci-
dente may be the more redylie found without protractinge
all or parte of the voyage : in which variatyons I hope I
haue not much erred from the truth, comminge nearer then
some which haue beene imployed that way heretofore.

And because your worships may more redylie see and
perseue howe far we haue beene, I haue heare following
placed a small mapp, and it is to be noted that within the

ILE OF RESOLUTYON wee sawe no more land then that I haue colored with greene, besides ilands. And heare is traced out our ships waye, with the red prickle lyne, notynge euery place wheare we came on shore (to make tryall of the tyde) with a red crosse, and for the tyme of high water at those places they are on the next page.

Thus bouldly haue I presumed on your worships cle- mencie in two respectes, the one in consideration of your selues, beinge so well acquaynted with these matters (as hauinge payde so deare for them) would in respect (not of the writer) but of the accion, vouchsafe the readinge there- of; the other, that beinge in duty bounde to be at your worships pleasure, I knowe not howe to shewe my selfe more dutyfull affected, then by giuinge in an accounte how we haue spent, or mis-spent our tyme; beseechinge your wor- ships to accept them, not as my worke, but as my will and affection. And so with my daylie prayers to GOD for your health and prosperous successe in all your accions, I rest,

YOUR WORSHIPS, most dutyfullie to be commanded
to his best endeuoures, WILLIAM BAFFIN.

The LONGITUDE *and* LATITUDE *of* SUCH PLACES *wheare we haue beene on shore within* RESOLUTION ILAND *& what Moone doth make a full sea, or the* TYME OF HIGH WATER *on the* CHAINGE DAYE. *And allso there distance from* RESOLUTION ILAND.

	[1]*	[2]*	[3]*	[4]*	[5]*
Resolution Iland . . .	66 . 26	61 . 30	E.S.E.	7½	legues.
Saluage iland . . .	72 . 00	62 . 30	S.E. 4 E.	8¾	58
nine legues ½ beyond . .	73 . 00	62 . 40	S.E.	9	67½
Broken ilands . . .	74 . 30	63 . 46	S.E.by S	9¾	87
North Shore . . .	80 . 30	64 . 40	S.S.E.	10½	142
6 leagues short of Cape Comfort	85 . 20	64 . 45	S. 5 E.	11¾	180
At Cape Comfort . .	85 . 22	65 . 00	S. 5 E.	11¾	186
Sea Horse Poynt . .	82 . 30	63 . 44	S. by E.	11¼	154
Sir Dudly Diggs iland .	79 . 40	62 . 45	S.S.E.	10½	123
Nottyngam iland . .	80 . 50	63 . 32	S.S.E.	10½	13†

* BLANK IN THE ORIGINAL. ? 1, *Long.:* 2, *Lat.:* 3, *Bearing:* 4, *Time:* 5, *Distance.*   † This corner of the page is torn.

II. THE BREEFE IOURNALL.

Dayes.	THE Tru course.	Leagues.	windes by the compas.	Latytude.	Longitude from London.	Variatyon.	
APRIL							
7	...	...	...	...	...	... E.	This morne wee sett sayle from Silly.
8	...	...	...	...	...	7 . 00	We came to anchor this eveninge att Padstowe.
18	...	...	S.E.	50 . 30	7 . 00	...	This morning wee sett sayle from Padstowe.
19	...	...	S.E.	50 . 30	7 . 00	...	
20	...	41	E.S.E.	50 . 38	10 . 15	...	
21	W.¼ N.	37	E.S.E. : S.S.E.	51 . 12	13 . 00	6 . 50	
22	W. by N ¾ N.	45	E.S.E. : E.N.E.	52 . 44	15 . 20	...	
23	N.W.¼ N.	50	E.N.E.	54 . 05	19 . 20	...	
24	N.W. by W.	44	E.N.E.	54 . 50	22 . 40	5 . 30	
25	W.N.W.¾ N.	24	N.N.E.	55 . 25	24 . 35	1 . 16	
26	W.N.W.½ N.	36	E.N.E.	56 . 28	27 . 24	...	
27	N.W. by W.	13	E.N.E. : N.W.	57 . 00	28 . 00	...	
28	N.W. by N.	10	N.W. : E.N.E.	57 . 28	28 . 15	...	
29	N.W. by W.¾ W.	24	E.N.E. : W.	58 . 30	29 . 25	...	
30	N. 20 E.	10	variable but W. ward.	59 . 00	29 . 00	...	
MAYE							
1	N. ⅓ by w.	17½	W N.W.	59 . 50	29 . 26	1 . 30 w.	
2	W N.,W.¼ w.	24⅔	W N.W. : S.E.	60 . 24	31 . 40	...	
3	W., by N.	35	S.E. : S.W.	60 . 43	35 . 15	...	
4	w. 3 s.	25½	S.S.E.	60 . 40	38 . 00	...	This afternoone a storme att south-east.
5	W. 26 s.	25½	S S.E.	60 . 04	40 . 24	9 . 24	We suppose a currante sett to the south-west.
6	W. 12 s.	28	S.S.E. : S.E. : N.E.	59 . 45	43 . 00	10 . 30	This forenoone wee sawe land.
7	S.-w. by s.	21	N.N.W. : N. : W.	58 . 56	44 . 15	...	This night a storme.

							Remarks
8	w. 13 s.	13	w. by n.	58 . 46	45 . 20	11 . 30 w	Cape Farewell bore north 15 leg. east at noone.
9	w. 25 s.	7	n. by w.	58 . 32	46 . 00	12 . 00	
10	w. 15 n.	15	n.n.e.	58 . 40	47 . 30	...	
11	w. 20 n.	38	e.s.e. : s.e.	59 . 16	51 . 00	...	
12	w. 20 n.	39	s.s.e : s. by e.	59 . 48	54 . 40	...	
13	w. 18 n.	45	s. : s. by e.	60 . 30	58 . 50	...	
14	n.w.	9	n.w. : n. by e.	60 . 50	59 . 30	...	
15	w.n.w.	15	n.n.e.	60 . 55	61 . 00	19 . 26	
16	w.n.w.	4½	e.	60 . 58	61 . 15	20 . 18	
17	w.n.w.	25	e.n.e.	61 . 27	63 . 40	...	At noone we put into the ice.
18	...	...	s.s.e.	...	...	...	
19	...	...	s.s.e.	...	...	...	
20	...	...	s. by e.	...	...	...	
21	...	...	w.s.w.	...	...	...	
22	...	...	w.n.w.	61 . 20	64 . 33	22 . 36	This eveninge at 8 a clock we weare forth of the ice.
23	n.e. by n.	13	w.n.w.	61 . 18	64 . 26	...	
24	n.e. by n.	12½	n.n.w.	61 . 50	63 . 30	21 . 00	
25	w.	21	n. by w.	62 . 20	62 . 40	...	
26	...	...	n.e. : e.	62 . 21	64 . 40	23 . 40	
27	...	...	e. : e.n.e.	62 . 12	65 . 20	...	At 5 a clock this afternoone, we saw the iland of Resolution.
28	...	...	w. by n.	61 . 40	66 . 30	24 . 6	
29	...	...	w. by n.	...	...	...	
30	...	...	s.s.e.	...	...	...	
31	...	...	n.n.w.	61 . 18	66 . 50	24 . 8	This morne we weare sett within the entraunce of the Strayts.
IVNE							
1	...	...	w.n.w.	61 . 20	66 . 50	...	Wee came to anchor on the west side of Resolution ile.
2	...	...	e. : n.n.w.	...	...	...	Att noone we sett sayle.
3	...	...	n.w.	61 . 35	67 . 56	...	
4	w. 4 n.	10½	w.s.w.	61 . 38	68 . 04	...	
5	n.w. 6 w.	17	s.s.e. : w.s.w.	62 . 10	69 . 34	...	
6	w.n.w. 4 n.	19	w.s.w.	62 . 32	71 . 30	26 . 26	
7	s.w. by s.	4	w.n.w. : n.w.	62 . 21	71 . 40	27 . 10	

Dayes.	THE Tru course.	Leagues.	windes by the compas.	La ty. tude.	Longitude from London.	Vari aty on.	
8	N. 40 w.	5	N.W.	62 . 27	72 . 00	27 . 20	We came to anchor at Saluage iles, at 8 a clock this night.
9	N.W.	1½	N.N.W.	62 . 30	72 . 06	...	This morne we set saile, and in the afternoone came to
10	W.N.W.	9½	E. : N.W.	62 . 40	73 . 04	...	anchor agayne 9 leagues w.n.w. of
11	...	...	N.W.	62 . 40	73 . 04	...	This eueninge we sett sayle.
12	...	...	W.W.	62 . 40	73 . 04	...	
13	W.N.W.	9	variable.	62 . 48	74 . 00	...	
14	...	...	N. : N.N.W.	...	...	...	
15	...	...	S.S.E.	...	...	...	This eueninge we anchored among diuers iles.
16	...	...	S.S.E. ; W.N.W.	63 . 22	74 . 05	27 . 45	
17	...	...	N.W. by W.	63 . 26	74 . 45	...	At eleven a clock we sett sayle.
18	...	...	variable.	63 . 26	74 . 45	...	We made fast to a piece of ice wheare we stayed 8 dayes.
19	W.N.W.	12½	S.E.	63 . 40	76 . 14	28 . 30	This daye I obserued the moones comminge to the meridian and found the longitude 74° 5′ west from London, and 91° 35′ from Wittenberg.
22	...	...	...	...	...	...	
24	...	...	N.N.W.	63 . 28	76 . 18	...	
25	...	...	N.W. by N.	63 . 28	76 . 20	...	
26	...	...	N.W. by N.	63 . 18	...	...	This eueninge we set sayle ; hauinge had calme whether since the 19 daye.
27	...	...	S.E.	63 . 30	76 . 32	...	
28	...	...	S.E.	63 . 30	77 . 32	...	Att noone we sawe Salisburie island.
29	W.N.W.	13	S.E.	63 . 42	78 . 30	...	
30	W. 3 s.	5	variable.	63 . 40	...	28 . 34	
IVLY 1	w.	11½	S.S.E.	63 . 40	79 . 45	...	
2	N. 31 w.	6½	N.N.W.	63 . 55	80 . 10	28 . 10	
3	W. 24 N.	10	W.S.W.	64 . 05	81 . 13	28 . 28	
4	N.W.	28	S.W.	64 . 54	82 . 45	...	
5	N.W. by N.	5	N. : N.N.W.	65 . 00	83 . 00	...	This morne we weare by a smale iland, we called it Mill ile. At night our ship was in great distress with ice.
6	N.E.	5	N.N.E.	65 . 10	82 . 40	... w.	

										Remarks
7	S.E. by E.	11	N.W.	64 . 48	81 . 28	28 . 20	This eueninge we anchored near the north shore.
8	S.	3½	W.	64 . 46	81 . 28	:	
9	S.E.	3	W. : N.W.	64 . 36	80 . 40	:	
10	S.W.	5	S.W.	64 . 24	81 . 04	:	
11	W. 6 N.	18	W.S.W. : N.N.W.	64 . 30	83 . 08	:	We sent our bote ashore 6 leagues south of Cape Comfort : att 6 a clock this eueninge we returned.
12	W. 3 N.	12	W. : W.S.W.	64 . 33	84 . 48	:	
13	N. 36 w.	17½	S.W.	65 . 18	85 . 56	:	
[14]	:	:	S.E.	65 . 18	85 . 56	:	We anchored neare Cape Comfort. At night wayed anchor.
[15]	:	:	S.E.	65 . 02	85 . 22	:	We came to anchor at Sea Horse Point this eueninge.
[16]	:	:	Variable.	63 . 54	82 . 50	:	This morne we wayed anchor and stood for Nottinghams ile, wheare this night we anchored.
17	W.S.W.	6½	N.W. by W.	63 . 38	82 . 00	:	
18	W.S.W.	8½	N. : N. by E.	63 . 36	81 . 00	:	
19	:	:	N.W.	:	:	:	
20	:	:	S.W. by S.	:	:	:	
21	:	:	W.N.W.	:	:	:	
22	:	:	N.N.W.	:	:	:	
23	:	:	N.N.W.	:	:	:	
24	:	:	Southward.	:	:	:	
25	:	:	W.S.W. : W. by S.	:	:	:	
26	:	:	N.N.W.N.:N.N.E.	63 . 30	80 . 00	:	We passed betweene Nottinghame and Salisburies ile. At night we came to anchor.
27	E.N.E.	2	E. : E.N.E. : N.E.	:	:	:	This day stood ouer for Sea Horse Point agayne.
28	E.N.E.	13	N.E.	:	:	:	This morne we returned for Digges ile.
29	:	:	N.E.	62 . 44	80 . 05	:	We came to anchor at Digges ile, foule wether.
30	E. 8 N.	:	N.E. by N.	62 . 44	80 . 05	:	We wayed and sett sayle for homewards.
31	...	18	S.	62 . 56	75 . 45	:	
Avg.							
1	E. by S.	15	S.S.W. : S.W.	62 . 46	76 . 5	:	This afternoone we came to anchor on the north shore among diuers ilands, 30 leagues within Resolution ile.
2	E. 19 S.	38	S.W. : N.W. by W.	62 . 16	72 . 6	:	
3	E. 17 S.	19	N.W. : S.E.	62 . 20	70 . 15	:	This day we sett sayle.
4	...	:	...	:	:	:	

Dayes.	THE Tru course.	Leagues.	windes by the compas.	Latytude.	Longitude from London.	Vari aty on.	
				° ′	° ′	° ′	
5	E. 32 S.	45	N.W.	61 . 00	65 . 30	⋯ . 30	We past by the ile of Resolution, but sawe it nott.
6	E. 20 S.	46	N.W.	60 . 20	61 . 00	19 . 30	
7	E. 18 S.	43	N.W.	59 . 36	57 . 00	⋯	
8	E. 13 S.	29	N.W. : s. by w.	59 . 14	54 . 14	⋯	
9	E.	26	s.s.w. : s.	59 . 15	51 . 40	⋯	
10	E. 7 S.	32	N.N.W.	59 . 4	48 . 52	⋯	
11	E. 34 S.	46	N.W.	57 . 32	45 . 40	⋯	We came through som smale ice, of Cape Farewell, but saw no land.
12	E. 7 S.	40	w.s.w.	57 . 18	42 . 00	⋯	
13	E. 8 S.	38	w.s.w. s. by E.	57 . 6	38 . 25	⋯	
14	E. 40 N.	20	S.E. by E.	57 . 42	36 . 56	⋯	
15	N. 22 E.	11	E. by s.	58 . 15	36 . 35	⋯	
16	S.S.E.	7	E.	58 . 5	36 . 15	⋯	
17	E.N.E.	8	s.E.	58 . 20	35 . 35	⋯	
18	N. 30 E.	22	s.E.	59 . 20	34 . 30	⋯	
19	S. 25 E.	9	E.S.E. : E.	58 . 52	34 . 8	⋯	
20	S. 40 E.	14	N.N.E.	58 . 18	33 . 15	⋯	
21	S. 20 E.	20	E. : E.S.E.	57 . 22	32 . 30	⋯	
22	S.	4	E.	57 . 8	32 . 30	⋯	
23	S.S.E.	14	N.E.	56 . 30	32 . 6	⋯	
24	E. 25 S.	21	N.N.E.	56 . 5	30 . 20	⋯	
25	E. 30 S.	36	N. by E.	55 . 10	27 . 35	2 . 00	
26	E. 35 S.	38	N.N.E.	54 . 00	24 . 52	⋯	
27	S. 29 E.	39	N.E.	52 . 40	23 . 42	⋯	
28	S. 30 E.	18	N.E. by E.	52 . 18	23 . 5	⋯	
29	S. 30 W.	10	E.N.E.	51 . 25	23 . 30	⋯	A sore storme.
30	N. 30 E.	3	E.S.E.	51 . 32	23 . 25	⋯	
31	S.E.	20	N.E.	50 . 46	22 . 15	⋯	

[*Note.* Here the journal ends, at the bottom of a reverse page. Whether left incomplete, or whether the concluding portion be lost, must be left to conjecture.]

A TRU RELATYON OF SUCH THINGES AS HAPPENED IN
fourth voyage for the discouery of a passage to the
north west, performed in the yeare
1615.

After so many sundrye voyages to the north westward, to
the greate charge of the aduenturers, The last being under
the command of *Captaine* GIBBINS, in which by som sinister
accident, was little or nothinge performed.   Yett the right
worshipfull, *Sir* THO. SMITH, *knight;* SIR DUDLY DIGGES,
knight; Mr. JOHN WOSTENHOLME, *esquire; Mr.* ALDERMAN
JONES, with others, beinge not theare with discouraged,
this yeare 1615 sett forth agayne the good shipp called the
DISCOUERARE, beinge of the burthen of 55 tonn or theare
aboute, (which ship had beene the three former voyages on
the accion).

MARCH.

The cheefe mr. and commander, vnder GOD, *was* ROBERT
BYLETH, *a man well experienced that wayes, (hauinge
beene imployed the three former voyages) my selfe beinge
his mate and assotiate, with fourteene other men and 2
boyes.   This ship being in redines, vpon the* 15th *daye*
15 *of March came abourd Mr.* JOHN WOSTENHOLME, esquire,
one of the cheefe aduenturers, and with him Mr. ALLWIN
CARYE *(husband for the voyage).   Who hauinge deliuered
our mr. his commission, and reade certayne orders to be
obserued by vs in the voyage, giuing vs good exortations,
and large promyses of reward, as treble wages to all, if
the accion weare performed, they departed, charginge vs
to make what speede we could away.   So the next day,*
16 *beeing thursdaye, we wayed anchor at* ST. KATHERINS,
17 *and that tyde came to* BLACK WALL, *and the next day to*
18 GRAUES ENDE; *and the morrow after to* LEE.

19 *Sondaye the* 19 *it blu hard at south west and by south,*
    yet this daye we came to anchor neare the BOOY *on the*
    NOURE ENDE. *The* 20 *daye the winde variable, but by* 2
    a clock this afternoone we came to the NORTH FORLAND,
22 *wheare we stayed all the* 22 *daye, which day we wayed and*
23 *that night anchored in the* DOUNES. *The* 23 *in the morne*
    we wayed anchor, the winde att east, and east and by south :
26 *thus with indifferent windes and wether we came to anchor*
    in SILLY *the* 26 *daye.*

APRILL.

7   *Heare we stayed for a fayre winde till the* 7 *day of Aprill,*
    being Good Frydaye, which day we wayed anchor in the
    morne, the winde south south east.   We had not stoode on
    our course aboue 10 *or* 12 *leagues, but the wind came to*
    south, then to south south west and blu extreme hard, which
    encreased so sore, that we weare not able to beare any sayle
    at all.
8   *The next morning we stood for* PADSTOW *in* CORNEWALL,
    because we could not fetch Silly agayne, and about 10 *a*
    clocke we came to anchor in the entrance of the harbour,
9   *and the next daye, being Easter Sonday, in the forenoone*
    we moored our ship in the harboure.   Heare we stayed till
    the 19 *daye, hauinge had much foule wether and contrary*
    windes.   While heare we stayed we found much kindness at
    the handes of Mr. RICHARD PENKEWILL, *who, beinge will-*
    inge to further vs with what things we wanted, or that
    place could afford, as with beefe and porke, and also with
    a capstand which we wanted, haueing broke ours in the
    storme when we came from Silly.   And also he was de-
    sirous his eldest sonn should goe alonge with vs, to which
    our mr. and the rest of the company agreed, because he
19 *layd in all prouition fitt for the voyage.   So the* 19 *of*
    Aprill in the morne we wayed anchor, the winde south east
    a good gale, we keepinge our courses as in the breefe Jarnall

you may more conueniently see. And seinge fewe thinges of note happened in our outward bound voyage, I refer all other thinges to that table before noted.[1]

MAYE.

6 We haueing had an indifferent good passage, vpon the 6 of Maye we sawe land on the coste of GROYNLAND on the east side of CAPE FAREWELL; and that night we had a storme. So keeping a southwardly course to gett about the ice which lay on that coste, we kept on our course tyll the 17 daye of Maye: all which forenoone we sayled through many greate ilands of ice. Som of them were 200 foot aboue water, as I proued by on shortly after, which I found to be 240 foote high aboue water. And if reporte of some men be tru which affirme that there is but on seuenth part of it aboue water, then the height of that peece of ice I obserued was 140 [? 280] fathoms, or 1680 foote, from the top to the bottome. This proportion doth hould I knowe in much ice, but whether in all, or no, I know nott.

17 This 17 of May aboute noone, wee weare come to the firme ice as it shewed to sight, *although in deede it was many peeces drauen together:* wheare our mr. asked my opinion conserninge the puttinge into the ice. My judgment was it would be best for vs to stand somwhat more north ward, to se if we could find any more likley place, for heare we could not disserne wheare to put in the ships head. Hee answered we weare as for [far] to the north ward as the south end of RESOLUTION ILAND, and now had all the south channell southward of vs; and through much ice we must goe. Supposinge that, if

[1] The British Museum manuscript was very carefully collated with the narrative in Purchas, by Mr. Randall, and the foot-notes pointing out the differences are by him. The italic print denotes the matter *omitted* by Purchas. *Material alterations* or *additions*, in the version given by Purchas, are noticed in the foot-notes.

I

we could gett som 3 or 4 leagues within the ice, at euery
tyde it would open and we should gett somthinge on our
waye, it being now fayre wether, and if it should chance
to blo hard, we should then be forced to enter in. *I
could not much say agaynst his opynion, beinge indeede
in the latitude of* 61 *deg.* 26', *and hee knew the manner
of this ice better then my selfe, so presently we resolved to
put into the ice. (This first entrance I liked not uery well,
the ice being so uery thick, and by all our accounte and
reconinge we were* 30 *leagues from shore, which after we
found to be tru).*

After we weare entred a little into the ice, it was not
longe before we weare fast sett vp, but sometymes of
the tyde the ice would a little open, then we made our
way as much to the north-west as we could, yet we
playnlie found that we weare sett to the southward,
although the wind weare southwardly.

22 Nowe vpon the 22 daye the wind came to north north-
west, then we determined to gett forth agayne, fearinge
the wind should com to the north-east, for then it would
be hard for vs to fetch any part of the Straytes mouth :
seinge this aboundance of ice and knowing that it must
haue some time to dissolue, our mr. was determyned
to run up DAUIS STRAYTES and to spend some 20 dayes
therein, to trye what hopes that wayes would afford,
supposinge by that tyme we myght come near RESOLU-
TION ILE. This purpose of our mr. contynued no longer
but tyll we weare forth of the ice, which by God's assist-
23 ance was the 23d daye about 8 a clock att night, the
wind at N.W. and by W. When we weare cleare of
the ice, we stood to the northwarde, as much as the ice
and winde would suffer vs, running about 13 leg. north
east and by north ; by the next day at noone, beinge in
the latytude of 61° 50' and fayre weather.

25 The 25 daye we made our waye and course weare as

we did the daye before, namely N.E. and by N., 13 legues.[1]

26 The 26 daye all the forenoone fayre wether and could, but in the afternoone it blew uery hard, and close haysey wether, that about 2 a clock we weare forced to take in our sayles. All the tyme that we sayled this daye we passed through much ice, lyinge in longe driftes and ledges, hauing made a west way about [?] leagues.[2]

27 The 27 daye aboute 4 in the morninge we sett sayle. Most parte of the day proued close and foggy, with much snowe, freesinge on our shroudes and tackle, that the like we haue not had this yeare; but toward 5 a clock in the afternoone it cleared vp and we sawe the ILAND OF RESOLUTION, it bearinge west from vs about 13 or 14 leagues, and at night moored our ship to a peece of ice.[3]

28 The 28 daye, beinge Whitsondaye, it was fayre wether, but the winde at west and west by north, that we weare forced all this daye to make our shipp fast to a peece of ice, yet we playnlie perceued that we sett more into the straytes with one tyde of floud, then we sett forth in 2 ebbs, although the wind blu contrary.

29 The 29 the winde variable and fayre wether. About eleuen a clock we sett sayle and tacked too and fro

30 along the iland. And the next morne, about two a clocke, the winde came to the south south-east, but we hauinge so much ice we could doe but little good nowe we had a faire wind.[4] This night (or rather eueninge, because it was not darke), we were sett *within the*

---

[1] [About twelve leagues and an halfe, our latitude at noone 62 degrees 20 minutes. At sixe a clocke the winde was north north east. P.]

[2] [Havinge runne about twenty one leagues true vppon a west course. And note when I put this word true, I meane the true course, the variation of the compasse and other accidents considered. P.]

[3] [The winde being at west. P.]

[4] [The wind continued all this day and night a stiffe gale. P.]

poynt of the iland, so that nowe we weare within the
straytes, playnly prouinge what is sayd before, namely,
that one tyde of floud setteth more in then two tydes of
ebb will sett forth.

31 The last daye of Maye also faire weather, the wind for
the most part north north-west. The afternoone being
cleare, we saw the point of the South shoare[1] bearing
from vs south by the compas, which is indeed south
south-east, somewhat eastward, because here the compas
is varied to the west 24 degrees.

IVNE.

1 The first day of June some snowe in the forenoone, but
afterward it proued very faire, the wind west north-west;
and perceiuing the ice to be more open neare to the
shore we made the best waye we could to get in, and to
com to anchor if the place weare conueniente; seeinge
the wind was contrary and also to make tryall of the
tyde.   And by seuen a clock we weare at anchor in a
good harbour, on the west side of RESOLUTION ILAND,
wheare an east south-east moone maketh a full sea, or
halfe an houer past seuen on the chainge day, as seamen
acounte.   At this place the water doth rise and fall
about 22 or 23 foote; the compas doth vary 24...6'
west, and it is in longitude west from LONDON 66 degrees 35'.   The latytude of the north ende of the iland
is 61...36', *and the latytude of the south end is* 61...26'.
The bredth of the south channell, or the distance betweene the iland and the south shore is 16 leagues, and
the bredth of the north channell is aboute 8 miles in
the narrowest place.

Vpon this iland we went on shore, but found no certaine
signe of inhabitants, but only the tracke of beares and

---

[1] [Called *Button's Iles*. P.]

foxes. The soyle is only rocks and stonie ground, hardly any thinge growinge thearon which is greene. It is indifferent high land to the north, hauinge one high hill or hummocke to the north east side, but toward the southward it falleth away uery low.

2 The 2 June in the forenoone the wind came to east south east with snowe and foule wether. About noone we wayed and stood vp along by the iland¹ to the north ward. This afternoone it proued foule wether, but toward eueninge it cleared vp and we saw the north shore. But heare to wright of our often mooringe to ice, takinge in sayles, and fast inclosinge, would prooue but tedious to the reader, as it was troublesom to vs; so therefore I referre it: but our course, and waye we made from noone may be seene else wheare.

We continuing our courses so neare to the north shore as conueniently we could, with much variable wether and 8 windes, but stedfast in contynuance among ice, till the 8 daye. Then hauinge the winde contrary to vs, being somewhat neare a poynt of land (or rather a company of ilandes),² we determyned to come to anchor³ among them *if possible we could. About 6 a clock we weare come to anchor,* and as we weare busy *in makinge vp our sayles and fittinge our ship,* we hard a great houlinge and noyse, as we supposed of doggs vpon the ilande neare to vs.

So soon as the ship was moored, we sent our bote somewhat nearer the shore, to see if they could perceue any people, who returninge, they tould vs they sawe tentes and botes, with a number of doggs, but people they sawe none.

¹ [So well as the ice would giue vs leaue to gett. P.]
² [Which after we called *Savag Isles*, hauing a great sound, or indraught betweene the north shoare and them. P.
³ [Neere one of them, being the eastermost saving one. P.]

Then by and bye we went to prayer, and after our men had supt, we fitted our bote and selues with things conuenient; then my selfe and seuen other landed, and went to the tents, wheare findinge no people, we went to the top of the hill (being about a flite shot of) wheare we sawe one great cannoo, or bote, hauinge aboute four-teene personns in it; they being on the furthest, or north-west side theareof, beinge from vs somewhat aboue a musket shott of. Then I called vnto them (using some words of *Groynlandish* speeche), makinge signes of friendship. They did the like to vs; but seeing them *to be* fearefull of vs, and we not willinge to trust them, I made another signe to them, shewinge them a knife and other small thinges, which I left on the top of the hill, and returned doune to their tents agayne.

Beinge returned to theare tents, we found some whale finnes to the number of 14 or 15,[1] which I tooke aboard, leauinge kniues, bedes, and counters insteede thereof. And among other of theare househould, I found in a smale lether bagg a company of little images of men; and one the image of a woman with a child at hir backe: all the which I brought awaye.

Among there tents (being fiue in number) all couered with seale skinnes, weare runninge up and done, about 35 or 40 dogs, most of them mussled. They are most of them about the bigness of our mungrell mastives, being a brinded black culler, lookinge almost like wolues. These doggs they vse instede of horses, or rather as the *Lappians* doe theare deare, to draw theare sledes from place to place ouer the ice. Theare sleds beinge shod, or lined, with bones of great fishes to keepe them [from] wearinge, and the doggs have collers and furni-ture uery fittinge.

These people haue their apparell, botes,[2] tentes, with

---

[1] [Fortie or fiftie with a few scale-skinnes. P.]
[2] [Boots. P.]

other necesaryes, muche like to the inhabitaunte of
Groyneland, sauing that they are not so neate and arte-
fitiall, seminge to bee more rude and vnciuill, raynginge
vp and doune as theare fishinge is in season. For in
most places wheare we went ashore, we sawe wheare
people had beene, although not this yeare, but wheare
theare dwellinge or abode in winter is, I cannot well
9 coniecture. The next morninge we fetcht 2 botes
ladinge of stones aboard, because our ship was very
light, keepinge a good watch on shore, for feare the
people should come doune vpon vs while we weare busie.
By noone our ship was fitted. Then afterward we
marched aboute the island, but could see no people.

This iland lyeth in the latytude of 62...30', and in
longitude west from *London* aboute 72 degrees,[1] being
60 leagues within the entrance of the straytes. Here
the compas doth varye 27.30', and a south-east 4 degrees
east moone maketh a full sea. It doth ebb and flowe
almost as much water as it doth at RESOLUTION ILE ; and
heare the floud commeth from the eastward, although
our Master was confidente to the contrary.

10 The 10 daye,[2] in the morninge, we set sayle, the winde
north, which contynued not longe, but was very variable
tyll noone, and then it came to north-west, we hauinge
sayled along by the shore, about $9\frac{1}{2}$ leagues north north-
west, the ice lyinge so thicke in the offen that we could
not gett of. Then perceuinge a good harbour betweene
the mayne and 2 smale ilandes, we went in with the
ship, wheare we moored her, and stayed till the 12 day
at night.

---

[1] By the observations made on board the *Fury* and *Hecla* (July 24,
1821), this anchorage was made $2\frac{1}{2}$ miles to the northward, and 1° 52' to
the eastward of the position assigned to it by Baffin. Variation 52° 37'.
—*Voyage of the Fury and Hecla* (*Parry*), 1821, etc. P. 16. (*Chart.*)
London : 1824. 		[2] [At sixe a clocke. P.]

In this place it is high water on the chaunge day, at
9 a clock, or a south-east moone maketh a full sea.[1]
Here the floud commeth from the south-east, as it did
at SALVAGE ILAND,[2] *and because our Mr. was conceued*
otherwise, I tooke our surgeon (a man of good iudgment)
to the top of the ile, where most apparently we saw the
tru sett of the tyde by the ice dryvinge in the offen. For
all the tyme the water doth rise by the shore, the ice did
sett in to the straytes ; aad as soon as the water fell it
returned. But the truth of this was made more apparent
by other places after ward.[3]

12 The 12 day after we had doone som busines in our ship,
as cleared our pumps and such lyke, seinge the ice to
driue in more then vsuall it did before, about 8 a clock
we set sayle, it being almost calme. Shortly after the
winde came to south west and by south, which contynued but till 12 a clock; then it came to west with
snowe and foule wether.

13 The 13 aboute noone we tooke in our sayles, and made
the ship fast to a peece of ice, beinge some 9 leagues
14 from our last harbour. All this daye and the next the
wind was contrarye, and foule wether, we driuinge too
and fro with the wind and tide.

15 The 15 in the morne, the wind came to the south south
east; then we set sayle, and made the best waye we
could through the ice, and in the afternoone it blu uery
much winde, and was foule wether, so that at 8 a clocke
we weare forced to take in our sayles and to make the
ship fast to ice agayne, it beinge a storme and amounge
much ice.

16 The 16 day, lying still in the ice, the wether close and
hasye (as it hath beene these six dayes) we being neare

---

[1] [The latitude of the place is 62° 40'. P.]
[2] [Although our master was perswaded otherwise. P.]
[3] [In this place is no sign of people, as we could perceive. P.]

a greate company of ilandes, and the wind at north north west, this afternoone wee stood towards these ilandes : and at night came to anchor neare one of them, in a small coue, the better to defend the ship from danger of
17 the ice. In this place we stayed all the next day : but
18 vpon the 18 being Sonday, at eleuen a clocke we set sayle, it beinge allmost calme, we makinge the best way we could gett from a monge those ilands, being more safe further *of* then neare them : for these iles lye in a bay (as it weare), being many of them, and euery one hath his seuerall sett and eddy, carryinge the ice to and fro, that a ship is allwaye in danger of some hurte. The latytude of the place is 63...26′ ; and west from *London,* neare 74...[1] 25′ : the compas doth vary 27...40′ ;[2] and a south east and by south moone[3] maketh a full sea.
19 *This evening and the next forenoone we had a fine gale of wind at south east, we standinge alonge the lande, it being all broken ground and ilandes to the sea ward. By noone we weare come to the poynt of those ilandes, and being not past a league or 4 miles distant, we weare fast sett vp with ice, the wether very fayre and allmost calme. This poynt of ilands I after called Fair Ness,[4] by reason of the fayre wether we had at this place, for from this 19 daye till the 27 daye (yea till the 30) the wether was so faire, cleare and calme, that it was more then extraordinary in this place, and we so fast closed vp with ice, that many tymes one could not well dip a payle of water.*

[1] [72. P.] [2] [46. P.]
[3] [And a quarter of an houre after nine on the chainge day. P.]
[4] [This evening, and the next morning, we had a faire steering gale of winde at south east, wee standing along by the land, it being all small broken ilands, to a point of land about twelve leagues in distance from the ile wee put last from : which point I called BROKEN POINT, it being indeede a point of broken iles. On the nineteenth day, by twelue a clocke at noone, wee were about foure miles from the point before named, fast inclosed with ice, very faire weather ; and well might wee have called this point FAIRNESSE, or, POINT. P.]

And some dayes while heare we stayed we shott at butts
with bowe and arrows, at other tymes at stoole ball, and
some tymes at foote ball. And seinge I haue begun to
speake of exercise, I think it not amiss to relate one dayes
exercise of my owne.

While we weare thus fast inclosed with ice, and the
21 wether fayre and cleare (as is sayd before) vpon the 21
daye I sawe both the sonn and moone very cleare. Then
thinkinge it a fit tyme to be doinge of somthinge to
imploy myself vpon, I fitted my instruments to take
both the Almycanter and Azimuth of the sonn and also
of the moone : fearinge I should not see them so well
agayne. Which obseruations I think it not much unfitt
heare to sett doune (although I neuer wrought it, because I had another the next daye, better to my contentment, otherwise I would have spent some tyme in
this), as heare they followe :

		deg.				deg.
The	Sonns Almycanter ...	25 . 5		The	Moones Almycanter	32 . 5
	Sonns magne. Azimuth	29 . 00			Mones Azimuth ...	43 . 00
	w. of N.				s. of w.	

butt heare is to be noted that the moones Almycanter
and Azimuth weare taken 4 minites 30 seconds of tyme
after the sonns.[1]

[1] Baffin took every opportunity of taking astronomical observations,
and especially of testing theoretical methods of finding longitude. His
first recorded observation for longitude was taken in Cockin Sound, on
the coast of Greenland, and is explained by him in his journal (see page
20). The first part of this Greenland observation is that for finding the
time and place from the altitude of a heavenly body, the latitude and
declination being known. But the method of finding the longitude by
lunar culmination is unsuited to purposes of navigation, owing to the
great error in longitude caused by a small error in the time of the moon's
culmination.

The observation which Baffin describes in the text, at page 122, is a
complete lunar observation. I have been favoured with the following
interesting note upon it by Mr. John Coles, R.N., the Instructor in
Practical Astronomy and Surveying to the Royal Geographical Society.

"This, in a very rough way, is a complete lunar observation. Baffin

22 The next morne being fayre and cleare, and allmost as
stedy as on shore, it was no neede to bid me haue my
instrument of uariation in redynes to take the time of
[the] moone's comming to the meridian, hauinge my
quadrant redy to take the sonnes Almicanter, it being
indifferent large, as of 4 foote semydiameter. I hauinge[1]

appears to have chosen the method of measuring the distance by the
difference of Azimuth, because, in all probability, he did not possess an
instrument with which he could measure so large an angle as 104°, that
being the computed distance from the Azimuths given; this distance
would, however, be greatly in error unless the declinations of both
heavenly bodies were the same. The Almicanters here mentioned are
small circles, parallel to and, in this case, above the rational horizon;
they are therefore the observed altitudes. Thus we have the following
lunar observation:

Obs. Alt. of ☉	Angular Distance.	Obs. Alt. of the ☽
25° 5′.	104° 0′.	32° 5′.

which observation, cleared from the effects of parallax and refraction,
would give the true distance, and the longitude could be found by using
the right ascensions of the moon and sun, without the aid of such tables
as are now given (of lunar distances) in the *Nautical Almanac.*

"Speaking of this observation, Baffin says, 'I never wrought it'; and,
indeed, had he computed this observation, it is not possible that he could
have got any satisfactory results. This will be the more clear when we
consider that an error of 1′ in this very roughly observed distance would,
under the most favourable circumstances, produce an error of 25′ in the
longitude.

"Judging from this record, it seems quite certain that Baffin was
acquainted with the theory of obtaining the longitude by observing the
altitudes of the moon and some other heavenly body, and measuring the
angular distance between them, this method of finding the longitude
having been proposed as early as 1514 by John Werner of Nuremberg,
and again, in 1545, by Gemma Frisius of Antwerp; but this observation
of Baffin's is, so far as I am aware, the first recorded attempt to put it
into actual practice at sea; and any one who will inspect Baffin's observations can scarcely fail to come to the conclusion that it is highly impro-
bable that a man, so far in advance of his time as a navigator, and so
intimately acquainted with the practical part of astronomy, would, in
his studies, have overlooked so important an observation, or that he
would have failed, when a favourable opportunity presented itself, to
make an attempt to put it into practice."   [1] [Haue. P.]

taken the uariation of my needle this forenoone and dyuers tymes before, which was 28...30′ W. Nowe hauinge all things in redynes (for I had tyme jnough) for it would be after foure in the afternoone before any thinge could be doone ; so hauing wayted till the moone was precisely on the meridian, and that instant tooke the height of the sonn,[1] which was 26° 40′. *The latytude of the place is* 63...40′, and the sonns declination for that tyme 23 degrees 6 minites. By which three things giuen I haue found the houre to be fiue a clocke 4′...52″ ...1‴...4⁗ or 76 degrees 13′...16″ of the equinoctiall afternoone. Nowe according to *Searle's Ephemeris*,[2] the moone came to the meridian at LONDON at 4 a clocke 54′...30″ : and after *Origanus*,[3] the moone came to the meridian at WITTENBERGE at 4 a clocke 52′.5″, the same day. Nowe hauinge this knowne, it is no hard matter to finde the longitude of the place sought for. For according to the moones ordinary meane motion, which is 12 degrees ech day, which is in tyme 48 minites : and [?] to this account, if the moone be on the meridian at 12 a clock this day, tomorrowe it will be 48 minites past 12.[4]

[1] [The sunnes Almicanter, at the instant when the moone was on the meridian, was 26°. P.]

[2] John Searle received his licence to practise chirurgery in 1607, and published, in 1609, *An Ephemeris from* 1609 *to* 1617, *whereunto is annexed three succinct Treatises of the use of an Ephemeris of the fixed Starres, and foure Sections of Astrologie* (4to., London). The book contains, among other tables, a correction of time in respect of difference of meridians ; a list of places, with latitude and longitude in time ; a table for converting degrees and minutes into time; eclipses; and a table of the inequality of days, and the equation or correction of them.

The copy of Searle's *Ephemeris* at the British Museum wants the title page ; that at the Bodleian Library is a perfect copy.

[3] David Origanus was the author of an *Ephemeris* for the years 1595 to 1650. His meridian was Wittenberg. (Frankfort, 1599, 4to.)

[4] This is the same method he adopted in Cockin Sound for finding the longitude (see page 20), namely, by lunar culmination. Mr. Coles ob-

Nowe I hauinge the time at this place found by obseruation, which was 5 a clocke 4′...52″...1‴...4⁗ (but
in this I neede not be so precise): and at LONDON
4 a clocke 54′...30″: which, substracted from the former,
leaueth 10′...22″...1‴...4‴; and the moone's motyon for
that 24 houers was 12¹...38 : which conuerted into tyme
is 50′...25″...20‴. This beinge knowne, the proportion
is as follows: If 50′...25″...20‴ giue 360, what shall 10′
...22″...1‴.. 4⁗ giue ? The fourth proportionall will
be 74 degrees 5′, which is the longitude of this place
west from LONDON : because the moone was later on the
meridian at this place by 10′...22″.

*And by the same forme of working by Origanus Ephe-
merides, the distance is* 91 *degrees* 35 *minites west from
the place Origanus Ephemerides is supputated for, but
for to decide which is the truer I leaue to others : but neyther
of them is much different from my supposed longitude
according to my iurnall which was* 74...30′.[2] And seeing

serves:—" It is most surprising that Baffin should have obtained even
such an approximation as he did, and his method of observing with two
plumb lines set in the meridian, is both original and ingenious."

[1] [22. P.]

[2] [And by the same working of *Origanus Ephemerides*, the distance is
91 degrees, 35 minutes west of west. But whether be the truer, I leaue to
others to iudge :—and in these workings may some errour be committed,
if it be not carefully looked vnto: as in the obseruation, and also in finding what time the moone commeth to the meridian at the place where
the ephemerides is supputated for, and perchance in the ephemerides
themselves : in all which the best iudicious may erre; yet if observations
of this kinde, or some other, were made at places far remote, as at the
Cape Bonasperanza, Bantam, Japan, Noua Albion, and *Magellan Strayts*,
I suppose wee should haue a truer Geography than wee haue. P.]

Alluding to Broken Point, Captain Parry remarks: " On the 29th we
were off a point of land having several islands near it, and exactly
answering the description of that called by Baffin, in the year 1615,
Broken Point, it being indeed a point of broken islands. This headland
is memorable on account of a lunar observation made off it by this able
and indefatigable navigator, giving the long. 74 05′ which is not a degree to the westward of the truth." Parry had only seen Purchas. But

I am entred to speake of celestiall obseruations, I will
note another which I made at sea the twenty six of
April, by the moones comminge in a right, or strayte
line with two[1] starres; the one was the *Lyons heart*, a
starre of the first magnitude; the other a starre in the
Lyons rumpe, being of the second bignes. *These 2 stars
makinge a right line with the outward* edge, or circumference of the moone, at the instante I tooke the height
of one of them, namely the *Lyons harte*, because I would
haue the houer of tyme:[2] but in this obseruation it is
good to attend for a fit tyme : as to haue the moone in
a right line with two starres not far distante and those
not to be much different in longitude, because then the
moone will soone alter the angle or position, and such a
tyme would also be taken when the moone is in or neare
the 90 degree of the eclipticke aboue the horizon, for
then there is no paralax[3] of longitude, but only of latytude : but who is so paynfull in these busines shall
soone see what is needefull, and what is not : but the
notes I tooke are as followeth :—

		°	′	″
Lyons heart ♋	Right assention	146[4] 28	30
	Declination	13	57	30
	Longitude	24	29	45
	Latytude	00	26	30
	Almycanter	33	40	00
Lyons rumpe ♍	Right assention	163	23	00
	Declination	12	38	00
	Longitude	5	53	45
	Latytude	14	20	00

Baffin's manuscript gives 74° 30′ for the longitude, which is still more
correct.—See *Voyage of the Fury and Hecla*, 1821-23. P. 21. London:
1824.   [1] [Fixed. P.]
  [2] [The circumference, or outward edge, of the moone, being in a right
or straight line with these two starres before named : at the instant I
tooke the altitude of the south ballance, which was 2° 38′, because I
would haue the time. P.]
  [3] [Paralell. P.]   [1] [46. P.]

		°	′	″
	Paralax	00	47	46
The Moone	Låtytude	03	20	00
	Almycanter	37	00	00

Latytude of the Place, 56° 43′ 00″. *After Tycho Brahe.*

These notes I haue set doune, that if any other be desirous to spend a little tyme therein they maye ; my selfe haue spent some therein, and more I would haue spent, if other busines had not letted. I haue not heare set downe the pertyculer worke, because I found it not altogither to my mynde. The working of this proposition I receued from Master *Rudston.*

But if it had pleased God that we had performed the accion we intended, I would not feare but to haue brought so good contentment to the aduenturars, concerning the tru scituation of notable places, that smale doubt should haue beene thereof : but seeing so smale hopes are in this place, I haue not set doune so many obseruations as otherwise I would.

We lying heare inclosed with ice, hauing fayre and
27 calme wether (as before is said) till the 27 day at eueninge ; which tyme we sett sayle, the winde at south
28 east an easie gale. All the 28 and 29 dayes, we made
29 the best waye we could[1] through the ice. At noone this day we sawe SALISBURY ILAND.[2]
30 *The last of June the wind variable ; but our daylie object was still ice. All this day we stood toward the foresaid iland.*

IVLY.

1 The first of *July* close, haysie, wether, with much raine, the winde at south south east. By noone this daye we weare some 3 leagues from SALISBURY ISLAND ; but

---

[1] [But the nine and twentieth day the ice was more open then it had been these ten dayes before, and at noone....... P.]
[2] [It bearing due west from vs. P.]

hauinge much ice by the shore stood alonge to the
northward ; and the next morninge we weare fayre by
another smale ile (or rather a many of small ilandes),
which we afterward called MILL ILAND by reason of the
greate extremetye and grindinge of the ice, as this night
we had proofe thereof. At noone beinge close by this
ile we took the latytude thereof, which is near to
64 . . 00', *but how it lyeth may be better seene in the
mapp then heare nominated with writinge.* Heare driuinge to and fro with the ice most parte of this daye till
7 or 8 a clocke, at which time the ice began somewhat
to open and separate. Then we set sayle and hauinge
not stood[1] past an houer : but the ice came driuinge
with the tyde of floud from the south east with such
swiftnesse, that it ouerwent our shippe, hauinge all our
sayles abroad and a good gale of winde, and forced her
out of the streame into the eddy of these iles.

The ilande or iles, lying in the middle of the channell, hauinge many sounds runninge through them, with
dyuers points and headlands, encountering the force of
the tyde, caused such a rebounde of water and ice,[2] *that
vnto them that saw it not is almost incredible. But our
ship being thus in the pertition, between the eddy which
runne on waye, and the streame which runne another,
endured so great extremytie, that vnless the Lord himselfe
had beene on our side we had shurely perished ; for sometymes the ship was hoysed aloft ; and at other tymes shee
hauinge, as it were, got the vpper hand, would force greate
mighty peeces of ice to sinke doune on the on side of hir,*

---

[1] [Along by the ile, on the east side thereof. P.]

[2] [(Which ran one way and the stream another) our ship hauing met
the ice with the first of the floud, which put her so neere the shoare, that
she was in the partition betweene the ice, which the eddy caused to
runne one way and the streame the other, where she endured great distresse ; but God, which is still stronger than either ice or streame,
preserued vs and our shippe from any harme at all. P.]

and rise on the other. But GOD, *which* is still stronger
then either *rocks*, ice, *eddly*, or streame, preserued vs
and our shippe from any harme at all. *And I trust will
still contynue his love to vs, that we may performe some
more acceptable seruis to his glory, and to the good of our
common welth.*

This continued till towards high water, which was
aboute one a clocke. Then with no smale trouble we
got into the channell and stood away to the *north ward.*[1]
When we had passt some distance from the ilande we had
the sea more cleare of ice then it was since we came into
3 these straights; and sayled all the next day through an
indifferent cleare sea, with the winde at south west : but
towards 8 a clocke at night, we weare come agayne into
much ice, it being thicker and bigger than any we came
amonge yet. This place[2] is distant from Mill ilande som
26 leagues, and the tru course north west and by west.[3]
4 The next morne we sounded, and had ground at 120
fathoms, soft osey ground. Then standinge more north-
5 erly, the fifth day in the forenoone we had ground at 80
fathoms, which day the winde came to the north, and we
settinge som thinge more southward, had ground at 110
fathoms. Thus seeing this great aboundance of ice in
this place, and notinge that the more we get to the
northward,[4] the more shoalder the water was, the ice
also beinge foule and durtye, as not bred far from shore,
our mr. determined to stand to the eastward, to be cer-
tainely informed of the tyde.
6 The sixth day in the forenoone (as we stood to the eastward) we broke in a planke and two tymbers in the ships

---

[1] [North-*west*-ward. P.]
[2] [Where we began to be inclosed againe. P.]
[3] [After wee were fast in the ice, we made but smale way, yet we perceiued a great tyde to set to and fro. P.]
[4] [North-*west*-ward. P.]

K

bow, which after we had mended we proceeded[1] forward.

7 The next forenoone, we saw the shore, it being but low land *(in respect of the other)* and *toward this side* the sea is *more* shoald *then at other places :* but excellent good channell ground, as smale stones and shels ;[2] and also heare is a very great tide both of ebb and floud. But no other floud then that which commeth from Resolution ilande ; for about 7 a clocke, we beinge neare the shore, hoysed forth our bote, then 5 other and myselfe wente on shore found it ebbinge water. We staied on shore about an houer and a halfe, in which time the water fell about $3\frac{1}{2}$ foote, *all the ice in the offen setting to the southward*. A south south east moone maketh a full sea, or halfe an houre past tenne[3] *on the chainge day.* Here we sawe no signe of people to be this yeare, but in yeares heretofore they have beene, as we might well see by dyuers things, as wheare their tents had stood, *and such like ;* perchance theare tyme of fishing was not yet come, theare being so great aboundance of ice.

8. 9. The 8 day the winde was at west, and the next almost calme, we *keepinge*[4] not far from the shore, our mr. determined to stand over for Nottyngam Iland, to make triall of the tyde theare ; but the winde being at south west we weare forced all this day to[5] *tack to and fro, whereby we had more proofe of the settynge of the tyde.* Towards the night the winde came to the north north west ; then we stood away to the westward (leauing the search of Nottyngam ile) hauing a great swellinge sea out of the west with the winde which had blowne : which put vs in some hope.

---

[1] [For to get to the east side, which we called the north shore, because it is the land stretching from *Resolution*, on the north side of the straits. P.]

[2] [Some twelue or fourteene leagues from shore but the further off more osey. P.]   [3] [As the seamen account. P.]

[4] [Reeking. P.]   [5] [Turne. P.]

11 The eleuenth day, in the forenoone, we sawe land west
from vs, but no ground at 130 fathoms: so standinge
alonge by the land which here lay about north-west and
12 by north. And by the next morne we weare thwart of
a bay, or *sound runninge into the land. In the bottom
thereof the ice was not yet broke vp.* Then standing ouer[1]
that bay towards a faire cape, or headland, in the afternoone it was almost calme, and we beinge almost a league
from shore hoysed forth our bote, and sent six of our
men to see howe the tyde was by the shore.[2] They went
from the ship at 5 a clocke and came aboord agayne at
8, who brought vs word that it was falling water, and
that it had ebbd while they weare on shore somewhat
about 2 foote. Also they affirmed that the floud came
from the northward in this place, the which we also
sawe by the ship driuinge to the northward, and it being
calme (the cause thereof I suppose to be the indraft of
the bay) but this put vs in great hope of a passage this
waye, wherefore our Mr. named the poynte of land that
was some 6 leagues to the northward of vs CAPE COMFORT.
It lyeth in the latytude of 65de. 00[3] and is 85de. 20[4]
west from LONDON, and heare we had 140 fathoms water
13 not a league from shore. There our sudden hopes weare
as soon quayld, for the next morninge hauinge dubbled
the cape, when we supposed (by the account of the tyde)
we should be sett to the northward, it beinge little or
no winde, we weare sett to the contrary, and that day
hauinge a good gale of winde we had not proceeded on
our course past 10 or 12 leagues, but we sawe the land
trendinge from the cape, round aboute by the west tyll
it bore north-east and by east, and very thick pestred

---

[1] [To the northwards. P.]   [2] [And from whence it came. P.]
[3] [26'. P.] According to *Parry*, lat. " 64° 54'". — *Voyage of the
Fury and Hecla*, 1821-23, p. 33. London : 1824.
[4] [86°. P.] According to *Parry*, long " 82° 57'". — *Ibid.*

with ice, and the further we proceeded the more ice and shoalder water, with smale showe of any tyde.[1] We seeing this, our mr. soone resolued theare could be no passadge in this place, and presently we bore vpp the healme and turned the ships head to the southward. *This was about 6 a clock. The land which we sawe beare north and north-east was about 9 or 10 leagues from vs, and shurely without any question this is the bottom of the baye, on the west side; but howe far it runneth more eastward is yet uncertayne.*

14 The 14, the winde was for the most parte at south east, so that we could make but small waye backe agayne;

15 and the next morninge very foule wether, we comming to anchor in a smale coue near Cape Comfort, on the north west side thereof. Heare we found (as on the

[1] [At sixe a clocke this afternoone we sounded and had ground in 130 fathoms, soft osey, hauing had at noone 150 fathoms. P.]

In this vicinity, at 7 P.M. on the 5th of August 1821 (lat. 65° 22′ 50″ N., long. 81° 24′ 00″ W., var. 55° 05′ 30″), Captain Parry found the tide set E. by S. at the rate of half a mile an hour; and by observation, he ascertained and confirmed the truth of Baffin's remark respecting "the small show of any tide".

The following day, the *Fury* and *Hecla* were two miles and a quarter (lat. 65° 28′ 15″ N.) to the northward of the locality in which Bylot and Baffin left off their search for the North-west passage. Parry says "the reasons which induced Baffin to relinquish the enterprise at this place were the increased quantity of ice, the water becoming less deep, and his seeing land bearing N.E. by E. from him: circumstances which led him to conclude that he was at the mouth of a large bay." "The same land," Captain Parry continues, "which we had now in sight, proved to be one of several islands, and I gave it the name of BAFFIN ISLAND, out of respect to the memory of that able and enterprising navigator". On the 15th of the same month, the expedition was within a league of a remarkable headland on Southampton Island, which was named by Captain Parry, CAPE BYLOT, as being "probably the westernmost land seen by that navigator".—*Voyage of the Fury and Hecla*, 1821, etc., pp. 31-33-37. London: 1824. Baffin Island and Cape Bylot, named by Parry, are on each side of the entrance to Frozen Strait; the latter on Southampton Island.

other side) a south ½ east moone maketh a full sea, *or halfe an houre past* 11 *on the chainge daye :* but howe the floud doth set we could not well see, it beinge so foule wether at sea, *and so fogge.* In the afternoone the wind came to north by west, then we wayed anchor, and stood along by the land to the southward, with a stiffe

16 gale of winde and very hasey. By the 16 at noone we met with a great quantitie of ice lying som 7 or 8 leagues within the point of the land. Among this ice we saw som store of MORSE, *som vppon the ice and other in the water, but all so fearefull that I thinke little good would be expected in hope of killinge them. They are so beaten with the* SALUAGES *they will not suffer nether ship nor bote to com neare them.* By eight a clocke we were com to this southern point, which I called SEA HORSE POINT, wheare we anchored open in the sea, the better to proue the sett of the tyde.

Heare we found, most apparently to all our companies sight, that in this place the tyde of floud doth come from the south east, and the ebb from the north west, *being the certaynest sett of tyde we haue yet made proofe of ; playnelie perceuing the sett of the ships ridinge at anchor, and also by the settinge of the ice. And for our better assurance, our mr. went himselfe on shore to make proofe thereof. The tyme of high water on the chainge daye is about eleuen a clocke, something past : keping a proportion of tyme in all places as we haue beene at since we came into the strayts, all concurringe of the floud to come from the south east, and no place else, sauinge* 6 *leagues short of Cape Comfort, but the cause thereof I suppose to be nothing but the indraft of the baye.*

17 *The next morning our mr. asked our opinion whether it weare better for vs to seeke out some harboure heareaboute to see if we could kill any of those* MORSE *we sawe, or presently to go for* NOTTYNGAMS ILANDE *to make proofe of the*

*tyde of floud theare, which was the place wheare formerly
was affirmed the floud to come from the north west.*

*My answear and most of the companies was, that see-
inge we are bound for discouery, it could not be our best
waye to spend any tyme in search for these morse, they
being so fearefull and beaten with the saluages. And yf
we should kill some fewe of them they would not be worth
the tyme we should spend. Seeinge we knewe not wheare
to harboure our ship, and when shee is in harboure, we
haue no other botè but our ships bote, which we dare not
send far from the ship. And those morse we sawe weare
in the sea, and what tyme or wheare they would com on
shore was vncertayne.*

These thinges considered I thought it better to go for
NOTTYNGAM ILANDE, *and so to prosecute our uoyage as
theare we shoulde find occation, and if theare our hope of
passadge was voyde, and the weather prooue fayre, we
might soon com back to this place agayne, it beinge nott
past 16 leagues distante.*

*When I had spoke, our mr. sayd he was also of that
minde, and so* we wayed *anchor presently* and stood ouer
with a stiffe gale of winde, which continued; and toward
night a very foule wether, and a sore storme. By tenne
a clocke we weare com to anchor on the north west
side of NOTTYNGAM ILE, where are 2 or 3 smale iles
lye off from the greater, which make very good sounds
and harbours. About this ile we found some store of
ice, but nothing in comparison of that which heretofore
we haue had.

We staied about this island till the 27 day, hauinge
much foule wether, many stormes, often foggs and vncertaine windes. Dyuers tymes we set sayle to goe to
that side of the ile where the ship rode when CAPTAINE
BUTTON was in her: findinge in other places of this
iland the floud to com from the south eastward, and the

tyme of high water on the chainge day to be at half
an houer past ten, and not at halfe an houer past seuen,
as some supposed. In these ten dayes we staied about
this ile, we fitted our ship with ballast, and other
necessaries we had neede of; and then proceeded as
followeth.

26 The 26 daye, being indifferent faire wether, we passed
between NOTTYNGAM ILE and SALISBURYS ILANDE at the
south point thereof (I mean of Nottyngam Ile), wheare
are many small, low, *broken* iles, without the which had
beene a fit place for vs to haue anchord, to haue found
out the tru sett of the tyde. But our mr. desirous to
com to the same place wheare they had rode before,
stood along by this ile to the westward, and came to an
anchor in the eddy of these broken groundes, wheare
the ship rode at no certaintie of tyde at all.

27 The next morning the wether proued very foule and
much rayne and winde, so that our *kedger*[1] would not
hold the ship,[2] but was driuen into deepe water, that we
weare forced to set sayle, the winde beinge at east, and
then east-north-east, and at noone at north-east, still
foule weather. Being vnder sayle, we stood away towards SEA HORSE POINT. Our mr. (as I suppose) was
perswaded that there might be som passadge between
SEA HORSE POINT and that land which they called SWAN
ILANDE: so this afternoone we saw both SEA HORSE
POINT and NOTTYNGAM ILE. The distance is about 15
leagues, bearinge the one from the other north west
and south east.

28 The 28 in the morninge we weare neare the former
point, *being somwhat southward of it,* trendinge away
west south west so farre as we sawe; and very much
pestred with ice. At seuen a clocke we tacked about
and stood south east and by south.

[1] [Reger. P.]   [2] [At eightie fathoms' scope. P.]

29   The next day at eleuen a clocke we came to anchor at
DIGGES ILE, hauinge very foule weather. At this place
wheare we rode, it lyeth open to the west, hauinge two
of the greatest iles which breake off the force of the
floud till the tyde be well bent; for after the water
beinge risen by the shore about an houer and a halfe,
then the ship *doth wind vpp and* ride truly on the tyde
of floud all the tyde after. Now the tyme of high water
on the chainge daye is halfe an houer past ten,[1] *nearest
eleuen, whom hearetofore was taken to be halfe an houer
past seuen, or an east south east moone, by which mistake
I suppose hath growne the erroure at Nottyngam iland,
affirminge the floud to com from the north west, makinge
account that it would be high water at both places alike (as
indeede it is), but the mistakinge of the tyme was all, for
it is an easey thinge to make a man beleeue that which he
desireth.*

30   The 30, being fayre weather, about noone we set
sayle,[2] wheare we presently perceued the saluages to
be close hid on the top of the rockes; but when they
see we had espyed them, dyuers of them came runninge
downe to the water side, calling *and weauinge* vs to com
to anchor, which we would haue done if conueniently we
could. But heare the water is so deepe, that it is hard
to find a place to ride in, which we seeinge, lay to and
fro with our ship, while som of our men in the bote
killed 70 fowle, for in this place is the greatest quantitie
of these fowle (whom we call WILLOCKS), that in few
places else the like is to be seen : for if neade were we
might haue killed many thousands, almost incredible to
those which haue not seene it. Heare also we had sufficient proofe of the tyde, as we lay to and fro with the
ship, but when our men weare com aboord agayne, we

---

[1] [Or neerest thereabout. P.]
[2] [And stood along close by Digges Ile. P.]

set all our sayles for homeward, makinge the best expedition we could.

AVGVST.

3 But on the third of August we were forced to com to anchor agayne about thirtie leagues within RESOLUTION
4,5 ILAND, on the north shore. The next day we set sayle, and the 5th in the forenoone we past by RESOLUTION ILAND, without sight thereof: thus continuing our course (as in the breefe iournall may be seene) with much contrarie windes and foule wether.

SEPTEMBER.

6 We had sight of CAPE CLEERE in Ireland the sixt of September. The next morninge by daylight we were faire by SILLY, and that night, at two a clocke the next morne, we came to anchor in PLYMOUTH SOUND, *without the loss of one man. For these and all other blessings the Lord make us thankfull.*[1]

And now it may be that som expect I should give my opynion conserninge the passadge. To those my answere must be, that doubtles theare is a passadge. But within this strayte, whome is called Hudson's Straytes, I am doubtfull, supposinge the contrarye. But whether there be, or no, I will not affirme. But this I will affirme, that we haue not beene in any tyde then that from Resolutyon Iland, and the greatest indraft of that commeth from Dauis Straytes; and my judgment is, if any passadge within Resolution Iland, it is but som creeke or in lett, but the mayne will be vpp fretum Dauis; but if any be desirous to knowe my opynion in pertyculler, I will at any tyme be redy to showe the best resons I cann, eyther by word of mouth, or otherwise.

[1] [With all our men liuing, hauing onely three or four sicke, which soone recouered. P.]

THE FIFTH RECORDED VOYAGE

OF

WILLIAM BAFFIN.[1]

A briefe and true Relation or Journall, contayning such accidents
as happened in the fift voyage, for the discouerie of a passage to
the North-west, set forth at the charges of the Right Worshipfull
SIR THO. SMITH, Knight; SIR DUDLEY DIGGES, Knight;
MASTER JOHN WOSTENHOLME, Esquire; MASTER ALDERMAN
JONES, with others, in the good ship called the *Discouerie*, of London; ROBERT BILETH, Master;
and myselfe Pilot, performed in the yeere
of our Lord, 1616.

March 26.   IN the name of God, Amen. The forenamed ship being
in full readinesse vpon the twentie sixe of March, we set
saile at Grauesend, being in number seuenteene persons,
hauing very faire weather, which continued till the second
of Aprill: by that time we were off Portland, then the
winde comming westward, with foule weather, we kept sea
till the fourth day, then being not able to fetch Plimouth,
bore roome for Dartmouth, where wee stayed eleuen dayes,
in which time was much foule weather and westerly windes.

The fifteenth day of Aprill, being cleere of Dartmouth,
we were forced the next day to put into Plimouth. The
nineteenth day we set saile from thence, and the twentieth,
in the morning, we past betweene the Lands end and
Silly, with a faire winde. Continuing our course, as in
the briefe Table or Journall is set downe, with euery particular from noone to noone, that here I need not make a

---
[1] From *Purchas*, Part III, lib. IV, cap. xix, p. 844.

tedious repetition, nothing worthy of note hapning, but that we had a good passage, and the first land we saw was in Fretum Dauis, on the coast of Groinland, in the latitude of 65° 20′.[1] On the fourteenth of May, in the forenoone, then sixe of the people, being a fishing, came to vs, to whom we gaue small pieces of iron, they keeping vs companie, being uery ioyfull, supposing wee had intended to come to anchor; but when they saw vs stand off from shoare, they followed vs a while, and then went away discontented, to our seeming. Groinland.

We prosecuting our voyage, were loth to come to an anchor as yet, although the winde was contrarie, but still plyed to the northward, vntill we came into 70° 20′; then wee came to an anchor in a faire sound (neere the place Master Dauis called London Coast).[2] The twentieth of May at euening, the people espying vs, fled away in their boates, getting on rocks, wondring and gasing at vs, but after this night we saw them no more, leauing many dogs running to and fro on the iland.[3] Men and dogs

At this place we stayed two dayes, in which time wee tooke in fresh water and other necessaries; here we had some dislike of the passage, because the tydes are so small as not arising aboue eight or nine foot, and keepe no certaine course; but the neerest time of high water, on the change day, is at a quarter of an houre past nine, and the flood commeth from the south.

The two and twentieth day, at a north sunne, wee set saile and plyed still northward, the winde being right against vs as we stood off and on. Vpon the sixe and twentieth day, in the afternoone, we found a dead whale, Dead Whale.

[1] This would be Sukkertoppen, or the Cockin Sound visited by Baffin during his first voyage. See page 16.
[2] The north point of Disco Island is in 70° 20′ N. Hare Island, north of Disco, is in 70° 26′ N. Baffin may have anchored on the north shore of the Waigat, in this latitude, near Noursak.
[3] Probably Hare Island.

about sixe and twentie leagues from shoare, hauing all her
finnes.[1] Then making our ship fast, wee vsed the best
means wee could to get them, and with much toile got a hundred and sixtie that euening. The next morning the sea
went uery high, and the winde arising, the whale broke
from vs, and we were forced to leaue her and set saile, and
hauing not stood past three or foure leagues north-westward, came to the ice, then wee tacked and stood to the
shoare-ward, a sore storme ensued.

By the thirtieth day, in the afternoone, wee came faire
by Hope Sanderson, the farthest land Master Dauis was at,[2]
lying betweene 72 and 73°; and that euening, by a north
sunne, we came to much ice, which we put into, plying all
the next day to get through it.

The first of June, we were cleere of the ice before named,
and not farre from shoare, the winde blowing very hard at
north north-east, then we put in among diuers ilands ; the
people seeing vs, fled away in all haste, leauing their tents
behinde, and vpon a small rocke they hid two young
maides, or women. Our ship riding not farre off, we
espyed them, to whom our master, with some other of our
companie, went in the boate, they making signes to be
carried to the iland, where their tents were close adioyning.
When they came thither they found two old women more,
the one uery old, to our estimation little lesse than fourscore, the other not so old. The next time we went on
shoare, there was another woman with a child at her back,
who had hid herselfe among the rocks, till the other had
told her how wee had vsed them, in giuing them pieces of
iron and such like, which they highly esteeme ; in change
thereof they gaue vs seales skinnes ; other riches they had

*Hope
Sanderson.*

*Tents, men
and women.*

---

[1] That is, whale-bone.
[2] On the 30th of June 1587. See *Voyages of John Davis* (Hakluyt
Society, 1880), pp. xxx, and 44. Davis gives the latitude of Hope
Sanderson at 72° 12′ N.

none, saue dead seales, and fat of seales, some of which
fat or blubber afterward we carried aboord. The poore
women were very diligent to carry it to the water side, to
put into our caske, making shew that the men were ouer
at the mayne, and at another small iland something more
eastward. Then making signes to them that wee would
shew them our ship, and set them where the men were, the
foure youngest came into our boate; when they were
aboord, they much wondred to see our ship and furniture;
we gaue them of our meat, which they tasting, would not
eate. Then two of them were set on the iland, where they
supposed the men to be; the other two were carried to
their tents againe. Those that went to seeke the men
could not finde them, but came as neere the ship as they
could, and at euening wee set them ouer to the other.

This place wee called Womens Ilands; it lyeth in the Womens
Ilands.
latitude of 72° 45′;[1] here the flood commeth from the southward at nep tydes; the water ariseth but sixe or seuen
foote, and a south south-east moone maketh a full sea. The
inhabitants very poore, liuing chiefly on the flesh of seales, The people
described.
dryed, which they eate raw; with the skinnes they cloathe
themselues, and also make couerings for their tents and
boats, which they dresse very well. The women, in their
apparell, are different from the men, and are marked in the
face with diuers blacke strokes or lines, the skin being
rased with some sharpe instrument when they are young,
and black colour put therein, that by no means it will be
gotten forth.

Concerning their religion I can little say; onely they Religion.
haue a kinde of worship or adoration to the sunne, which
continually they will point vnto, and strike their hand on

---

[1] These islands are Upernivik, now a Danish settlement, and the sur-
rounding islets and rocks. Upernivik is in 72° 48′ N. The most northern
Danish station is at Kingitok, in 72° 55′ N.; where a very interesting
runic stone was found in 1824. See *R. G. S. J.*, viii, p. 127.

their breast, crying "Ilyout"; their dead they burie on the side of the hils, where they live (which is commonly on small ilands), making a pile of stones ouer them, yet not so close but that wee might see the dead body, the aire being so piersing that it keepeth them from much stinking sauour. So likewise I haue seene their dogs buried in the same manner.

Vpon the fourth day wee set sayle from thence, hauing very faire weather, although the winde were contrary, and plyed to and fro betweene the ice and the land, being as it were a channell of seuen or eight leagues broad: then on the ninth day, being in the latitude of 74° 4',[1] and much pestered with ice, neere vnto three small ilands, lying eight miles from the shore, we came to anchor neere one of them.

These ilands are vsed to be frequented with people in the latter part of the yeare, as it seemed by the houses and places where the tents had stood; but this yeare, as yet, they were not come. Here the tides are very small, especially the floud, which ariseth not aboue fiue or sixe foot, yet the ebbe runneth with an indifferent streame, the cause thereof (in mine opinion) is the great abundance of snow melting on the land all this part of the yeare.

The tenth day wee set sayle from thence, and stood through much ice to the westward, to try if that further from the shoare, we might proceede; but this attempt was soone quailed, for the more ice we went through, the thicker it was, till wee could see no place to put in the ships head.[2]

Seeing that as yet we could not proceede, we determined

[1] Probably those now known as the Baffin Islands, north of Cape Shackleton. They are in 73° 54' N.
[2] This attempt to take the middle pack is very perilous. Parry succeeded in 1819, and Nares in 1875. But it is always safer to stick to the land-floe in passing through Melville Bay.

to stand in for the shoare, there to abide some few dayes, till such time as the ice were more wasted and gone (for we plainely saw that it consumed very fast; with this re-solution we stood in, and came to anchor among many ilands, in the latitude of 73° 45',[1] on the twelfth day, at night. Here wee continued two dayes without shew or signe of any people; till, on the fifteenth day in the morning, about one a clocke, there came two and fortie of the in-habitants in their boates or canoas, and gaue vs seale skinnes, and many peeces of the bone or horne of the sea vnicorne, and shewed vs diuers peeces of sea mors teeth, making signes that to the northward were many of them; in exchange thereof we gaue them small peeces of iron, glasse beads, and such like. At foure seuerall times the people came to vs, and at each time brought vs of the aforesaid commodities, by reason thereof we called this place Horne Sound.[2]

42 Inhabit-ants.

Vnicornes hornes.

Horne Sound.

Here we stayed six dayes, and on the eighteenth day, at night, we set sayle, hauing very little winde; and being at sea, made the best way we could to the northward, although the winde had beene contrary for the most part of this moneth; but it was strange to see the ice so much con-sumed in so little space, for now we might come to the three ilands before named, and stand off to the westward almost twenty leagues, without let of ice, vntill we were more north (as to 74° 30'), then we put among much scat-tered ice, yet euery day we got something on our way, nothing worthy of note happening, but that at diuers times we saw of the fishes with long hornes, many and often, which we call the sea vnicorne: and here, to write particu-larly of the weather, it would be superfluous or needelesse,

They see many Sea Vnicornes.

[1] Islands off Cape Shackleton, which is 1400 feet high, and nearly perpendicular.

[2] The name is not retained on modern maps. It should be placed just north of Cape Shackleton, where there is a loomery.

because it was so variable, few dayes without snow, and often freezing, in so much that on Midsummer day, our shrowds, roapes, and sailes were so frozen that we could scarce handle them ; yet the cold is not so extreame, but it may well be endured.

Sharp frost on Mid-Summer Day.

The first of July we were come into an open sea, in the latitude of 75° 40′, which anew reuiued our hope of a passage ; and because the winde was contrary, wee stood off twenty leagues from the shoare before we met the ice ; then standing in againe ; when we were neare the land, we let fall an anchor to see what tyde went, but in that we found small comfort. Shortly after the winde came to the south-east, and blew very hard, with foule weather, thicke and foggie; then we set sayle, and ran along by the land ; this was on the second day, at night. The next morning we past by a faire cape or headland, which we called Sir Dudley Digges Cape ; it is in the latitude of 76° 35′, and hath a small iland close adioyning to it ;[1] the winde still increasing, we past by a faire Sound twelue leagues distant from the former cape, hauing an iland in the midst, which maketh two entrances.[2] Vnder this iland we came to anchor, and had not rid past two houres but our ship droue, although we had two anchors at the ground ; then were we forced to set sayle and stand forth. This Sound wee called Wosten-holme Sound; it hath many inlets or smaller sounds in it, and is a fit place for the killing of whales.[3]

Sir Dudly Digs his Cape.

Wosten-holme Sound.

The fourth day, at one a clocke in the morning, the

---

[1] The cape with the small island off it, now called Cape Dudley Digges, and probably the one Baffin alludes to, is only in 76° 8′ N. Saunders Island, off the entrance of Wolstenholme Sound, is in 76° 35′ N.

[2] Saunders Island.

[3] Here H.M. ship *North Star*, commanded by Mr. Saunders (Master, R.N.), wintered in 1849-50. She was sent out with stores for the expedition of Sir James Ross, but was unable to get through the ice of Melville Bay until late in the season, and eventually wintered in Wolstenholme Sound.

storme began againe at west and by south, so vehement, that it blew away our forecourse, and being not able to beare any sayle, wee lay a drift till about eight a clocke, then it cleared vp a little, and we saw our selues imbayed in a great Sound; then we set sayle, and stood ouer to the south-east side, where, in a little cove or bay we let fall an anchor, which we lost with cable and all, the winde blowing so extreamely from the tops of the hils, that we could get no place to anchor in, but were forced to stand to and fro in the Sound, the bottome being all frozen ouer; toward two a clocke it began to be lesse winde, then we stood forth.

In this Sound we saw great numbers of whales, therefore we called it Whale Sound, and doubtlesse, if we had beene prouided for killing of them, we might haue strooke very many. It lyeth in the latitude 77° 30'. All the fift day it was very faire weather, and wee kept along by the land till eight a clock in the euening, by which time we were come to a great banke of ice, it being backed with land, which we seeing, determined to stand backe some eight leagues to an iland we called Hakluits Ile—it lyeth betweene two great Sounds, the one Whale Sound, and the other Sir Thomas Smith's Sound; this last runneth to the north of 78°, and is admirable in one respect, because in it is the greatest variation of the compasse of any part of the world known; for by diuers good obseruations I found it to be aboue fiue points, or fifty-six degrees varied to the westward,[1] so that a north-east and by east is true north, and so of the rest. Also, this Sound seemeth to bee good for the killing of whales, it being the greatest and largest in all this bay. The cause, wherefore we minded to stand to this iland, was to see if we could find any finnes or such like on the shore,

Sir Thomas Smith's Sound, in 78°. Variation of the compasse 56° to the West, which may make questionable D. Gilberts rule, tom. i, l. 2, c. i, that where more earth is more attraction of the compasse happeneth by variation toward it. Now the known continents of Asia, &c., must be unspeakably

---

[1] The variation at Port Foulke in Smith Sound (lat. 78° 19' N.) was 110°W., on July 28th, 1875; as observed by Captain A.H. Markham, R.N. See note at page 154.

more than
here there
can be, and
yet here is
more varia-
tion then
about Jepan
or Brasil,
Peru, &c.[1]
and so, indeed, this night wee came to anchor, but with foule weather, that our boat could not land. The next day wee were forced to set sayle, the sea was growne so high, and the wind came more outward. Two dayes wee spent and could get no good place to anchor in; then, on the eight day it cleered vp, and wee seeing a company of ilands lye off from the shoare twelue or thirteene leagues, wee minded to goe to them to see if there we could anchor. When wee were something neere, the winde took vs short, and being loth to spend more time, we tooke opportunitie of the wind, and left the searching of these ilands, which
Caries
Ilands.
wee called Carys Ilands,[2] all which Sounds and ilands the map[3] doth truly describe.

So we stood to the westward in an open sea, with a stiffe gale of wind, all the next day and till the tenth day at one or two a'clocke in the morning, at which time it fell calme and very foggie, and wee neere the land in the en-
Alderman
Jones
Sound.
trance of a faire Sound, which wee called Alderman Jones[4] Sound. This afternoone, being faire and cleere, we sent our boat to the shoare, the ship being vnder sayle, and, as soone as they were on shoare, the winde began to blow; then they returned againe, declaring that they saw many sea morses by the shoare among the ice, and as farre as they were they saw no signe of people, nor any good place

---

[1] See note at page 154.

[2] Probably named after Mr. Alwyn Cary, the ship's husband, for this and the former voyage.

[3] "This map of the authour for this and the former voyage, with the tables of his iournall and sayling, were somewhat troublesome and too costly to insert." So says Master Purchas. His want of funds and of discernment resulted in an irremediable loss to posterity. The map of the "former voyage" has, fortunately, been preserved in manuscript, and a facsimile is given in the present volume. But that illustrating the important discoveries made in the voyage of 1616 is gone, without, it is to be feared, a hope of its ever now being found.

[4] For an account of Alderman Jones, see Introduction.

to anchor in along the shoare. Then hauing an easie gale
of wind at east north-east, we ranne along by the shoare,
which now trendeth much south, and beginneth to shew
like a bay.

On the twelfth day we were open of another great Sound,
lying in the latitude of 74° 20′, and we called it Sir James
Lancaster's Sound ;[1] here our hope of passage began to be Sir James
Lancasters
lesse euery day then other, for from this Sound to the Sound.
southward wee had a ledge of ice betweene the shoare and
vs, but cleare to the seaward, we kept close by this ledge
of ice till the fourteenth day in the afternoone, by which
time wee were in the latitude of 71° 16′, and plainely perceiued the land to the southward of 70° 30′; then wee
hauing so much ice round about vs, were forced to stand
more eastward, supposing to have beene soone cleare, and
to haue kept on the off side of the ice vntill we had come
into 70°, then to haue stood in againe. But this proued
quite contrary to our expectation, for wee were forced to
runne aboue threescore leagues through very much ice,
many times so fast that wee could goe no wayes, although
we kept our course due east; and when wee had gotten
into the open sea, wee kept so neere the ice that many
times wee had much adoe to get cleare, yet could not come
neere the land till we came about 68°, where indeede we
saw the shoare, but could not come to it by eight or nine They see
Land, and
leagues, for the great abundance of ice. This was on the find themselues em-
foure and twentieth day of July; then spent we three braced.
dayes more to see if conueniently wee could come to
anchor to make triall of the tides; but the ice led vs into
the latitude of 65° 40′. Then wee left off seeking to the
west shoare, because wee were in the indraft of Cumberland Cumberland Iles.

[1] Sir John Ross remarks upon the accuracy of Baffin's latitude of
Lancaster Sound. See page 3 for some account of Sir James Lancaster.

Iles, and should know no certaintie, and hope of passage could be none.

Now seeing that wee had made an end of our discouery, and the yeare being too farre spent to goe for the bottome of the bay to search for drest finnes; therefore wee determined to goe for the coast of Groineland to see if we could get some refreshing for our men; Master Herbert and two more hauing kept their cabins aboue eight dayes (besides our cooke, Richard Waynam, which died the day before, being the twenty-six of July), and diuers more of our company so weake, that they could doe but little labour. So the winde fauouring vs, we came to anchor in the latitude of 65° 45′, at six a clocke in the euening, the eight and twentieth day, in a place called Cockin Sound.[1]

The next day, going on shoare on a little iland, we found great abundance of the herbe called scuruie grasse, which we boyled in beere, and so dranke thereof, vsing it also in sallets, with sorrell and orpen, which here groweth in abundance; by meanes hereof, and the blessing of God, all our men within eight or nine dayes space were in perfect health, and so continued till our arriuall in England.

Wee rode in this place three dayes before any of the people came to vs; then, on the first of August, six of the inhabitants in their canoas brought us salmon peele, and such like, which was a great refreshment to our men; the next day following, the same six came againe, but after that we saw them no more vntill the sixt day, when we had wayed anchor, and were almost cleere of the harbour; then the same six and one more brought vs of the like commodities, for which we gaue them glasse beads, counters, and small peeces of iron, which they doe as much esteeme as we Christians do gold and siluer.

Cockin Sound.

Scuruy Grasse.

Six men.

[1] See note at page 16. Baffin, at page 16, gives the latitude of Cockin Sound at 65° 20′ N. Perhaps this 65° 45′ is a misprint for 65° 25′.

In this Sound we saw such great scoles of salmon swim- Plenty of Salmon.
ming to and fro that it is much to be admired; here it
floweth about eighteene foote water, and is at the highest
on the change day at seuen a clocke : it is a uery good harbour, and easie to be knowne, hauing three round high hils
like piramides close adioyning to the mouth of it, and that
in the middest is lowest, and along all this coast are many
good harbours to be found, by reason that so many ilands
lye off from the maine.

The sixt of August, by three a clocke in the afternoone,
wee were cleere of this place, hauing a north north
west winde, and faire weather, and the Lord sent vs a
speedy and good passage homeward as could be wished;
for, in nineteene dayes after, wee saw land on the coast of
Ireland, it being on the fiue and twentieth day; the seuen
and twentieth at noone we were two leagues from Silly,
and the thirtieth day, in the morning, wee anchored at
Douer in the roade, for the which and all other His blessings the Lord make vs thankfull.

Master BAFFIN *his Letter to the right Worshippfull Sir* JOHN
WOLSTENHOLME, *one of the chiefe Adventurers*
for the discovery of a passage to
the North-west.

Worthy Sir, there needs no filling a Journall or short
Discourse with preamble, circumstance, or complement;
and therefore I will onely tell I am proud of my remembrance, when I expresse your worth to my conceit; and
glad of my good fortune, when I can auoid the imputation
of ingratitude, by acknowledgeing your many favours; and
seeing it is not vnknowne to your worship in what estate
the businesse concerning the North-West hath beene heretofore; and how the only hope was in searching Fretum

Davis; which if your selfe had not beene the more forward, the action had wel-nigh beene left of. Now it remayneth for your worship to know what hath beene performed this yeere; wherefore I intreat you to admit of my custome, and pardon me if I take the plaine highway in relating the particulars, without vsing any refined phrases, or eloquent speeches.

Therefore briefly thus, and as it were in the fore-front, I entend to shew the whole proceeding of the voyage in a word : as namely, there is no passage nor hope of passage in the north of Davis Straights.   We hauing coasted all, or neere all the circumference thereof, and finde it to be no other then a great bay, as the voyage doth truely shew. Wherefore I cannot but much admire the worke of the Almightie, when I consider how vaine the best and chiefest hopes of men are in thinges vncertaine; and to speake of no other then of the hopeful passage to the North-West. How many of the best sort of men haue set their whole endeauoures to prooue a passage that wayes? not onely in conference, but also in writing and publishing to the world. Yea, what great summes of money haue been spent about that action, as your worship hath costly experience of. Neither would the vain-glorious Spaniard haue scattered abroad so many false maps and journals, if they had not beene confident of a passage this way; that if it had pleased God a passage had beene found, they might haue eclipsed the worthy prayse of the adventurers and true discouerers. And for my owne part I would hardly haue beleeued the contrary vntill my eyes became witnesse of what I desired not to haue found; still taking occasion of hope on euery likelihood, till such time as we had coasted almost all the circumference of this great bay.   Neither was Master Davis to be blamed in his report and great hopes, if hee had anchored about Hope Sanderson,[1] to haue taken notice

[1] See page 140 and note.

of the tydes. For to that place, which is 72° 12′, the sea is open, and of an vnsearchable depth, and of a good colour : onely the tydes keepe a certaine course, nor rise but a small height, as eight or nine foote ; and the flood commeth from the southward ; and in all the bay beyond that place the tyde is so small, and not much to be regarded. Yet by reason of snow melting on the land, the ebb is stronger then the floud ; by meanes whereof, and the windes holding northerly the fore part of the yeere, the great iles of ice are set to the southward, som into Fretum Hudson, and other into Newfoundland : for in all the channell where the sea is open, are greate quantities of them driuing vp and downe ; and till this yeere not well knowne where they were bred.

Now that the worst is knowne (concerning the passage) it is necessarie and requisite your worship should vnderstand what probabilitie and hope of profit might here be made hereafter, if the voyage might bee attempted by fitting men. And first, for the killing of whales ; certaine it is, that in this bay are great numbers of them, which the Biscayners call the Grand Bay whales, of the same kind as are killed at Greeneland, and as it seemeth to me, easie to be strooke, because they are not vsed to be chased or beaten. For we being but one day in Whale Sound (so called for the number of whales we saw there sleeping, and lying aloft on the water, not fearing our ship, or ought else) ; that if we had beene fitted with men and things necessarie, it had beene no hard matter to haue strooke more then would have made three ships a sauing voyage ; and that it is of that sort of whale theare is no feare. I being twise at Greeneland[1] tooke sufficient notice to know them againe ; besides a dead whale we found at sea, hauing all her finnes (or rather all the rough of her mouth),[2] of which with much labour we got one hundred and sixtie the same evening we found her : and if that foule wether and a

[1] Spitzbergen.　　　[2] Whale bone.

storme the next day had not followed, we had no doubt but to haue had all, or the most part of them : but the winde and sea rising, shee broke from vs, and we were forced to leaue her ther. Neither are they onely to be looked for in Whale Sound, but also in Smith's Sound, Wolstenholme's Sound, and others, etca.

For the killing of sea-morse I can give no certaintie, but onely this : that our bote being but once a shore in all the north part of this bay, which was in the entrance of Alderman Jones his Sound ; at their returne our men told vs they saw many morses alonge by the shore on the ice ; but our ship being under sayle, and the winde comming faire, they presently came aboord without further search : besides, the people inhabiting about 74°, tould vs by diuers signes, that toward the north were many of those beasts, having two long teeth ; and shewed vs diuers peeces of the same.

As for the sea-unicorne, it being a great fish, hauing a long horne or bone growing forth of his forehead or nostrils (such as Sir Martin Frobisher, in his second voyage, found one), in diuers places we saw of them : which, if the horne be of any good value, no doubt but many of them may be killed.

As concerning what the shore will yeeld, as beach-finnes, morse-teeth, and such like, I can say little, because we came not on shore in any of the places where hope was of findinge them.

But here som may obiect why we sought that coast no better ? To this I answere, that while we were thereabout, the wether was so exceeding foule, we could not ; for first we anchored in Wolstenholme Sound, where presently we droue with two anchors a head ; then were we forced to stand forth with a low saile. The next day, in Whale Sound, we lost an anchor and cable, and could fetch the place no more ; then we came to anchor neere a small iland, lying between Sir Thomas Smith's Sound and Whale

Sound : but the winde came more outward, that we were forced to weigh againe. Neuerthelesse, if we had bene in a good harbor, hauing but our ship's bote, we durst not send her farre from the ship, having so few men (as seventeen in all), and som of them very weake : but the chiefe cause we spent so little time to seeke a harbor, was our great desire to performe the discouery ; having the sea open in all that part, and still likelihood of a passage ; but when we had coasted the land so farre to the southward, that hope of passage was none, then the yeere was too farre spent, and many of our men very weake, and withall we hauing some beliefe that ships the next yeere would be sent for the killing of whales, which might doe better than we.

And seeing I have briefly set doune what hope there is of making a profitable voyage, it is not vnfit your worship should know what let or hindrance might be to the same. The chiefest and greatest cause is, that som yeere it may happen by reason of the ice lying betweene 72 and a halfe and 76 degrees, no minutes, that the ships cannot com into those places till toward the middest of July, so that want of time to stay in the countrey may be some let : yet they may well tarry till the last of August, in which space much businesse may be done, and good store of oile made. Neuertheless, if store of whales come in (as no feare to the contrarie) what cannot be made in oyle, may be brought home in blubber, and the finnes will arise to good profit. Another hinderance will be, because the bottome of the sounds will not be so soone cleere as would bee wished ; by meanes whereof, now and then a whale may be lost. (The same case sometimes chanceth in Greeneland.) Yet I am perswaded those sounds before named will all be cleere before the twentieth of July : for we, this yeere, were in Whale Sound the fourth day, amongst many whales, and might have strooke them without let of ice.

Furthermore, there is little wood to be expected either

for fire, or other necessaries; therefore coales and other such thinges must be prouided at home; they will be so much the readier there.

This much I thought good to certifie your worship, wherein I trust you will conceiue that much time hath not beene spent in vaine, or the businesse ouer carelessly neglected; and although we haue not performed what we desired (that is, to have found the passage), yet what we have promised (as to bring certaintie and a true description), truth will make manifest that I haue not much erred.

And I dare boldly say (without boasting) that more good discouerie hath not in shorter time (to my remembrance) beene done since the action was attempted, considering how much ice we have passed, and the difficultie of sayling so neere the pole (vpon a trauerse). And above all, the variation of the compasse, whose wonderfull operation is such in this bay, increasing and decreasing so suddenly, and swift, being in some part, as in Wolstenholme Sound and in Sir Thomas Smith's Sound, varied aboue fiue points or 56°, a thing almost incredible and matchlesse in all the world beside;[1] so that without great care and good obseruations, a true description could not have beene had.

[1] On the subject of Baffin's observations for variation see also page 145, and the marginal note there, referring to the work of Dr. Gilbert.

Baffin evidently paid much attention to questions relating to terrestrial magnetism and to phenomena connected with the magnetic needle. The variation had been observed in London since 1580, and in 1581 William Borough published his *Discourse of the Compass or Magnetical Needle*. A second edition appeared in 1596. This was followed in 1585 by a work entitled "*The newe Attractive*, containing a short discourse of the magnet, or loadstone, and among other his Vertues of a new discovered Secret and subtil propertie, concerning the declining of the needle touche, and therewith under the plaine of the horizon, now first found out by Robert Norman, Hydrographer". New editions of the *New Attractive* appeared in 1596 and 1604. The great work of Dr. Gilbert, of Colchester, referred to in the marginal note at page 145, was published in 1600. The title was, *De magnete, magneticisque corporibus, et de magno magnete tellure; Physiologia nova, plurimis et argu-*

In fine, whatsoeuer my labours are, or shall be, I esteeme
them too little to expresse my thankfull minde for your
many fauours, wherein I shall be ever studious to supply my
other wants by my best endeauours, and euer rest at your
worship's command,·

WILLIAM BAFFIN.

A briefe Discourse of the probabilitie of a passage to the Westerne
or South Sea, illustrated with testimonies : and a briefe
Treatise and Mappe by MASTER BRIGGES.

I thought good to adde somewhat to this relation of
Master Baffin, that learned-vnlearned mariner and mathematician, who, wanting art of words, so really employed
himselfe to those industries, whereof here you see so euident fruits. His mappes and tables would haue much

mentis et experimentis demonstrata. Dr. Gilbert pointed out, for the first
time, the magnetic properties of the earth, and showed that the earth,
by its directive force, performed, relating to the compass needle, the
office of a real magnet.

Baffin must have studied the works of Borough, Norman, and Gilbert ; and he strove diligently, by his own observations, to furnish new
materials for the study of magnetic phenomena. Thus the scientific
results of Baffin's voyages are still valuable, for the changes in the magnetic inclination and declination of places in the earth's surface make
the comparison of observations taken at different periods a most
important element in the study of terrestrial magnetism. In 1580, the
variation at London was 11¼ E. ; in 1818, it was 24¾ W. ; and in 1878,
it was 18½ W. At the Cape of Good Hope there was no variation in
1608 ; in 1840, it was 29 W. ; and in 1878, it was 30 W. It is due to
the first observers, such as Baffin, that these changes are known to us.
Without Baffin's observations, Professor Hansteen, of Christiania, could
not have constructed the first of his series of magnetic maps. It is a
variation map for 1600. *Abweichungskarte für das Jahr* 1600, the
second for 1700, the third for 1756, and the fourth for 1770. See *Mag-
netischer Atlas gehörig zum Magnetismus der Erde, von Chr. Hansteen,
Professor, Christiania,* 1819 (folio).

illustrated his voyages, if trouble, and cost, and his owne despaire of passage that way, had not made vs willing to content our selues with that mappe following of that thrice learned (and, in this argument, three times thrice industrious) mathematician, Master Brigges,[1] famous for his readings in both vniuersities and this honourable citie, that I make no further voyage of discouery to finde and follow the remote passage and extent of his name. Master Baffin told mee, that they supposed the tyde from the north-west, about Digges Iland, was misreported, by mistaking the houre, eight for eleuen, and that hee would, if hee might get employment, search the passage from Japan, by the coast of Asia (*qua data porta*) any way he could. But in the Indies he dyed, in the late Ormus businesse, slaine in fight with a shot, as hee was trying his mathematicall proiects and conclusions.

Now for that discouery of Sir Thomas Button, I haue solicited him for his noates, and receiued of him gentle entertainment and kinde promises : but being then forced to stay in the citie vpon necessary and vrgent affaires, he would at his returne home seeke and impart them. Since I heare that weightie occasions haue detained him out of England, and I cannot communicate that which I could not receiue : which if I doe receiue, I purpose rather to give thee out of due place, then not at all. Once he was uery confident in conference with me of a passage that way, and said that he had therein satisfied his Maiestie, who from

---

[1] Henry Briggs, a Yorkshireman, was born in 1556, and became professor of geometry at Oxford in 1596. He promoted the use of logarithms first explained by Lord Napier in 1614, and made a journey to Edinburgh on purpose to confer with the discoverer. In 1629 Briggs printed his *Arithmetica Logarithmica*. He also published the first six books of Euclid. He was a promoter of the voyage of N. W. Fox, but did not live to see its departure. The great mathematician died at Oxford on January 26th, 1630. Fox, who sailed in 1631, named a group of islands in Hudson's Bay " Brigges his Mathematickes".

his discourse in private inferred the necessitie thereof. And the maine argument was the course of the tyde : for wintering in Port Nelson (see the following mappe) hee found the tyde rising euery twelue houres fifteene foote, (whereas in the bottome of Hudsons Bay it was but two foote, and in the bottome of Fretum Davis, discouered by Baffin, but one) ; yea, and a west winde equalled the nep tydes to the spring tydes : plainely arguing the neighbour-hood of the sea, which is on the west side of America. The summer following, he found, about the latitude "of 60°, a strong race of a tide, running sometimes eastward, sometimes westward ; whereupon Josias Hubbard in his plat called that place Hubbarts Hope, as in the map appeareth. Now Hubberts Hope. if any make scruple because this discouery was not persued by Sir Thomas Button, let him consider that, being Prince Henries seruant, and partly by him' employed (whence I thinke he named the country New Wales), the vntimely death of that prince put all out of ioint ; nor was hee so open that others should haue the glory of his discouerie.[1]

[1] There was, for some unexplained reason, a good deal of obstruction placed in the way of those who sought for information respecting Sir Thomas Button's voyage. The instructions were drawn up by Henry, Prince of Wales, in 1612. Button was ordered to make the best of his way up Hudson's Strait to Digges Island, carefully observing the tides and currents, the elevation and variation of the compass, and the latitude, as well as the distance of the moon from any fixed stars of note. All observations were to be entered in a book, to be delivered to the Prince on the return of the expedition. Digges Island was appointed as the rendezvous for the two ships.

The two ships were the *Resolution* (commanded by Sir Thomas Button) and the *Discovery* (Captain Ingram). After a stay of eight days at Digges Island, the expedition steered N.W., and fell in with land which Button named " Cary's Swan's Nest", on August 13th, 1612. They then anchored at the mouth of a river which was named Port Nelson, after the Master of the *Resolution*, who died there. Button was thus the first navigator who reached the western side of Hudson's Bay. Here the expedition wintered. The men suffered severely from sickness, although they seem to have obtained great numbers of ptarmigan. Josias Hubart was the pilot of the *Resolution*, and, on the breaking up of the ice, he

And if any man thinke that the passage is so farre, as the maps vse to expresse America, running out into the west, it is easily answered, that either of negligence, or ouer-bisie diligence, maps by Portugals in the east, and Spaniards in the west, haue beene falsely proiected. Hence, that fabulous strait of Anian, as before by Francis Gaule's testimonie and navigation is euident.[1]   And hence the Portugals, to bring in the Moluccas to that moity of the world, agreed vpon betwixt the Spaniards and them, are thought to haue much curtailed Asia and the longitude of those ilands, giuing fewer degrees to them then in iust longitude is requisite. So the older maps of America make the land from the Magelane Straits to the South Sea runne much west, when as they rather are contracted somewhat easterly from the north.   The like is iustly supposed of their false placing Quinira,[2] and I know not (nor they neither) what countries they make in America to run so farre north-westward, which Sir Francis Drake's voyage in that sea (his Nova[3] Albion being little further westward than Aquatulco)[4] plainely euince to be otherwise.   Yea, the late map of California, found to be an iland, the sauages discourses in all the countries northwards and westwards from Virginia, fame

advised that a north-westerly course should be steered.   They got as far north as 65° on July 29th, 1613, and then turned southwards, discovering Mansel's Islands on August 4th.   The return of Sir Thomas Button did not discourage the adventurers, who considered that his discoveries gave fresh hopes for a north-west passage.

[1] This is Francisco de Gali, a Spanish pilot, who made a voyage from Acapulco to Manilla, in 1583, returning so as to strike the coast of California in 37° 30' N.   His narrative is given in Linschoten (1598) and Hakluyt.   He proved that there was no Strait of Anian where it had been placed in 38° N., but a wide ocean between Japan and California.   The question is discussed by Davis in his *Worlde's Hydrographical Description* (p. 211).

[2] On the coast of Drake's " New Albion", near Cape Mendocino.

[3] " This easily appeareth in obseruing his voiage, and comparing that before of Fr. Gaul therewith."

[4] On the coast of Mexico.

whereof filled my friend Master Dermer with so much confidence, that hearing of strange ships which came thither
for a kind of yre or earth, the men vsing forkes in their
diet, with caldrons to dresse their meate, etc., things
nothing sutable to any parts of America, hee supposed
them to come from the east, neere to China or Japan,
and, therefore, he made a voyage purposely to discouer,
but, crossed with diuers disasters, he returned to Virginia,
frustrate of accomplishment that yeare, but fuller of confidence, as in a letter from Virginia he signified to me,
where death ended that his designe soon after. But how
often are the vsuall charts reiected by experience in naui-
gations in this worke recorded? Painters and poets are
not alwayes the best oracles. For further proofes of a
passage about those parts into the West Sea (or South, as
it is called from the first discouery thereof to the south,
from the parts of New Spain, whence it was first descried
by the Spaniards), there is mention of a Portugall (and
taken in a carricke in Queene Elizabeth's dayes, of glorious
memory) confirming this opinion. Sir Martin Frobisher,
also from a Portugall in Guinie, receiued intelligence of
such a passage, he saying he had past it. The pilots of
Lisbone are said generally to acknowledge such a thing,
and the Admirall of *D. Garcia Geoffroy Loaisa*, of Cite-
Real, in the time of Charles the Fifth, is reported by the
coast of Baccalaos and Labrador to haue gone to the
Moluccas. Vasco di Coronado writ to the emperour that
at Cibola he was one hundred and fiftie leagues from the
South Sea, and a little more from the North.[1] Antonio de
Herera, the king's choronista maior (part of whose worke
followeth) maketh with vs also in the distances of places by
him described. But to produce some authority more full, I
haue here presented Thomas Cowles, a marriner, and Master

[1] All this is discussed in the *Worlde's Hydrographical Description* by
Davis. (See *Voyages of Davis*, p. 212 and note.)

Michael Locke, merchant, and after them a little treatise ascribed to Master Brigges, together with his map. And if any thinke that the Spaniard or Portugall would soone haue discouered such a passage, these will answere that it was not for their profit to expose their East or West Indies to English, Dutch, or others, whom they would not haue sharers in those remote treasures by so neere a passage. First, Thomas Cowles auerreth thus much :—

"I, Thomas Cowles, of Bedmester, in the countie of Somerset, marriner, doe acknowledge that six years past, at my being at Lisbon, in the kingdome of Portugall, I did heare one Martin Chacke, a Portugall of Lisbon, reade a booke of his owne making, which he had set out six yeares before that time, in print, in the Portugale tongue, declaring that the said Martin Chacke had found, twelue yeares now past, a way from the Portugall Indies through a gulf of the Newfound Land, which he thought to be in 59° of the eleuation of the North Pole. By meanes that hee, being in the said Indies, with foure other shippes of great burden, and he himselfe in a small shippe of fourscore tunnes, was driuen from the company of the other four shippes with a westerly winde, after which hee past alongst by a great number of ilands, which were in the gulfe of the said Newfound Land. And after hee ouershot the gulfe, he set no more sight of any other land vntill he fell with the north-west part of Ireland ; and from thence he took his course homewards, and by that meanes hee came to Lisbone foure or fiue weekes before the other foure ships of his company that he was separated from, as before said. And since the same time, I could neuer see any of those books, because the king commanded them to be called in, and no more of them to be printed, lest in time it would be to their hindrance. In witnesse whereof I set to my hand and marke, the ninth of April Anno 1579.

A Note made by me, Michael Lok the elder, touching

the Strait of Sea, commonly called Fretum Anian, in the
South Sea, through the North-west passage of
Meta Incognita.

WHEN I was at Venice, in Aprill 1596, happily arriued
there an old man, about threescore yeares of age, called
commonly Juan de Fuca, but named properly Apostolos
Valerianos, of nation a Greeke, borne in the Iland Cefalonia, of profession a mariner, and an ancient pilot of
shippes. This man being come lately out of Spaine, arriued first at Ligorno,[1] and went thence to Florence, in
Italie, where he found one John Dowglas, an Englishman,
a famous mariner, ready comming from Venice, to be pilot
of a Venetian ship, named *Ragasona*, for England, in whose
company they came both together to Venice. And John
Dowglas being well acquainted with me before, he gaue me
knowledge of this Greeke pilot, and brought him to my
speech ; and in long talke and conference betweene vs, in
presence of John Dowglas, this Greeke pilot declared, in
the Italian and Spanish languages, thus much in effect, as
followeth :—

First he said, that he had bin in the West Indies of
Spaine by the space of fortie yeeres, and had sailed to and
from many places thereof, as mariner and pilot, in the
seruice of the Spaniards.

Also he said, that he was in the Spanish shippe, which,
in returning from the Ilands, Philippinas and China, towards
Noua Spania, was robbed and taken at the Cape California,

---

[1] Here we see the commencement of the gradual process of corrupt-
ing Livorno into Leghorn.

Captaine
Candish.

by Captaine Candish, Englishman, whereby he lost sixtie thousand duckets, of his owne goods.[1]

Also he said, that he was pilot of three small ships, which the Vizeroy of Mexico sent from Mexico, armed with one hundred men, souldiers, vnder a captaine, Spaniards, to discouer the Straits of Anian, along the coast of the South Sea, and to fortifie in that strait, to resist the passege and proceedings of the English nation, which were feared to passe through those straits into the South Sea. And that by reason of a mutinie, which happened among the souldiers, .for the sodomie of their captaine, that voyage was ouerthrowne, and the ships returned backe from California coast to Noua Spania, without any effect of thing done in that voyage: and that after their returne, the captaine was, at Mexico, punished by iustice.

Also he said, that shortly after the said voyage was so ill ended, the said Vizeroy of Mexico sent him out againe, Anno 1592, with a small carauela, and a pinnace, armed with mariners onely, to follow the said voyage, for discouery of the same Straits of Anian, and the passage thereof, into the sea which they call the North Sea, which is our northwest sea. And that he followed his course in that voyage, west and north-west, in the South Sea, all alongst the coast of Noua Spania and California, and the Indies, now called North America (all which voyage hee signified to me in a great map, and a sea-card of mine owne, which I laied before him) untill hee came to the latitude of forty-seuen degrees, and that there finding that the land trended north and north-east, with a broad inlet of sea, betweene forty-

Land trending in 47°. seuen and forty-eight degrees of latitude, hee entred thereinto, sayling there in more then twentie dayes, and found that land trending still sometime north-west, and north-east and north, and also east and south-eastward, and very much

[1] Cavendish captured this prize off Cape San Lucas, on November 14th, 1587.

broader sea then was at the said entrance, and that hee passed by diuers Islands in that sayling. And that, at the entrance of this said strait, there is, on the north-west coast thereof, a great hedland or iland, with an exceeding high pinacle, or spired rocke, like a piller thereupon.

Also he said, that he went on land in diuers places, and that he saw some people on land clad in beasts skins; and that the land is very fruitfull, and rich of gold, siluer, pearle, and other things, like Noua Spania.

And also he said that he being entred thus farre into the said strait, and being come into the North Sea already, and finding the sea wide enough euery where, and to be about thirtie or fortie leagues wide in the mouth of the Straits, where he entred, hee thought he had now well discharged his office, and done the thing which he was sent to doe; and that hee not being armed to resist the force of the saluage people that might happen, hee therefore set sayle, and returned homewards againe towards Noua Spania, where hee arriued at Acapulco, Anno 1592, hoping to be rewarded greatly of the Viceroy, for this seruice done in this said voyage.

The mouth of the Straight where he entred 30 or 40 leagues broad.

Also he said, that after his comming to Mexico, hee was greatly welcommed by the Viceroy, and had great promises of great reward, but that hauing sued there two yeares time, and obtained nothing to his content, the Viceroy told him that he should be rewarded in Spaine of the king him-selfe very greatly, and willed him, therefore, to goe into Spaine, which voyage he did performe.

Also he said, that when he was come into Spaine, he was greatly welcommed there at the Kings Court, in wordes after the Spanish manner; but after long time of suite there also, hee could not get any reward there neither, to his content. And that, therefore, at the length he stole away out of Spaine, and came into Italie, to go home againe and liue among his owne kindred and countrimen, he being very old.   M 2

Also he said, that hee thought the cause of his ill reward, had of the Spaniards, to bee for that they did not vnderstand very well, that the English nation had now giuen ouer all their voyages for discouerie of the North-West Passage, wherefore they need not feare them any more to come that way into the South Sea, and therefore they needed not his seruice therein any more.

Also he said, that in regard of this ill reward had of the Spaniards, and vnderstondinge of the noble minde of the Queene of England, and of her warres maintayned so valiantly against the Spaniards, and hoping that her Maiestie would doe him iustice for his goods lost by Captaine Candish, he would bee content to goe into England, and serue her Maiestie in that voyage, for the discouerie, perfectly, of the North-West Passage into the South Sea, and would put his life into her Maiesties hands to performe the same, if shee would furnish him with onely one ship of fortie tunnes burden, and a pinnasse, and that he would performe it in thirtie days time, from one end to the other of the Streights, and he willed me so to write into England.

The straight to be discouered in 30 dayes.

And vpon this conference had twise with the said Greeke pilot, I did write thereof accordingly into England, vnto the right honourable the old Lord Treasurer Cecill, and to Sir Walter Raleigh, and to Master Richard Hakluyt, that famous cosmographer, certifying them hereof by my letters. And in the behalfe of the said Greeke pilot, I prayed them to disburse one hundred pounds of money, to bring him into England with my selfe, for that my owne purse would not stretch so wide at that time. And I had answere hereof by letters of friends, that this action was very well liked, and greatly desired in England to bee effected; but the money was not readie, and therefore this action dyed at that time, though the said Greeke pilot perchance liueth still this day at home, in his owne countrie in Cefalonia, towards the which place he went from me within a fortnight after this conference had at Venice.

And in the meane time, while I followed my owne businesse in Venice, being in law-suit against the Companie of
Merchants of Turkie, and Sir John Spencer, their Gouernour, in London, to recouer my pension due for my
office of being their Consull at Aleppo, in Turkie, which
they held from me wrongfully. And when I was (as I
thought) in a readinesse to returne home into England, for
that it pleased the Lords of her Maiesties honourable Priuie
Counsell in England to looke into this cause of my law-suit
for my reliefe, I thought that I should be able, of my owne
purse, to take with me into England the said Greeke pilot.
And therefore I wrote unto him from Venice a letter, dated
in July 1596, which is copied here-vnder.

*"Al Mag^{co.} Sig^{or.} Capitan Ivan De Fvca Piloto de Indias
amigo mio char^{mo.} en Zefalonia.*

" Mvy honrado Sennor, siendo yo par a bueluerme en In-
glatierra dentre de pocas mezes, y accuerdandome de lo
trattado entre my y V. M. en Venesia, sobre el viagio de las
Indias, me ha parescido bien de scriuir esta carta à V. M.
par aque si tengais animo de andar con migo, puedais es-
cribirme presto, en que maniera quereis consertaros. Y
puedais embiarmi vuestra carta, con esta nao Ingles que
sta al Zante (sino hallais otra coientur a meier) con el sobre-
scritto que diga, en casa del Sennor Eleazar Hycman Mercader Ingles, al tragetto de San Thomas en Venisia. Y
Dios guarde la persona de V. M. Fecha en Venesia al primer
dia de Julio, 1596, annos.

"Amigo de V. M. MICHAEL LOK, Ingles."

And I sent the said letter from Venice to Zante, in the ship
Cherubin. And shortly after I sent a copie thereof in the ship
Mynyon. And also a third copie thereof by Manea Orlando,
Patron de Naue Venetian. And vnto my said letters he
wrote mee answere to Venice by one letter which came not

to my hands. And also by another letter which came to my hands, which is copied here-vnder.

"*Al Illmo.* Sig^{or.} MICHAL LOCK, Ingles, *in casa del* Sig^{or.} LASARO *Mercader Ingles, al tragetto de San Thomas en Venesia.*

"Mvy Illustre Seg^{or.} la carta de V. M. receui à 20 dias del Mese di Settembre, por loqual veo Loche V. M. me manda, io tengho animo de complir Loche tengo promettido à V. M. y no solo yo, mas tengo vinte hombres para lieuar con migo, porche son hombres vaglientes; y assi estoi esperando, por otra carta che avise à V. M. parache me embiais los dinieros che tengo escritto à V. M. Porche bien saue V. M. como io vine pouer, porche me glieuo Capitan Candis mas de sessanta mille ducados, come V. M. bien saue; embiandome lo dicho, ire à seruir à V. M. con todos mis compagneros. I no spero otra cossa mas de la voluntad è carta de V. M. I con tanto nostro Sig^{or.} Dios guarda la illustre persona de V. M. muchos annos. De Ceffalonia à 24 de Settembre del 1596.

"Amigo and seruitor de V. M.,

"JUAN FUCA."

And the said letter came to my hands in Venice, the 16 day of Nouember, 1596; but my law suite with the Companie of Turkie was not yet ended, by reason of Sir John Spencers suite made in England at the Queenes Court to the contrarie, seeking onely to haue his money discharged which I had attached in Venice for my said pension, and thereby my owne purse was not yet readie for the Greeke Pilot.

And, neuerthelesse, hoping that my said suite would haue shortly a good end, I wrote another letter to this Greeke Pilot from Venice, dated the 20 of November, 1596, which came not to his hands, and also another letter dated the 24 of Januarie,

1596, which came to his hands. And thereof he wrote me answere, dated the 28 of May 1597, which I receiued the first of August 1597, by Thomas Norden an English merchant yet liuing in London, wherein he promised still to goe with me into England to performe the said voyage for discouerie of the north-west passage into the South Sea, if I would send him money for his charges according to his former writing, without the which money, he said he could not goe, for that he said he was vndone vtterly, when he was in the ship *Santa Anna,* which came from China, and was robbed at California. And yet againe afterward I wrote him another letter from Venice, whereunto he wrote me answere, by a letter written in his Greeke language, dated the 20 of October 1598, the which I haue still by me, wherein he promiseth still to goe with me into England, and performe the said voyage of discouerie of the north-west passage into the South Sea by the said streights, which he calleth the Streight of Noua Spania, which he saith is but thirtie daies voyage in the streights, if I will send him the money formerly written for his charges. The which money I could not yet send him, for that I had not yet recouered my pension owing mee by the Companie of Turkie aforesaid. And so of long time I stayed from any furder proceeding with him in this matter.

The Ship *Santa Anna.*

The Streight of Noua Spania thirtie dayes iourney in the Streight.

And yet, lastly, when I my selfe was at Zante, in the moneth of June 1602, minding to passe from thence for England by sea, for that I had then recouered a little money from the Companie of Turkie, by an order of the Lords of the Priuie Counsell of England, I wrote another letter to this Greeke Pilot to Cefalonia, and required him to come to me to Zante, and goe with mee into England, but I had none answere thereof from him, for that as I heard afterward at Zante, he was then dead, or very likely to die of great sicknesse. Whereupon I returned my selfe by sea from Zante to Venice, and from thence I went by land

through France into England, where I arriued at Christmas,
An. 1602, safely, I thanke God, after my absence from
thence ten yeeres time; with great troubles had for the
Company of Turkies businesse, which hath cost me a great
summe of money, for the which I am not yet satisfied of
them.

A Treatise of the North-west passage to the South Sea, through the Continent of Virginia, and by Fretum Hudson.

By HENRY BRIGGS, the Mathematician.

THE noble plantation of Virginia hath some very excellent prerogatiues aboue many other famous kingdomes, namely, the temperature of the aire, the fruitfulnesse of the soile, and the commodiousnesse of situation.

The aire is healthfull and free both from immoderate heate, and from extreme cold; so that both the inhabitants and their cattell doe prosper exceedingly in stature and strength, and all plants brought from any other remote climate, doe there grow and fructifie in as good or better manner, then in the soile from whence they came. Which though it doe manifestly prooue the fruitfulnesse of the soile, yelding all kindes of graine or plants committed vnto it, with a rich and plentifull increase; yet cannot the fatnesse of the earth alone produce such excellent effects vnlesse the temperature of the aire be likewise so fauourable, that those tender sprouts which the earth doth abundantly bring forth, may be cherished with moderate heate and seasonable moisture, and freed both from scourching drought, and nipping frost.

These blessings are so much the more to be esteemed, because they are bestowed vpon a place situated so conueniently, and at so good a distance, both from Europe and the West Indies, that for the mutuall commerce betwixt these great and most rich parts of the habitable world, there cannot bee deuised any place more conuenient for the succour and refreshing of those that trade from hence

thither, whether they be of our owne nation, or of our
neighbours and friends; the multitude of great and nauigable
rivers, and of safe and spacious harbours, as it were inuiting
all nations to entertaine mutuall friendship, and to partici-
pate of those blessings which God, out of the abundance
of his rich treasures, hath so graciously bestowed some
vpon those parts of Europe, and others no lesse desired
vpon these poore people, which might still haue remayned
in their old barbarous ignorance, without knowledge of
their owne miserie, or of Gods infinite goodnesse and
mercy, if it had not pleased God thus graciously, both to
draw vs thither with desire of such wealth as those fruitfull countries afford, and also to grant vs, too, easie, certaine,
and safe a meanes to goe vnto them, which passage is, in
mine opinion, made much more secure and easie by the
commodious harbours and refreshing which Virginia doth
reach out unto vs. The coasts of Florida, to the west,
being not so harberous ; and of New England to the east,
somewhat more out of the way, amongst so many flats and
small ilands, not so safe. Neither is the commodiousnesse
of Virginia's situation onely in respect of this West At-
lanticke Ocean, but also in respect of the Indian Ocean,
which we commonly call the South Sea, which lyeth on the
west and north-west side of Virginia, on the other side of
the mountaines beyond our Falls, and openeth a free and
faire passage, not onely to China, Japan, and the Moluc-
caes ; but also to New Spaine, Peru, Chili, and those rich
countries of Terra Australis, not as yet fully discouered.
For the sea wherein Master Hudson did winter, which was
first discouered by him, and is, therefore, now called Fretum
Hudson, doth stretch so farre towards the west, that it
lyeth as farre westward as the Cape of Florida. So that,
from the Falls aboue Henrico Citie, if we shape our iourney
towards the north-west, following the riuers towards the
head, wee shall, vndoubtedly, come to the mountaines,

which, as they send diuers great riuers southward into our
Bay of Chesepiock, so likewise doe they send others from
their further side north-westward into that bay where
Hudson did winter. For so wee see in our owne countrie,
from the ridge of mountaines continued from Derbishire
into Scotland, doe issue many great riuers on both sides
into the East Germane Ocean, and into the Westerne Irish
Seas; in like sort from the Alpes of Switzerland and the
Grizons, doe runne the Danubie eastward into Pontus
Euxinus, the Rhene into the North Germane Ocean, the
Rhone west into the Mediterranean Sea, and the Po south
into the Adriaticke Sea. This bay, where Hudson did
winter, stretcheth itself southward into forty-nine degrees,
and cannot be, in probabilitie, so farre distant from the
Falls as two hundred leagues; part of the way lying by
the riuers side towards the mountaines, from whence it
springeth, and the other part on the other side cannot want
riuers likewise, which will conduct us all the way, and I
hope carry vs, and our prouisions, a good part of it. Besides that bay, it is not vnlikely that the Westerne Sea, in
some other creeke or riuer, commeth much neerer then that
place. For the place where Sir Thomas Button did winter,
lying more westerly then Master Hudsons Bay, by one
hundred and ninetie leagues in the same sea, doth extend
it selfe very neere as farre towards the west as the Cape of
California, which is now found to be an Iland stretching
it selfe from twenty-two degrees to forty-two, and lying
almost directly north and south; as may appeare in a map
of that Iland, which I haue seene here in London, brought
out of Holland; where the sea, vpon the north-west part,
may very probably come much neerer then some doe
imagine; who, giuing too much credit to our vsuall globes
and maps, doe dreame of a large continent, extending it
selfe farre westward to the imagined Streight of Anian,
where are seated (as they fable) the large kingdomes of

Cebola and Quiuira, hauing great and populous cities of
ciuill people; whose houses are said to bee fiue stories
high, and to haue some pillars of Turquesses, which relations are cunningly set downe by some vpon set purpose,
to put us out of the right way, and to discourage such as
otherwise might be desirous to search a passage by the
way aforesaid into these seas.

Gerardus Mercator, a very industrious and excellent
geographer, was abused by a map sent vnto him, of foure
Euripi meeting about the North Pole; which now are found
to bee all turned into a mayne icie sea. One demonstration
of the craftie falsehood of these vsuall maps is this, that
Cape Mendocino is set in them west north-west, distant
from the south Cape of California about seuenteene hundred leagues, whereas Francis Gaule, that was imployed in
those discoueries by the Vice-roy of New Spaine, doth in
Hugo Linschotten, his booke, set downe their distance to
be onely fiue hundred leagues.

Besides this, in the place where Sir Thomas Button did
winter in fifty-seven degrees of latitude, the constant great
Tydes euery twelue houres, and the increase of those tydes
whensoeuer any strong westerne winde did blow, doe
strongly persuade vs that the maine westerne ocean is not
farre from thence; which was much confirmed vnto them
the summer following; when sayling directly north, from
that place where they wintered, about the latitude of sixty
degrees, they were crossed by a strong current, running
sometimes eastward, sometimes westward. So that if we
finde either Hudsons Bay, or any other sea more neere vnto
the west, wee may assure our selues that from thence we
may, with great ease, passe to any part of the East Indies.
And that, as the world is very much beholding to that
famous Columbus, for that he first discouered vnto vs the
West Indies; and to the Portugal for the finding out the
ordinarie, and as yet the best way that is knowne to the

East Indies, by Cape Bona Speranza, so may they and all the world be in this beholding to vs in opening a new and large passage, both much neerer, safer, and farre more wholesome and temperate through the Continent of Virginia, and by Fretum Hudson, to all those rich countries, bordering vpon the South Sea, in the East and West Indies. And this hope that the South Sea may easily from Virginia be discouered ouer land, is much confirmed by the constant report of the sauages, not onely of Virginia, but also of Florida and Canada; which, dwelling so remote one from another, and all agreeing in the report of a large sea to the westwards, where they describe great ships not vnlike to ours, with other circumstances, doe giue vs very great probabilitie (if not full assurance) that our endeavours this way shall, by God's blessing, haue a prosperous and happy successe, to the encrease of his kingdome and glorie amongst these poore ignorant Heathen people; the publique good of all the Christian world, the never-dying honour of our most gracious Soueraigne, the inestimable benefit of our nation, and the admirable and speedie increase and advancement of that most noble and hopefull plantation of Virginia; for the good successe whereof all good men with mee, I doubt not, will powre out their prayers to Almightie God. H. B.

INSTRUCTIONS

TO

WILLIAM BAFFIN,

A.D. 1616.

(From Purchas, iii, p. 842.)

"For your course you must make all possible haste to
Cape Desolation; and from thence you, William Baffin, as
pilot, keep along the coast of Greenland and up *Fretum
Davis*, until you come toward the height of eighty degrees,
if the land will give you leave. Then, for feare of inbaying,
by keeping too northerly a course, shape your course west
and southerly, so farre as you shall thinke it convenient, till
you come to the latitude of sixtie degrees; then direct your
course to fall in with the land of *Yedzo*, about that height,
leaving your further sayling southward to your owne discretion, according as the time of the year and windes will
give you leave; although our desires be, if your voyage
prove so prosperous that you may have the year before you,
that you goe so farre southerly as that you may touch the
north part of *Japan*, from whence, or from *Yedzo*, if you
can so compasse it without danger, we would have you
bring home one of the men of the countrey; and so God
blessing you, with all expedition to make your return home
againe."

BAFFIN'S SHIPS.

I. 1612.—*Patience* (140 tons), forty men and boys.

James Hall (General).
WILLIAM BAFFIN (Pilot).
William Gordon (Master's Mate).
John Hemsley (Master's Mate).

William Huntriss (Master's Mate).
John Gatonby (Quarter Master).
Mr. Wilkinson (Merchant).
James Carlisle (Goldsmith).

II. 1613.—*Tiger* (260 tons).

Benjamin Joseph (General).
Thomas Sherwin (Master).

WILLIAM BAFFIN (Pilot).
Master Spencer (Master's Mate).

III. 1614.—*Thomasine*.

Thomas Sherwin (Master).
WILLIAM BAFFIN (Pilot).

Robert Fotherby (Master's Mate).
Robt. Hambleton (Master's Mate).

IV. 1615.—*Discovery* (55 tons), fourteen men and two boys.

Robert Bylot (Master).

WILLIAM BAFFIN (Pilot).

V. 1616.—*Discovery* (55 tons), fourteen men and two boys.

Robert Bylot (Master).
WILLIAM BAFFIN (Pilot).

Master Herbert.
Richard Waynam (Cook).

VI. 1617-19.—*Anne Royal* (1057 tons).

Andrew Shilling (Master).
WILLIAM BAFFIN (Master's Mate).
Edward Haynes (Merchant).

Joseph Salbanke (Merchant).
Richard Barber (Merchant).

VII. 1620-22.—*London*.

Andrew Shilling (General).
WILLIAM BAFFIN (Master).
Bartholomew Symonds (Surgeon).
Nicholas Crispe (Purser).
John Woolhouse (Chaplain).

Archibald Jennison (Master's Mate).
Edwyn Guy (Purser's Mate).
John Barker (Merchant).
Edward Monox (Merchant).
Robert Jefferies (Merchant).

INDEX.

CONTENTS OF THE INDEX.

I.

LIST OF PERSONS MENTIONED IN BAFFIN'S VOYAGES.

Baffin, William, *passim.*

Ball, Richard, 3. A London merchant, adventurer in the Greenland voyage of 1612. Ball's river, a fiord opening on Godthaab harbour was named after him.

Barker, Andrew, 13, 24, 26. Master of the *Heart's Ease* in the Greenland voyage of 1612, and took chief command on the death of Hall. An old and experienced seaman. Warden of the Hull Trinity House, 1606, 1613, 1618.

Bonner, Thos., 44, 50, 52, 72. Master of an Amsterdam ship² in Spitzbergen in 1613, which was captured by the English, and sent northward for discovery under Captain Marmaduke.

Button, Sir Thomas, 134. Commander of an expedition of discovery in Hudson's Bay in 1612-13, wintering to Nelson River. His ship was the *Discovery*, the same ship in which Baffin made his two voyages in 1614 and 1615.

Bylot, Robert, 111, 138. Master of the *Discovery* when Baffin was pilot in 1615 and 1616. He also served with Hudson in his last voyage, and with Button and Gibbons, always in the *Discovery.*

Carlisle, James, 25, 33. Goldsmith in Hall's Greenland expedition, 1612.

Cary, Allwyn, 111, 146. Ship's husband for the *Discovery* in the voyage of 1615 and 1616.

Cockayne, Sir William, 4. Adventurer for Hall's Greenland voyage of 1612. For a notice of him, see note at p. 4.

Cooper, Master, 49. In the Spitzbergen voyage of 1613. Complaint against him by the master of the French ship who had been allowed to fish.

Cudner, Master, 52. Merchant on board a ship of Alborough called the *Desire*, in Spitzbergen in 1613.

Davis, John, 8, 139, 140, 150. References to his discoveries of Cape Farewell, London Coast, and Hope Sanderson, and to his views respecting a passage.

Digges, Sir Dudley, 103, 111, 138. See his life in the Introduction, p. x to xvi.

Edge, Thomas, 49, 50. In 1611 he went to Spitzbergen in command of the *Mary Margaret*. The fleet of 1613 was under the joint command of Joseph and Edge. Edge made several other voyages to Spitzbergen down to 1616.

Fisher, Thos., 42. Gunner on board a French ship at Spitzbergen, 1613.
Fletcher, 52. Master of a ship from Alborough called the *Desire*, 1613.
Fopp, Captain, 40, 42, 43. Captain of a ship of Dunkirk, in Spitzbergen, 1613.
Fotherby, Robert, 54-79, 80-102. Author of the two narratives, 1613 and 1614, with Baffin, and of another, 1615. For a notice of him and his family, see note at p. 80.
Frobisher, Sir Martin, 152. Reference to his bringing home a narwhal's horn.
Gatonby, John, 1, 26, 27. Quartermaster of the *Patience*, in Hall's Greenland voyage of 1612, of which he wrote a narrative published in Churchill. He went home master's mate of the *Heart's Ease*.
Gibbons, Captain, 111. Sent out in command of an expedition in 1614, but did nothing. Bylot was with him in the *Discovery*.
Gordon, William, 26, 52. Master's mate of the *Patience* in Hall's Greenland voyage of 1612. He was afterwards employed in Spitzbergen voyages.
Green, Mr., 68. One of the master's mates of the *Mathew* in the Spitzbergen voyage of 1613, who died on the way home.
Hall, James, 3, 15, 22, 24, 25. Commander of the Greenland expedition of 1612, who was murdered by the Eskimo on July 22. For an account of his former services with the Danes, see Introduction, p. xviii.
Hambledon, Robert, 88. Master's mate of the *Thomasine*, with Baffin, in the Spitzbergen voyage of 1614.
Hemsley or Hemstay, John, 10, 26. Master's mate of the *Patience* in Hall's Greenland voyage of 1612. He displayed some insubordinate feeling when Andrew Barker succeeded to the chief command.
Herbert, 148. Master Herbert is mentioned as suffering from scurvy on board the *Discovery* in the voyage of 1616.
Hildyard, Sir Christopher, 1. Gatonby dedicated his narrative to Sir C. Hildyard of Winestead; for a notice of him, see note at p. 1.
Hubbard, Josiah, 157. With Hall in his third voyage with the Danes, and drew sketches of land. After-

wards he was pilot with Sir T. Button, and drew a chart, now lost.
Huntriss, William, 24, 27, 32. A Yorkshire lad of Scarborough, the faithful follower of Hall, both in the Danish voyages and in 1612. On Hall's death, he became master of the *Heart's Ease*.
Jones, Sir Francis, 111, 138, 146, 152. Adventurer in the voyages of 1615 and 1616. For an account of him, see Introduction, p. x.
Joseph, Benjamin, 38 (*n.*), 40, 55, 81, General of the Spitzbergen voyages of 1613 and 1614. For some account of him, see note at p. 39.
Lancaster, Sir James, 3, 13, 147. An adventurer in the expeditions of 1612, 1615, and 1616. See note at p. 3.
Marmaduke, Master, 50 (*n.*), 60, 61, 72, 93, 99. A captain from Hull, who made several voyages to Spitzbergen, and explored part of the north coast in 1612.
Martin, Clais, of Horn. In command of a pink from Dunkirk, 1613.
Mason, John, 49, 86, 88, 91, 99. In the Spitzbergen voyages of 1613 and 1614. Master of the *Gamaliel*.
Origanus, David, 124, 125. Reference to his *Ephemeris*, by Baffin.
Penkewill, Richard, 112. A gentleman from Padstow, who showed kindness to the crew of the *Discovery*, 1616.
Prestwood, Lawrence, 93. Served with Marmaduke in Spitzbergen in 1612, and set up a cross on Red Beach.
Pullay, James, 14, 15. One of the crew of the *Patience*, in Hall's Greenland voyage of 1612. Killed by the Eskimo at Godthaab.
Rudston, Master, 127. A mathematician, who worked out some of Baffin's observations.
Sallowes, Allen, 40, 42. (Allane Sallis.) An English pilot on board a French ship at Spitzbergen, 1613.
Searle, John, 124. His *Ephemeris* referred to by Baffin. For some account of him, see note at p. 124.
Sherin or Sherwin, Thomas, 45, 81, 89, 99. Master of the *Tiger* in Spitzbergen in 1613, and again in the *Thomasine* with Baffin in 1614.
Silvator, Pierce de, 60. Captain of a Bordeaux ship, 1613, allowed to fish on conditions.

N

II.

ANIMALS AND PLANTS MENTIONED IN BAFFIN'S VOYAGES.

MAMMALS.

Bear (*Ursus maritimus*), 35, 62, 65, 71.

Dog (*Canis familiaris*), 35, 118, 142.

Fox (*Vulpes lagopus*), 18, 35, 62, 71.

Grampus (*Orca gladiator*), 7.

Hare (*Lepus glacialis*), 35.

Morse (*Odobœnus rosmarus*), 36, 47, 48, 61, 62, 71, 78, 133, 146, 152.

Reindeer (*Rangifer tarandus*), 35, 47, 57, 62, 70, 71.

Seal (*Phoca*), 35, 36, 61, 71.

Unicorn (*Monodon Monoceros*), 13, 17, 71, 143, 152.

Whale (*Balæna mysticetus*), 7, 46, 47, 49, 59, 71, 72, 73, 78, 88, 99, 139, 143, 144, 151, 152.

White Whale (*Beluga leucas*), 71.

BIRDS.

Culverdumes, 62 ; Cuelverduns, 71. Probably a corrupt form. *Culver* suggests a pigeon.

Geese (*Bernicla Brenta*), 62, 71.

Gulls (*Larus ?*), 71.

Partridges (*Lagopus rupestris*, Ptarmigan), 17, 71.

Sea Pigeons (*Uria grylle*, Dovekeys), 71.

Sea Parrots (*Fratercula Arctica*, Puffins), 71.

Stints (*Tringa*, Sandpipers), 71.

Willocks (*Uria arra*, Guillemots), 62, 71, 136.

FISH.

But Fish, Halibut (*Pleuronecthes hippoglossus*) (Torbut ? *Egede*, p. 91), 19.

Cod (*Gadus*), 19. 71.

Musk Fish (?), 19.

Salmon (*Salmo salar*), 36, 71.

Salmon Trout (*Salmo carpio*), 18, 19.

Salmon Peel, 148.

PLANTS.—GREENLAND.

Angelica (*Archangelica officinalis*, Quan), 34.

A little branch running along the ground, bearing a black berry (*Empetrum nigrum*, Crowberry), 34.

Grove of small wood, 6 or 7 feet high (*Betula alpestris*, dwarf birch), 34.

Scurvy Grass (*Cochlearia officinalis*), 148.

Sorrel (*Oxyria reniformis*), 148.

Orpen, 148. (A yellow flowered *sedum*.) Name from orpine (orpiment), gold pigment. There are three *sedums* (stonecrops), but all in South Greenland: *Sedum annuum*, *sedum rhodiola*, *sedum villosum*).

PLANTS.—SPITZBERGEN.

A white moss. 70.

Straggling grass, with a bluish flower, like young heath, 70. (*Silene acaulis?* a little purple flower, grows level with the moss, or, perhaps, *Saxifraga oppositifolia*).

III.

SPITZBERGEN NAMES MENTIONED BY BAFFIN AND FOTHERBY.

Fair Haven, "Gansen Eyl" of Van Keulen.

Sea Horse Bay, 49.

Sir T. Smith's Bay, 51, 56, 59, 60, 85. The channel between Prince Charles Island and the main; now called Foreland Fiord.

Sir T. Smith's Inlet, 94, 97, 100. The Hinlopen Strait of modern charts; or, possibly, Wiide Bay. On the map of Porchas, it is certainly in the position of Hinlopen Strait. But Baffin and Fotherby say they saw the end of it, 30 miles distant, and this answers better to Wiide Bay.

Trinity Harbour, 86. In Magdalena Bay (or Maudlin Sound), so named by Fotherby, who took possession there, in the name of King James, on June 22nd, 1613.

Wiche's Sound, 92, 94. This appears to be the Wiide Bay of modern charts, on the north coast. Baffin and Fotherby crossed it, and climbed a high hill, whence they saw a point of land, E.N.E., 18 or 20 leagues. They would have been on a hill over Mossel Bay, whence 60 miles E.N.E. would just reach the North Cape of North-East Land.

IV.

NAMES IN HUDSON'S STRAIT MENTIONED BY BAFFIN.

Broken Islands, 105. Baffin's latitude, 63° 46′ N.

Broken Point, 121, 125. So named by Baffin in 1614. On the north side of Hudson Strait. Sir Edward Parry (Second Voyage, p. 21) says the spot is memorable, because here Baffin took the first lunar ever observed at sea, giving his longitude 74° 30′ W. Parry was there on July 29th, 1821.

Comfort, Cape, 104, 131, 132, 133. Baffin's latitude, 65° N. So named by Bylot. Parry gives the latitude 64° 54′ N. He sighted it on August 6th, 1821. It is on Southampton Island.

Digges Island, 105, 136. Baffin's latitude, 62° 45′ N. On the south side of the western entrance to Hudson Strait. It was here that the villains, Green and Jewett, who abandoned Hudson, were murdered by Eskimo, 1615.

Fair Ness, 121, named by Baffin in 1614.

Mill Island, 128. So named by Baffin from "the greate extremetye and grindinge of the ice". His latitude is 64° N. It is on the north side of the western entrance of Hudson

Strait, west of Salisbury and Nottingham Islands.

Nottingham Island, 105, 130, 133, 134, 135. Baffin's latitude, 62° 45′ N. Nottingham and Salisbury Islands are at the western end of Hudson Strait, on the north side.

Resolution Island, 105, 113, 114, 115, 116, 137. Baffin's latitude, 61° 30′ N. He sighted it on May 27th, 1615. Parry sighted it on July 6th, 1821. This island is at the eastern entrance of Hudson Strait, on the north side. Discovered by Davis.

Salisbury Island, 127, 135. Sighted by Parry on July 31st, 1821. At the western end of Hudson Strait. So named by Hudson, who thought it was a cape on the main land.

Savage Islands, 105, 117, 120. Baffin's latitude, 62° 30′ N. Named by Baffin in June 1614. Parry was off them on July 22nd, 1821 (p. 16). They are on the north side of the entrance to Hudson Strait.

Sea Horse Point, 105, 135. Baffin's latitude, 63° 44′ N. The eastern point of Southampton Island.

Swan Island, 135.

v.

GREENLAND AND BAFFIN'S BAY NAMES MENTIONED BY BAFFIN.

VI.

GENERAL INDEX.

184

INDEX.

Cary, Allwin, ship's husband, 111
—— Islands, liii, lv-lvi, 146
—— Swan's Nest, 157 (*n.*)
Cavendish, prize taken by, with Juan de Fuca on board, 162, 164
Chacke, Martin, a Portuguese, as to North-west Passage, 160
Chester, Colonel, aid from, in searching for name of Baffin, xxiii
Chichelay, Sir Robert, ancestor of Sir T. Smith, ii
Chilham, home of Sir Dudley Digges, xv, xvi ; subsequent owners of, xv
Christian IV of Denmark, his expeditions to Greenland, xviii, xix ; gives up the Greenland enterprise, xx
Churchill, "Voyages and Travels," Gatonby's narrative of Hall's Greenland voyage in, xxiv
Cibola, 139, 172
Coard, John, slain in action with Portuguese, xli
Cockayne, Sir William, vi, xvii ; notice of, and family, 4 (*n.*); adventurer in Hall's Greenland voyage, xxi
Cockin Sound, 16 (*n.*) ; Baffin's observations at, xlviii, 20, 21 ; named after Alderman Cockayne (Cockin), 22 ; *Discovery* in, liii, 148 ; salmon in, 149 ; Baffin's Greenland narrative commences at xxiv
Cod, 19, 71
Cold Cape, Spitzbergen, 52
Colebrookes, owners of Chilham, xv
Colepeppers of Leeds Castle, iii
Comfort, Land of, 10 (*n.*)
—— Cape, position. 104 ; named, 131 ; at anchor near, 132, 133
Cooper, Master, 49
Coronado, Vasco de, 159
Corpo Santo seen, 102
Cove, Nicke's, 41, 46
Cowles, Thomas (mariner), evidence as to North-west Passage, 160
Crispe, Nicholis, power of the *London*, xl
Cromwell, family, kinship with Sir T. Smith, ii (*n.*)
Cross Road, Spitzbergen, 85
Cudner, Master, 52
Cuelverduns, birds in Spitzbergen, 62, 71
Cullen, Viscount, title of the Cockayne family, 4 (*n.*) See Cockayne
Cumberland Isles, 147
Cunningham, John, General of the Danish Greenland expedition, xviii
—— Mount, xviii, 18
—— Fiord, xx, 23

Danish voyages to Greenland, xviii, xix ; manuscript accounts of, first printed by Pingel, xix (*n.*)
D'Anville, map of Baffin Bay, lvi
David, Walter, slain in action with Portuguese, xlii
Davis, John, inlets seen by, xxix ; named Cape Farewell, 8 ; "London Coast" of, 139 ; his furthest at Hope Sanderson, 140 ; not to be blamed for believing in a passage, 150
—— Strait, 114, 137, 139 ; Baffin on a passage by, 150, 174
Deceit Point, named by Fotherby, 99
Declination of the needle (or Dip), 39, 44
Denmark Haven, 18
Deptford, house of Sir T. Smith at, iii ; burnt, vi
Dermer, Master, 159
Desire, ship in Spitzbergen fleet, 38, 41, 42, 45, 81, 82, 84 ; Basques on board, 49 ; homeward bound, 67
Desolation land sighted, 9, 174
De Wit, Atlas, map of Baffin's Bay in, lv
Digges, Sir Dudley, ancestry, x ; birth, xi ; embassies, xii, xiii ; parliamentary life, xiii ; marriage and children, xiv ; death, xiv ; home at Chilham, xv ; monument, xvi ; director of North-West Company, xxix ; Baffin's letter to, 109, xxxi ; Not discouraged by failure of Captain Gibbon's, 111 ; adventurer in expedition of, 1616, xxxii, 138
—— Cape, lii, lv, 144
—— Island, position, 105, 136 ; Button at, 157, (*n.*)
—— Leonard, his works, x, xi
—— Thomas, father of Sir Dudley, xi
—— West, xiv
Dip of the magnetic needle, xlviii, 39, 44
Discovery, Hudson's ship, xxix ; Ingram's ship in Button's expedition, 157, (*n.*) ; Bylot and Baffin in 1615 ; liii, 111 ; sails, 111 ; in 1616, xxxii, 138 ; illness on board, 148 ; return of, 149
Dogs, Eskimo, 35, 118, 142
Dolphin. (*See* Ships.)
Dovekeys, or sea pigeons,71
Drake, Sir Francis, his discoveries do not show that America extends north-west, 158
Dunkirk ships in Greenland, 40, 42
Dutch ships at Spitzbergen, 41, 48, 64; two appointed for discovery, 95 ;

For EU product safety concerns, contact us at Calle de José Abascal, 56–1°,
28003 Madrid, Spain or eugpsr@cambridge.org.

www.ingramcontent.com/pod-product-compliance
Ingram Content Group UK Ltd.
Pitfield, Milton Keynes, MK11 3LW, UK
UKHW010345140625
459647UK00010B/842